**Before the gates of excellence**

# Before the gates of excellence

---

*The determinants of creative genius*

R. OCHSE

The right of the
University of Cambridge
to print and sell
all manner of books
was granted by
Henry VIII in 1534.
The University has printed
and published continuously
since 1584.

**Cambridge University Press**

*Cambridge*

*New York   Port Chester*

*Melbourne   Sydney*

Published by the Press Syndicate of the University of Cambridge
The Pitt Building, Trumpington Street, Cambridge CB2 1RP
40 West 20th Street, New York, NY 10011, USA
10 Stamford Road, Oakleigh, Melbourne 3166, Australia

First published 1990

Printed in Great Britain by J. W. Arrowsmith Ltd., Bristol

*British Library cataloguing in publication data*
Ochse, R.
Before the gates of excellence: the determinants of creative genius.
1. Creativity
I. Title
153.3'5

*Library of Congress cataloguing in publication data applied for*

ISBN 0 521 37557 6 hard covers
ISBN 0 521 37699 8 paperback

AS

This book is dedicated to:

**Dick**

and

**The Memory of Lenchen von Willich**

With thanks to those on whose moral and practical support I have depended while it was written and published – especially

Dick Ochse

Peter von Willich, Bernie Gultig, Betty Rothman, Caryl Moore, Jane Matjiane, at home, and Judy Rissik and Anne McKane, abroad;

Peter, Michelle, Charlie, Eddie and Ryno at PC Maintenance;

Jenny Potts and Judith Ayling, at Cambridge University Press;

James Kitching and others at the Unisa library – which lies *within* the Gates of Excellence.

# Contents

## PART III CREATIVE THINKING AND INSPIRATION

# Prologue

In 1957 Royce remarked that the literature of psychology was much like a mail-order catalogue, 'loaded with many individually accurate items, some of them even grouped under major headings or domains, but [with] little system within each domain, and little relationship between the various parts' (p. 402). In somewhat similar vein Irving Taylor (1959/1972) later described the literature on creativity as an increasing body of 'unintegrated theoretic and research material'.

Today this is no less true. Recently Pezdek (1987) remarked that cognitive psychology has been acquiring more trees without gaining more or better forests – and this applies particularly well to research on creativity. An enormous body of findings has accumulated in this area. But even though we have gathered numerous isolated facts and ideas, relatively little has been done to integrate them into a meaningful whole. Many narrowly focussed theories have been put forward to explain some or other aspect of the creative person, process or product. But none has been wide enough to reveal the connections between them. None, for example, has shown how various life experiences and personal characteristics of creative people relate to creative thinking processes.

The most difficult task that behaviour scientists have, said Royce (1957), is 'to pull the facts together and try to make some sense of them [but this needs to be done] because most of our facts simply lie around, and have little or no relationship to each other' (p. 402). To tackle part of that task, this book tries to pull together and make sense of facts and ideas that have emerged from studies of highly creative people. Theories put forward in the past are examined in the light of the facts – and some new theory is presented, in an attempt to provide answers to the old question of what makes people creative.

What makes people creative? This question can be interpreted in various ways. For one, it might mean '*who* is creative (on what basis should people be called creative)?' – and the answer to this is of course a matter of opinion. But the question might also ask 'what are the determinants of creative ability or what causes creative inspiration?' – and the answers to these will depend on who one decides to call creative. We address the question of who should be designated as creative in this Prologue, and consider the other versions of the question at some length in the rest of the book.

## Modern conceptions of creativity

The word 'create' derives from the Latin 'creare' which means 'to bring into being'. In modern parlance it has numerous denotations and connotations, and in psychological literature it has been defined in literally hundreds of ways. But although psychological definitions of creativity vary to some extent, a common pattern may be seen running through them. Most suggest something to the effect that creativity involves

> *bringing something into being* that is
> *original* (new, unusual, novel, unexpected) and also
> *valuable* (useful, good, adaptive, appropriate).

This still helps little to explain exactly what creativity means in practical terms however, as the 'something', the 'original' and the 'valuable' to which most definitions refer may be construed in various ways. In psychological literature one is likely to find that the something brought into being by creativity is anything from a toddler's finger painting to Einstein's theory of relativity. 'Original', may refer to something that is merely new to the person concerned – such as a child's solution to a problem he has never been shown how to solve, but it may also refer to something that is new to the world – such as a radical departure from an existing scientific or artistic discipline. 'Valuable' may refer to answers that gain high marks on creativity tests or to inventions that change the quality of human life.

Readers embarking on a psychological study of creativity are therefore likely to find the literature rather bewildering. They are soon likely to realize that 'creativity' means different things to different people – even to different psychologists. Indeed it seems that 'creativity' means different things even to the same person, and that some writers are happy to ignore the distinction between their various conceptions of creativity – leaping blithely to conclusions about one type of creativity on the basis of facts relating to another.

Summing up a collection of articles recently published under the title of *The nature of creativity* (Sternberg, 1988) Tardif and Sternberg concluded: 'Creativity, like food, has many natures' (p. 440). This analogy is rather misleading. 'Creativity', does not refer to a supra-ordinate class of functionally related entities, as 'food' does. It refers to a variety of phenomena that have very little in common besides the words used when referring to them – and any discrepancies in conclusions of studies on creativity should therefore not be surprising.

From the above one can see that differing *concepts* of creativity should be distinguished before various *aspects* of a particular concept are integrated. I have therefore classified various types of people and behaviours commonly described as creative into three major categories.

1. In one category are people who are designated as creative because of their lifestyle, interpersonal functioning and attitudes. They cope well with life: they are imaginative, flexible, unstereotyped and non-authoritarian rather than rigid and conforming. Their behaviour is described as original because it does not adhere to social prescriptions or emulate the behaviours of others. This type of functioning is considered good or valuable in the sense that it involves healthy, adaptive, authentic, spontaneous responses rather than rigid, ritual or defensive reactions to the various demands of daily life.

2. A second category includes people designated as creative because they perform well on creativity tests or other given tasks that are described as creative. The superior performance of such people (in structured or controlled classroom situations) is judged to be creative because the tasks they are given are assumed to require the same mental processes as those underlying the generation of valuable new ideas and cultural products. The term 'original' refers to unusualness or novelty of responses, and responses are regarded as valuable if they are numerous, diverse, appropriate, adaptive, correct, or pleasing to teachers and others who score the performance.

3. In the third category are people who produce something of cultural value. In these terms 'Creative' is 'a medal which we pin on public products, not the name of private processes' (J. P. White, 1968, p. 126). 'Original' retains the meaning of the Latin word 'originalis' signifying 'first', 'beginning' or 'never having been before', suggesting that creative people excel – they go beyond what others have done. 'Valuable' implies that their products enrich the culture or otherwise improve the quality of life.

Although it is often taken for granted that the three types of creativity mentioned in the foregoing tend to occur in the same individuals and vary together, there is little convincing evidence to show this is true. One should therefore not take for granted that whatever applies to people who have an unstereotyped style of life also applies to people who are creative in the classroom, or to people who produce something of cultural value. There are indeed bound to be discrepancies in the findings of research on different categories of creativity – and it is *not* valid to generalize conclusions from one type of creativity to another.

## The focus of this book

There are of course no correct or incorrect answers to the questions of who and what should be called creative. Replies to these questions merely reflect choice or opinion. As I have chosen to focus on the third conception of creativity described in the foregoing, the answer given here to the question of who should be called creative is 'people who have been *recognized by expert opinion as having contributed something of original value to the culture*'. The relevant type of creativity is called 'productive creativity' or 'creative achievement' – some call it genius.

There are three parts to the book. Part I (chapters 1 and 2) provides a perspective. The first chapter presents an historical overview showing how various theoretical conceptions of creativity developed during the twentieth century, and the second discusses the various types of research that have been conducted to explore the nature of creative genius.

Part II (chapters 3 to 8 inclusive) focusses on various aspects of the social origins, life experiences, and personal characteristics that have been shown to be typical of eminent creators. It culminates in the author's theory explaining the determinants of genius and showing links between social origins, life experiences, personal characteristics and productive creativity.

Part III (chapters 9 to 12) focusses on the creative process. These chapters discuss existing theories of the creative process and then offer some new answers to the question of what causes inspiration. They also indicate how life experience and intellectual habits might affect the unconscious basis of creative thinking.

# Part I

## Perspective

# 1

## *Genius and creativity: historical perspective of theory and research*

Today the word 'genius' refers to intellectual excellence and creativity of the highest order – but it brings from the past some mystical connotations. Throughout the ages genius has been attributed to supernatural powers that inspire people with beautiful and excellent ideas – but also drive them out of their minds.

The word 'inspire' literally means 'blow into', conveying the suggestion that creative ideas are breathed into a human agent by some divine force, and for thousands of years this rather romantic mystical view of creative inspiration has been kept alive by creators themselves. Plato (circa 300 BC/1976) explained that inspiration charges poets with beauty and wisdom but leaves them otherwise bereft of their wits,

> in order that we listeners may know that it is not they who utter these precious revelations while their mind is not within them, but that it is god himself who speaks, and through them becomes articulate to us . . . the poets are nothing but interpreters of the gods, each one possessed by the divinity to whom he is in bondage. And to prove this, the deity on purpose sang the liveliest of all lyrics through the most miserable poet. (pp. 32–33)

Speaking of his own experience of inspiration more than two thousand years later, Friedrich Nietzsche (who was generally sceptical of supernatural explanations) confessed

> Provided one has the slightest remnant of superstition left, one can hardly reject completely the idea that one is the mere incarnation, or mouthpiece, or medium of some almighty power. The notion of revelation describes the condition quite simply; by which I mean that something profoundly convulsive and disturbing suddenly becomes visible and audible with indescribable definiteness and exactness. One hears – one does not seek; one takes – one does not ask who gives: a thought flashes out like lightning, inevitably without hesitation – I have never had any choice about it. (1954, p. 210)

Both Plato and Nietzsche eventually suffered mental breakdown. But other philosophers, as well as writers, mathematicians and scientists, who showed little sign of psychopathology, have also reported feeling as though they were affected by supernatural influences during moments of creative inspiration. Until a hundred years ago, it was indeed rather generally accepted that extraordinary qualities of the mind, whether excellent or otherwise deviant, might be attributed to divine intervention. The effects of early experiences and personal characteristics on the development of genius were seldom considered.

Scientific inquiry into the origins and nature of genius was initiated during the latter half of the nineteenth century, when it became recognized that the difference between geniuses and others might be a matter of degree rather than kind, and the origins and dynamics of genius were considered appropriate subjects for theory and research. Major influences on this shift in conceptualization were the works of Sir Francis Galton and Dr Sigmund Freud. In contrast to the ancients, both Galton and Freud accounted for genius in terms of biological energies residing within the individual, rather than external forces. But in other respects their approaches had little in common. Galton focussed on the effects of genetic determinants of *intellectual powers*; and Freud concentrated on the effects of instinctual needs on *emotional experience and imagination*.

## Galton's initiation of theory and research on genius and 'productive creators'

Francis Galton had an extremely wide range of scientific interests and knowledge. He studied colour blindness, mental imagery, and the employment of finger prints for the identification of criminals. He made the first serious attempts to chart the weather on an extensive scale, to establish a theory of anticyclones, and to design psychological tests, and he originated the technique of composite portraiture. But one would perhaps best describe Galton as an anthropologist. Inspired by Darwin's *Origin of species*, he began to use statistical techniques on measures of human attributes and laid the foundations for the study of eugenics (which has to do with improvement of the human species by control of hereditary factors). It was Galton's philosophy that, for their own good, humans should control their own breeding judiciously, as they control the breeding of domestic animals. Mates should be scientifically selected; the unfit should be restricted from breeding, and the productivity of the fit should be increased.

Galton's views on genius allowed for little mystique. He assumed that intellectual activity (whether in men of genius or idiots) depends on biological processes, the efficacy of which are genetically determined. Although he devised various measures of intellectual functioning, he was content to regard outstanding success in a profession or artistic field as a reliable measure of superior genetic potential. It seemed obvious to Galton that the ascent of a person with a high level of natural intellectual potential would not be deterred by social obstacles. Genius 'will out'. But he also believed that a tendency to persevere is a part of the genetic equipment of geniuses, and recognized the importance of some sort of motivating tendency that urges people to use their intellectual ability effectively – so that they reach the top of their fields and stay there. The determining factors that lead geniuses to 'perform acts that lead to reputation', said Galton (1869), are capacity, zeal and the tendency to work hard.

I do not mean capacity without zeal, nor zeal without capacity, nor even a combination of both of them without an adequate power of doing a great deal of very laborious work. But I mean a nature, when left to itself, will, urged by an inherent stimulus, climb to the path that leads to eminence and has strength to reach the summit – one which, if hindered, will fret and strive until the hindrance is overcome, and it is again free to follow its labouring instinct. (1869, p. 33)

It is possible that Galton's interest in eugenics and his tendency to attribute the determinants of genius to genetic factors were influenced not only by the spirit of his times, but also by his personal circumstances. There is no doubt that he was something of a genius himself – and few social obstacles were placed in the way of his own remarkable intellectual development. He came from a notable, rather inbred, family that included many eminent members with highly intellectual interests. Among them was his cousin Charles Darwin who, on reading Galton's *Hereditary genius* reacted enthusiastically, remarking 'I do not think I ever in all my life read anything more interesting and original' (e.g. Simonton, 1984, p. 31).

Galton set out to prove that genius is largely genetically transmitted by demonstrating that people who attain eminence in their professions have a significantly greater proportion of eminent relatives than others do. Among the subjects of his research were judges, politicians, noblemen, generals, admirals, authors, poets, scientists, musicians, painters, divines and athletes, many of whom held prominent positions in society. Through investigating the incidence of eminence in their families, Galton arrived at a set of estimates. The probabilities of various relatives of eminent personalities being eminent themselves were, briefly, as shown in table 1.1.

Table 1.1 Probabilities of eminence in various relatives of eminent creators

| Relative of eminent person | Probability of being eminent |
| --- | --- |
| Grandfather | 1 in 25 |
| Father | 1 in 6 |
| Son | 1 in 4 |
| Brother | 1 in 7 |
| Grandson | 1 in 29 |
| Uncle or nephew | 1 in 40 |
| Cousin | 1 in 100 |
| More remote relatives | 1 in 200 |

There were however certain differences to be seen in the families of eminent men in different fields. For example, eminence in art, music and poetry was rarely found beyond two degrees of kinship in the same family. Scientists differed from others in that fewer scientists had eminent fathers or grandfathers but a greater proportion of distinguished sons. There was a noticeable lack of eminent relatives along the female line of musical families. But in the case of scientists the importance of the female line was apparent.

Uncharacteristically, Galton, who tended to explain the effects of one generation on another in terms of genetic transmission, attributed the influence of the female line on scientists to social transmission of attitudes, explaining it is from his mother that a son learns his basic attitudes toward reality. She may encourage him either to accept dogma without question, or to adopt an attitude of scientific inquiry.

On the whole Galton's findings were apparently convincing, and his conclusions that genius is mainly determined by genetic endowment seem to be supported by the well-known fact that certain families have boasted a number of eminently creative members. Among those who readily spring to mind are Galton's own family and the Huxley family in Victorian England, who were eminently scientific; the Bachs in seventeenth-century Germany, at least twenty of whom are noted in histories of music; and the Bernoulli family in seventeenth- and eighteenth-century Switzerland, of whom eight members were exceptional mathematicians and many more gained some distinction in the field of mathematics.

Several arguments have, however, been raised against Galton's conclusion that genius is determined mainly by genetic transmission of intellectual potentials. For one, the transmission of creative ability from one generation to another within the same family need not be genetic. Family members may influence one another's intellectual development in various ways, and the superior intellectual development of children born into eminently intellectual families may be attributed to factors such as stimulation of interest, transmission of values and knowledge, and access to the necessary materials for exercising intellectual skill. One of Marie Curie's creative modern descendants, Robert Joliot (whose mother, father, grandmother and grandfather were all Nobel Prize winners) testified to the powerful effects of modelling and enthusiasm. He had grown up seeing a laboratory as a place where his parents and other adults were fascinated with what they were doing – 'they seemed to be having fun' he said, 'and I wanted to grow up and have fun too!' (personal communication to Wilson, 1972, p. 137). Adult relatives not only transmit enthusiasm, however, but also knowledge. What is more, eminence may breed eminence in the same family by providing influential social connections, which enable the promise in members of the younger generation to be recognized, nurtured, and used to noticeable effect in high positions.

Replications of Galton's study showed that the pattern of genetic relationships underlying scientific and artistic creativity was far less clear than Galton suggested, and did not clearly support the hypothesis that heredity is the major factor underlying the determination of genius. Only the eminence of judges clustered into clear family configurations (Bramwell, 1948; Simonton, 1984). Furthermore other researchers (e.g. Bullough, Bullough, & Mauro, 1981) found that, although crafts and artistic or scientific skills may be seen in succeeding generations of the same family, creative genius is infrequently found beyond one generation.

Nevertheless, even if Galton failed to consider the power of social influences on the development of genius, the findings of his research should not be ignored. *They give some reason to believe that the basis and promotion of creative intellect might somehow be affected by immediate members of the creator's family.*

## Galton's legacy

Among Galton's contributions to twentieth-century study of genius and creativity is the use of some form of reputation (rather than test scores) as a criterion of genius, and a systematic approach to the investigation of the correlates of creative achievement. His publications stirred interest in the natural bases of creative achievement, which lead at the beginning of the present century to a number of systematic retrospective studies of eminent historical figures. Like Galton, other early researchers into the determinants of eminence were largely concerned with genetic influences but, as time went by, psychological researchers began also to consider the effects of early experiences and personality characteristics.

Of special note are two monumental studies of genius published in 1925 and 1926 at Stanford University – volumes I and II of the five-volume *Genetic studies of genius* initiated by Lewis Terman. The first of these was a tremendously detailed and thorough study of the development of over 1300 intellectually gifted children selected from over a quarter of a million children of the same age in American schools. These subjects were subsequently repeatedly re-assessed, throughout adolescence and adulthood, and the findings cast considerable light on their mental and physical traits in childhood and later as adults (Feldman, 1984; Oden, 1968; Terman & Oden, 1959). Among the facts revealed by these studies are that the index of giftedness or intelligence (IQ as measured by tests) tends to remain fairly stable, but giftedness is *not* necessarily actualized in creative achievement in adulthood. After the study had been going for sixty years, Feldman (1984) compared twenty-six subjects who had an IQ above 180 with twenty-six drawn at random from the original sample, finding that the differences between the two groups were not as marked as one might expect. Feldman's overall impression was that neither group had in fact achieved as much as one might have expected on the basis of their IQs. He concluded that although IQ seems to predict advantages such as high income, marital happiness, health and stability, it does not predict transcendent achievement. Terman had reached a similar conclusion. Although some of the subjects of his study were extremely gifted, by 1947 he expressed the belief that none of them would be found among the most eminent persons in history a hundred years hence. Scores on IQ tests are not sufficient for predicting the adult achievements of the gifted, he said. Achievements in adulthood *must be attributed to non-intellectual factors.*

The second of the Terman studies of genius was a retrospective study under the direction of Catherine Cox (1926). Researchers involved in this study examined vast quantities of biographical materials, to gain systematic information about the early development of 300 famous historical figures who had made extraordinary contributions to their cultures. Descriptions of Cox's methods and findings are discussed in conjunction with those of later studies of 'productive' creators throughout later chapters of this book. But it is interesting to note here in passing that she too concluded that genius must be largely attributed to non-intellectual factors – and particularly to *perseverance.*

## Freud's initiation of theory and research into the psychodynamics of the creative personality

Although Sigmund Freud shared Galton's interest in the biological determinants of genius, he approached the subject from an entirely different point of view. Freud focussed on the influence of instinctual needs and unconscious emotional processes. Whereas Galton sought to discover similarities and differences between various groups of people, Freud examined the development of single creative individuals, such as Leonardo da Vinci (Freud, 1910/1973c) and Dostoevsky (Freud 1928/1973f).

It was Freud's contention that all human motivation is aimed at maximizing gratification of instinctual needs (especially sexual and aggressive needs) while minimizing the possibility of punishment and guilt. When social prescriptions or the realities of a situation do not allow gratification of instinctual needs, said Freud, then energy is diverted from the pursuit of the unattainable or forbidden pleasures into socially approved endeavours. He called this process 'sublimation'. 'Sublimation' means more than devising ways of achieving some satisfaction without too much opposition. It implies that the people concerned seek to release tension created by instinctual needs but do not allow themselves fully to recognize the nature of their own desires, and it was Freud's belief that the progress of civilization may be largely attributed to unconscious sublimation of energy generated by instinctual drives into creative work.

Somewhat paradoxically, although Freud attributed the motivation underlying creativity to the diversion of instinctual energy into work, he suggested the principles involved were similar to those involved in *childhood* play. Children engaging in play re-arrange the realities of their world in their imagination, so as to make circumstances more favourable and pleasing to themselves, allowing them to feel powerful – to be heroes – to be the kings of their 'castles in the air'. Freud explained that, although people cease to play as they grow up, they continue to gain this type of pleasure from fantasizing or daydreaming. Adult fantasies are however more secretive than childhood play. Although children at play may share their fantasies with other children, adults are usually ashamed of their daydreams and keep them hidden from others. The daydreams of adults are motivated by frustrated desires – and are mainly the products of unsatisfied erotic needs and ambitions to gain esteem. Freud pointed out that erotic needs and ambition are, moreover, often united, for in the majority of fantasies relating to ambition 'we can discover in some corner or other the lady for whom the creator of the phantasy performs all his heroic deeds and at whose feet all his triumphs are laid' (1908/1973b, p. 147).

Freudian theory suggests further that wishes arising from unfulfilled needs are often kept secret even from one's own consciousness. If wishful ideas arising from unconscious instincts are unacceptable to one's conscience, they are repressed during waking hours and emerge in dreams. Sometimes, when approved outlets for instinctual energies cannot be found and tensions have built up, conscious thought may regress from realistic logical thinking to a more primitive type of thinking known as 'primary process thinking' even while the person is awake. This is the unrealistic, illogical, fantastic thinking occurring during daydreaming and half-wakened states, where forbidden wishes are disguised by taking on symbolic forms. (Some revolutionary suggestions as to the nature of primary-process thinking and its relation to inspiration will be discussed in chapter 11.)

To Freud, creative writings, like daydreams, are a continuation and a substitute for the imaginative play of childhood. One of the main differences between creative people and others lies in the creators' ability to allow fantasies generated at an unconscious level to break through the repressive barrier into consciousness – but also to keep the fantasies under the control of the logical part of the psyche (the 'ego'). When uncomfortable amounts of emotion have accumulated, creators use such behaviour as an escape valve, allowing generally unacceptable fantasies to be consciously expressed, while keeping them under control and elaborating them into a form that is communicable, meaningful, and acceptable to others as well as themselves.

Freud's interpretations explain not only the motivations underlying creative writing but also the enjoyment of reading. By allowing forbidden wishes into daydreams in a softened and aesthetic form, said Freud, writers may enhance the pleasure of their readers' own daydreams. Disclosure of the writer's personal fantasies helps readers to liberate tensions by enjoying their own daydreams – without self-reproach or shame.

Among the slight ambiguities to be detected in Freud's explanations of the dynamics of creativity are his suggestions relating to creativity and pathology. On the one hand, Freud suggested that creativity is the outcome of sublimation: a healthy adaptive defence against fear of punishment and guilt. On the other he described creative imagination as a flight from reality and a possible path to neurosis – explaining that

an artist is once more in rudiments an introvert, not far removed from neurosis. He is oppressed by excessively powerful instinctual needs. He desires to win honour, power, wealth, fame and the love of women; but he lacks the means for achieving these satisfactions. Consequently, like any other unsatisfied man, he turns away from reality and transfers all his interest, and his libido too, to the wishful constructions of his life of phantasy, whence the path might lead to neurosis. (1917/1973d, p. 376)

Freud's suggestion that creative people are especially able to deliberately express unconsciously generated primary processes and to keep them under control of the rational 'ego' explained why creativity need not necessarily lead to psychopathology. But it did not explain why the creative person's controlled expression of fantasies would acquire any particular value. Freud gave little attention to the intellectual skills necessary for the creation of cultural products, and it is easier to understand why controlled expression of emotional fantasies might take the form of intimate diaries or paperback romances than to see how they result in the creation of significant philosophical writings or scientific theories. Even Freud (1925/1973e) admitted that psychoanalysis 'can do nothing toward elucidating the nature of the artistic gift, nor can it explain the means by which the artist works' (p. 65).

## Freud's legacy

Despite its limitations, Freud's work on creativity had several notable influences on later theoretical approaches to the subject. To this day psychoanalytical case histories of eminent creators continue to make their appearance. The creative process is still described in terms of the eruption of ideas generated at an unconscious level into the conscious mind, where they come under the control of the ego. The correspondence between this concept of the creative process and the ancient concept of 'inspiration' is notable. The difference lies in the fact that the ancients saw inspiration as an invasion of external forces whereas psychoanalysts see it as an invasion of internal (unconscious) forces into the conscious mind.

Freud's views on the role of the unconscious were, however, modified by later theorists of a psychoanalytic persuasion, including Kris (e.g. 1952) and Kubie (e.g. 1958), who shifted the focus from 'unconscious' to 'preconscious' processes. Consequently creative thinking is now often described as a purposeful blend of unconscious and conscious processes at a preconscious level rather than as a defensive reaction arising from unfulfilled unconscious needs. Attempts are made to stimulate creativity through relaxation and daydreaming, using visual imagery rather than verbal thinking (for references, see Suler & Rizziello, 1987).

In the last few decades attention has also been given to the effects of 'altered states' of consciousness on creative thought. This 'psychedelic' approach to creativity is based on the premise that people usually restrict their range of awareness, and never or seldom exploit the most potent dimensions of their minds. To remedy this supposed neglect, various practical techniques, such as transcendental meditation, ingestion of drugs, or sensory deprivation have been used for expanding awareness through altered states of consciousness. (Traditional views relating to the preconscious and unconscious processes in creative thinking are discussed in more detail in chapter 10, and are challenged by some new suggestions in chapter 11.)

Further influence of Freud's work is noticeable in subsequent theories relating to the psychodynamics or motivation underlying creativity. His suggestions concerning instinctual drives stimulated interest in the role played by natural urges in promoting creativity. Whereas Galton had suggested that certain individuals are endowed with intellectual capacities and natural urges that lead them to gain reputation and reach the top of their fields, Freud suggested that all people are endowed with natural emotional urges that may find creative expression.

This particular interpretation of the role of natural urges also began to lose favour in some quarters, however. Whereas Freud focussed on motives underlying the production of cultural works, attention shifted to motives underlying less productive forms of creativity; and, whereas Freud focussed on the influence of sexual needs, interest shifted towards other less primitive needs, such as the need for self-actualization. As explained in the following section, these shifts led to a Humanistic approach to creativity, which is relatively little concerned with creative products or excellence.

## The Humanistic approach to creativity

Around the middle of this century there was a general shift in psychological interest – from the maladapted or merely normal aspects of human functioning to positive aspects of mental health. Much of this shift may be attributed to the emergence of what has come to be known as the 'third force' in psychology or the 'Humanistic approach'. The new trend was a reaction on the one hand to the deterministic psychoanalytic approach, which had focussed largely on maladapted behaviour arising from conflict between instinctual needs and internalized social prescriptions. On the other hand there was a reaction to the previously popular 'behaviouristic' approach which had concentrated on isolated elemental behaviours (of people and animals), explaining them in terms of environmental stimuli. According to the new school of Humanistic psychologists, such deterministic, narrowly focussed and mechanistic explanations of behaviour deprive people of their human qualities.

The Humanistic approach to personality was partly influenced by the views of existentialists, who held that people are part of their own environment but are free to choose what to make of themselves and their world. To the existentialists and the Humanists, each person should be viewed as a unique whole, and never static. One is always in the process of 'becoming' – of transforming oneself and one's world. The Humanists moreover subscribed to Jean-Jacques Rousseau's (e.g. 1762/1957) view of man as essentially good, though often corrupted by social institutions. And they suggested that one will naturally actualize all one's true (good) potentials, develop an unstereotyped personality, and live an 'authentic' life if one reacts spontaneously to immediate perceptions and does not follow the dictates of society.

Among those whose works led to a Humanistic view of creativity were Alfred Adler (e.g. 1935) and Otto Rank (e.g. 1932/1960). Both were originally disciples of Freud, but they rejected Freud's suggestion that creativity resulted from the sublimation of a sexual drive, and suggested instead that it was the successful expression of a positive drive to improve the self and gain mental health.

### Adler's views of the creative self

Although Alfred Adler's works were published several decades before the emergence of the Humanistic school, Maslow regarded him as a member of the third force in psychology (Ansbacher, 1971). Adler's theory of personality centres upon his concept of a 'creative self' that affects one's style of life, one's goals and the way in which one reaches those goals. Throughout one's life, said Adler, the creative self guides one's interactions with the environment and people, attempting to compensate for one's real or imagined inferiorities that usually stem from physical weaknesses or one's position and role in the family.

According to Adler, many great artists and philosophers developed their skills to compensate for physical or intellectual disability. For example, scientific creativity may be engendered by a need to overcome feelings of imperfection or ignorance through gaining superior knowledge. Eminent creators may also be motivated by an unconscious fear of death that inspires people to compensate for their feelings of impending extinction by producing something of lasting value to survive them.

The way in which people compensate for real or imagined inferiorities, said Adler, is largely determined by the family atmosphere. Coping through creativity is characteristic of what he called an 'active constructive' style of life – the style of people who are ambitious but eager to serve the human race and largely concerned with the welfare of others. According to Adler, the choice of such a lifestyle is engendered by a family atmosphere of co-operation, mutual trust, respect and understanding.

Although Adler's remarks about scientists and philosophers refer to productive creativity, it is notable that he failed to draw a clear distinction between motives underlying their ambition to overcome ignorance and achieve immortality and motives underlying a desire to serve the human race through care and cooperation. Adler apparently assumed that all the behaviours he labelled 'creative' are directed by social concerns and subserve the major goal of overcoming personal inadequacies by bringing the personality to healthy completion. His theory of the creative self consequently implies that creative achievers are naturally *altruistic, public spirited and mentally healthy.*

### Rank's and Fromm's notions of balance between belonging and independence

As MacKinnon (1965) pointed out, Rank sometimes referred to the development of a creative personality in terms of three stages of development and sometimes in terms of three types of person – the normal or average man, the neurotic or conflicted man, and the 'artist' or man of will and deed – each of whom typify the characteristics of a particular developmental stage.

It was Rank's opinion that, as people move through life, from the trauma of birth to the trauma of death, they have to contend with two opposing fears: the fear of life and the fear of death. The fear of life is a fear of separation, which is first and most traumatically experienced when the child leaves the comfort and security of the mother's womb. Throughout life it is experienced as a fear of differentiating oneself from others: a fear of standing alone, of being autonomous and independent. This fear gives rise to a desire to regress to earlier, more dependent stages of life and to depend on others more powerful than oneself.

In opposition to the fear of life, said Rank, is the fear of death, which is experienced throughout life as a fear of becoming enmeshed with others: a fear of renouncing one's freedom and individuality; of being controlled by others and becoming dependent upon them. This fear gives rise to a need for self-assertion, a tendency to separate and free oneself from others and a desire to develop one's individuality.

Rank (1945) called a person who is dominated by fear of life the *adapted* man – explaining that such people continually seek the security of belonging and unity with others. They tend to be dependent, and to conform. In contrast is what Rank called *the neurotic*, explaining that such people are dominated by fear of death, and continually trying to separate themselves from others, although they feel guilty for doing so, as children feel when exercising their own wills against their parents.

Rank's conception of the ideal personality is what he calls *the artist*. In people of this calibre the fear of life and the fear of death are balanced. They acquire discipline from others while preserving their own individuality. Although he called such a person 'the artist' Rank made it clear that the person need not however be involved in any artistic enterprise. To Rank, the development of artistic ability and a healthy personality have similar foundations. 'Creativity' lies at the root of both artistic production and life experience.

From the foregoing it is clear that, like Adler, Rank believed both creative achievement and a healthy personality to be the outcome of transcending difficulties or conflicts and adopting a healthy style of life. Further suggestions in this vein came from Fromm (1955), who proposed that the 'productive' or 'creative' person is one whose interactions with others are characterized by closeness as well as independence. To Fromm there are three types of interpersonal interaction. First there is *symbiotic relatedness*, which results in dependence and the 'swallowing up' of one person by another. A symbiotic relationship between a child and its parents may lead the child to an exploitive type of interpersonal functioning. The second type of interaction is *withdrawal-destructiveness*, which results in indifference or withdrawal, and this type of relationship between parent and child may lead a child to become distant and indifferent to others, or to adopt a more active form of withdrawal by being destructive. The third type of relationship is *love*. This type of interaction between parents and child offers both respect for personal freedom and support, said Fromm. It gives children no reason for not loving themselves and others. Loving interaction moreover promotes a tendency to transcend one's animal nature and to create purposeful goals, from whence arise reason, art and material production.

## Maslow's concept of creativity as self-actualization

Although he was not the first theorist to advocate a Humanistic psychology, Maslow is usually cited as the leader of the third force, and his theory is regarded as one of the most representative of the Humanistic school of thought.

Maslow's theory focusses largely on the 'need for self-actualization' in the development of a healthy personality. The term 'self-actualization, which was coined by Goldstein (e.g. 1939), refers to a drive to develop one's full potential. Goldstein saw it as a drive to overcome obstacles in a spirit of joy of conquest rather than anxiety. Before Maslow, Adler, Rank, Murray and others had already aligned such a motive to mental health and creativity: but it was Maslow who firmly established the use of the term in psychology and gave self-actualization the central role in the development of a healthy personality.

To Maslow, the need for self-actualization became expressed when lower needs, such as physiological needs, the need for security, social needs, and the need for esteem had been regularly satisfied. The personality is then no longer dominated by motives arising from deficits in these domains. Maslow explained that a person who lacks food, security or love is not likely to develop the more lofty desires for beauty or the need to express oneself and to create, which are contained in the need for self-actualization.

Maslow (e.g. 1968) described self-actualization as 'the process of becoming everything one is able to become' – an expression bound to elicit some argument, for the very idea of aspiring to become everything one is able to be seems not only unrealistic, but also perhaps unwise. The absurdity of such an ambition was amusingly illustrated by William James (1890) many years before the Humanists began to stress the importance of striving to actualize all one's potentials.

I am often confronted by the necessity of standing by one of my empirical selves and relinquishing the rest. Not that I would not, if I could, be both handsome and fat and well dressed, and a great athlete, and make a million a year, be a wit, a bon vivant, and a lady-killer, as well as a philosopher; a philanthropist, statesman, warrior and African explorer, as well as a 'tone poet' and saint. But the thing is simply impossible. The millionaire's work would run counter to the saint's; the bon vivant and the philanthropist would trip each other up; the philosopher and the lady killer could not well keep house in the same tenement of clay. Such different characters may well conceivably at the outset of life be *possible* to a man. But to make any one of them actual the rest must more or less be suppressed. (vol. 1, pp. 309–310; italics in the original)

However, it seems that, when speaking of everything one is able to become, Maslow was less concerned with the development of professional skills than with the ability to adapt to change. In referring to the challenges of the future, he pointed out that professional skills become obsolete, and that society needs a new kind of person: a person who enjoys change: a person who is able to improvise with confidence and courage in unexpected situations.

The Humanistic conceptions of the relation between mental health and creativity seems to have brought us a considerable distance from the ancient view of the relation between genius and madness. But Maslow (1967) seems to have recognized the ancient view, admitting that when formulating his theory of creativity he had to give up the idea that creativity, genius, talent and productivity were synonymous. He found himself forced to distinguish between two kinds of creativity, which he called 'primary' and 'secondary'. *Secondary creativity* corresponds to *productive creativity* or *creative achievement*. It involves the creation of outstanding artistic or scientific products, and to Maslow, this was secondary because it involves logical thought (secondary-process thinking). Secondary creativity should not be seen in the same light as inspiration, said Maslow, because it relies on 'plain hard work', discipline, and skill; and rests as much on stubbornness and patience as on the 'creativeness of the personality' (1967, p. 45).

Maslow's reluctance to acknowledge the value of secondary creativity, especially if it involved effort or occurred in someone with less-than-ideal personality characteristics, made him rather disparaging of any form of productive creativity. He lightly dismissed genius – as being unfathomable, and 'more or less independent of goodness or health of character' (p. 87). Although the sample of people he selected for his study of self-actualizing personalities included eminent productive creators such as Einstein (Maslow, 1954), he suggested that 'Nobel Prize winners, great inventors, and so on' are unsuitable examples of creative people,

The trouble is, if you know a lot of scientists, that you soon learn that something is wrong with this criterion because scientists as a group are not nearly as creative generally as you would expect. This includes people who have discovered, who have created actually, who have published things which were advances in human knowledge. Actually, this is not too difficult to understand. This finding tells us something about the nature of science rather than the nature of creativeness. If I wanted to be mischievous about it, I could go so far as to define science as a technique whereby noncreative people can create. (1967, 45–46)

Continuing in this vein Maslow explained that if scientists were unable to stand on the shoulders of their predecessors, they would be unable to achieve what they do, whereas spontaneously inspired creativity is independent of the influence of previous works. But although he apparently favoured artistic above scientific creativity, it is clear that Maslow also refused to see the production of culturally valuable art works as an important form of creativity. Their creation has also mainly to do with secondary creativity. To Maslow the source of inspiration and originality is primary creativity, which stems from the unconscious and has little to do with finished works of art. Unlike secondary creativity, said Maslow, primary creativity is inherent in all individuals, as is the tendency toward self-actualization.

Like Freud, Maslow compared creative behaviour to the play of children, commenting that primary creativity is 'in many respects like the creativeness of *all* happy and secure children . . . spontaneous, effortless, innocent, easy, a kind of "innocent" freedom of perception and "innocent" uninhibited spontaneity and expressiveness' (1976, p. 88; italics in original).

However, whereas Freud had regarded creative behaviour (and play) as a retreat from the frustrations arising out of reality and social prescriptions, Maslow assumed creativity, like play, to be a carefree unfettered expression of natural tendencies. To Maslow such tendencies are inherent in everyone, but are counteracted and blocked by socialization, education and the acquisition of skills. In males they may also be blocked by a tendency to regard imagination, fantasy, and artistic pursuits as feminine, and therefore not worthy of interest.

In Maslow's view, the term 'creative' would best be applied to those people who 'can see the fresh, the raw, the concrete, the idiographic, as well as the generic, the abstract, the rubricized, the categorized and the classified . . . [people who are] more "natural" and less controlled and uninhibited in their behavior, which seemed to flow out more easily and freely with less blocking and self-criticism' (Maslow, 1976, p. 88). The behaviour of such people is expressive and spontaneous. It is based on 'lack of willful trying, a lack of effortful striving or straining, a lack of interference with the flow of the impulse and the free "radioactive" expression of the deep person' (p. 54). Maslow confessed that it had indeed dawned on him that primary creativity and self-actualization were indeed much the same thing.

As to be expected, Maslow has been criticized for placing higher value on unproductive, uncontrolled 'creative' behaviour than on contributions to the culture. But it is at least in his favour that he attempted to draw a distinction between productive (secondary) creativity and his concept of self-actualizing (primary) creativity. He clearly pointed out that he wittingly used the term 'creativity' in more than one way. Nevertheless it is probable that he promoted the currently popular tendency to believe these two types of creativity vary together – a belief that is unambiguously reflected in the stated goals and design of creativity training programmes, which aim to foster productive creativity by encouraging the uninhibited expression of imaginative fantastic ideas during group training sessions.

Before leaving Maslow's views on creativity, it is interesting to note a rather strange twist in the last of his publications. A few days before he died, Maslow returned the corrected proof of a paper (Maslow, 1972) which begins with an expression of regret that despite the accumulations of methods, testing techniques and a vast quantity of information, the theory of creativity had not much advanced. He then expressed an intention to further advance theory, by integrating rather than choosing between various ideas that had already been put forward. Nevertheless, it is clear that his commitment to the idea that creativity is a manifestation of mental health had remained unshakable:

As I read the literature, it seems terribly impressive that the relationship [between creativity and] psychiatric health or psychological health is so crucial, so profound, so terribly important, and so obvious, and yet it is not used as a foundation on which to build theory. (p. 287)

This is much in line with his previous writings. His very last words on the subject are, however, rather surprising and particularly notable:

Some student tells me, 'No I don't want to do that because I don't enjoy it', and then I get purple in the face and fly up in a rage – 'Damn it, you do it, or I'll fire you' – and he feels I am betraying my own principles. In making a more measured and balanced picture of creativeness, we workers with creativity have to be responsible for the impressions we make upon other people. Apparently one impression we are making on them is that creativeness consists of lightning striking you on the head in one great glorious moment. The fact that the *people who create are good workers* tends to be lost. (p. 293, my emphasis)

There is little doubt that the Humanistic school's loss of the fact that people who create are good workers was largely due to Maslow's own description of the creative process – as effortless and easy, like the creativeness of all happy secure children. Only at the end of his life did he acknowledge what he had previously regarded as 'secondary' and unnecessary to inspiration – *plain hard work.*

### Rogers's conceptions of the development of a creative person

Although Rogers was in agreement with Maslow that creativity is the outcome of a fully functioning personality, he contended that for him, as a scientist,

there must be something observable, some product of creation. Though my fantasies may be extremely novel, they cannot be usefully defined as creative unless they eventuate in some observable product – unless they are symbolized in words, or written in a poem, or translated into a work of art, or fashioned into an invention. These products must be novel constructions . . . Creativity has the stamp of the individual upon its product, but *the product is not the individual*, nor his materials, but partakes of the relationship between the two. (1954/1976, pp. 296–297; my emphasis)

Here Rogers seems to be advocating the return to a 'productive' concept of creativity, and it is therefore somewhat surprising to find him proclaiming that

there is no fundamental difference in the creative process as it is evidenced in painting a picture, composing a symphony, devising new instruments of killing, developing a scientific theory, discovering new procedures in human relationships, or *creating new formings of one's own personality in psychotherapy.* (1954/1976, p. 297; my emphasis)

From this it appears that, unlike Maslow, who clearly distinguished between productive creativity and self-actualizing creativity, Rogers made a direct attempt to accommodate various conceptions of creativity under a single set of principles. The inclusiveness of his concept of creativity is clearly apparent in his remark to the effect that

the action of the child inventing a new game with his playmates; Einstein formulating a theory of relativity; a housewife devising a new sauce for the meat; a young author writing his first novel; all of these are, in terms of our definition, creative, and there is no attempt to set them in some order of more or less creative. (1954/1976, pp. 297–298)

Central to Rogers's theory of the development of a creative person is the notion that if 'conditions of worth' are placed upon growing children, the children will incorporate their parents' values into their own self-concepts. If parents make children feel unworthy for not complying with their wishes, then the children will see themselves as unworthy for not complying. Consequently children might not only behave in accordance with what parents expect, but will become defensive. They would value their own experience according to the conditions of worth placed upon them, rather than according to whether the experience 'enhances or fails to enhance [their] own organism' said Rogers (1959, p. 209). They will be inclined to deny or distort those aspects of their experience that are considered unworthy (by others and themselves). Thus conditions of worth lead to the development of a self-concept that does not faithfully correspond with a child's natural proclivities, and block the child's self-actualization.

Accordingly, Rogers (1959) maintained that the development of a healthy, self-actualizing personality depends on *lack of conditions of worth*. Children who have been led to realize that they are worthy even though their behaviour might be unacceptable, develop an open healthy attitude, he explained. They are self-accepting. As they have unconditional positive self-regard, there is no need for them to deny or distort any experience to defend their self-esteem, and they are therefore able to remain fully open to experience.

To Rogers, creativity is most likely to find expression in people who are fully open to experience – people who do not deny or repress anything they feel. This leaves them free to actualize their potential. Education might have an adverse effect on creativity, as the most dangerous enemies of the development of creativity are *exposure to evaluation and the setting of standards*. These of course imply conditions of worth, and it was therefore especially important to Rogers that such barriers to creativity be removed from educational programmes because 'for the individual to find himself in an atmosphere where he is not being evaluated, not being measured by some external standard, is enormously freeing. Evaluation is always a threat, always creates a need for defensiveness' (1954/1976, p. 303).

## The legacy of Humanistic psychology

Coupled with discussions of Freud's views on the psychodynamics of genius, descriptions of Humanistic views of creativity are likely to be somewhat confusing. Whereas Freud had depicted genius as a slightly pathological retreat from reality, the Humanists celebrated creativity as an unrestricted expression of mental health. Both Freud and the Humanists accused society of restricting the conscious expression of natural impulses. But to Freud *it was this very restriction that forced people to divert their energies into creativity* (whether or not they paid the price of neurosis). Like Freud, the Humanists recognized that frustration of natural impulses might lead to psychopathology. But their commitment to a positive view of human nature would not allow them to believe that any good could possibly come from restricting natural impulses. Certainly nothing as valued as creativity could be associated with unnatural controls.

Among the most well received of the Humanists' contributions to the field of creativity was this tendency to view creativity as a type of healthy personality functioning. It suggested that everyone is inclined and able to be creative. Creativity is a natural and universal tendency, awaiting only the appropriate conditions to be released and find expression. The suggestion that creativity is manifest as a spontaneous unstereotyped personality offered a welcome alternative to eminence as a criterion of creativity. Children, as yet unwarped by social controls, more spontaneous, more imaginative and more open to their own impulses than adults, were held up as examples of true creativity. Everyone, including the toddler was considered a suitable subject for creativity research – and this allowed for an extremely wide range of studies.

The tendency to view creativity as healthy personality-functioning also influenced the development of techniques for enhancing creative expression through preventing defensiveness. Laymen, teachers and psychologists, including Gowan (1972), Renzulli (e.g. 1979), Rogers (1954/1976, 1959), Sarnoff and Cole (1983), I. A. Taylor (1959/1972), Torrance (e.g. 1979), Treffinger, Isaksen and Firestien (e.g. 1982) expressed the belief that positively valued factors such as love, trust, unconditional acceptance, lack of judgment and/or freedom of expression in childhood are common to the development of both a healthy personality and productive creativity. In accordance with this belief, creativity programmes, particularly those that followed the examples developed by Gordon (e.g. 1961), aimed to develop psychological health. Trainees were taught to be non-evaluative, so as to reduce defensiveness (which would block creativity). They were encouraged to express themselves freely, in any way or in any type of language they chose. A specific rule in 'brainstorming' techniques (developed by Osborn, e.g. 1953) banned criticism, in the hope that this would encourage a free, easy-going atmosphere and allow the spontaneous expression of creative ideas. The stated aim of these programmes was, however, *not* merely to enhance personality functioning, but also to promote socially valuable creative production – and it is clear that the authors of the programmes assumed that healthy personal functioning and productive creativity vary together.

Although the Humanistic approach to creativity engendered a great deal of enthusiasm, it did not however escape criticism. Not all agree that children can be creative. Maddi (1965) sharply attacked the Humanistic view of creativity, referring to it as a set of 'old wives tales', the first of which is the tale that a person is unlikely to be creative when the environment is structured or evaluative. Rokeach (1965) and J. P. White (1968) asserted that creativity is not merely discovering something new, but also changing existing ideas and producing something valued by the culture. R. B. Cattell (1971) spoke out very strongly on the subject, suggesting that Maslow's theorizing had 'led to the picture of the creative person as an incontinent, unrestrained, over-self-expressive individual . . . one scarcely can escape the impression that, without some daily assault upon convention, such a person feels futile' (p. 410). Nicholls (1972b) pointed out that one might find a way to dignify all people without bestowing on them the virtue of creativity.

Albert declared that things had come to such a pass that

Nowadays when one thinks of such behavioral attributes as creative, novel, or original, the main emphasis is upon the personality and behavior of moderately intelligent contemporary persons, especially students and young children who, along with their accessibility, bring with them 'psychological' health. This may be, in part a reaction to earlier research on the extreme or clinical case, and is seen as part of the effort to develop a psychology of the 'normal'. While there is much to be said for such a strategy the study of intelligence and creativity may have suffered. (1969, pp. 743–744)

It is important to realize, however, that these criticisms were based mainly on the fact that the Humanists and their critics tended to use the term 'creative' to mean different things. The attacks might therefore be parried by pointing out that the term may be used in various ways (as long as one makes it clear what one means by it, and does not expect one type of creativity to be enhanced by promoting another). A more cogent criticism of the Humanistic approach is that *the Humanists tended to generalize from one concept of creativity to another without providing convincing evidence to show that they are indeed positively related.*

Moreover, despite their interest in the development of a 'creative personality', theorists of the Humanistic school of psychology did even less than Freud did to explain how the intellectual aspects of creative ability developed. Freud at least implied that creative people might develop skill because they tend to divert their instinctual energies into culturally valued work (instead of expending them on sexual and aggressive behaviours). But the Humanistic view of creativity offered no explanations for superior actualization of intellectual potential (or as Galton would have it actualization of superior potential).

## The 'intellectual process' approach to creativity

During the first part of this century psychologists who were concerned with intellectual functions began to examine aspects of creativity that Galton and Freud (and subsequently the Humanists) had neglected to consider. They set out to gain insights into the nature of the intellectual processes involved in creative thinking.

Followers of this 'intellectual process' approach construed creativity in terms of problem solving. They assumed that problem solving requires specific intellectual processes, and set out to show what these are. Originally researchers who followed this approach to creativity drew on information supplied by eminent creators who had examined and analysed their own thinking. For example, findings relating to the various stages in the creative process were based on self-reports of eminent mathematicians, inventors and scientists. These self-reports referred of course to the solution of problems that had taken exceptional people days or months to solve. But it was not feasible to use exceptional creators as subjects for all investigations of the creative process. Outstanding creative achievements do not occur to short order under the watchful eyes of researchers. Therefore subsequent work on stages and specific processes involved in problem solving had to be based on observations of unexceptional people (or even animals) working on simple practical problems in a classroom or laboratory.

In an attempt to construct a conceptual framework of intelligence, Guilford (e.g. 1967) arrived at the conclusion that it consisted of 120 minimally related intellectual abilities or *factors*. Some of these, which Guilford believed to be essential to creative problem solving, are collectively known as *divergent thinking*.

Other psychologists concerned with the intellectual aspects of creativity construed creative problem-solving in terms of specific mental processes rather than intellectual factors, and many focussed on the process of association. Over the ages, philosophers such as Plato, Aristotle, Francis Bacon, Hobbes, Locke, Hume and John Stuart Mill had suggested that learning and thinking involve forming new associations between items of existing knowledge. Twentieth-century psychologists came to describe creative thinking as a matter of forming 'remote' associations between concepts in different domains – which implies that creativity involves forming associations between concepts that have hitherto not been connected, although they do have something in common. Some theorists have concentrated on analogical or meta-phorical thinking, which may be regarded as a specific form of remote association.

Adopting a somewhat different approach, Max Wertheimer (1945), who was an intimate friend of Einstein and a principle exponent of the Gestalt school of psychology, argued that creative problem solving cannot be fully explained in terms of the traditional views of logic and association developed by philosophers. Problem solving, said Wertheimer, demanded not simply a *combination* but also a *reorganization* of existing knowledge or perceptual 'gestalts'.

The main thesis of Gestalt theory (originally formulated by von Ehrenfels) is that people have a natural inclination to organize perceptions into 'gestalts' or wholes, and tend to find meaning in what they perceive. The *relations* between the associated parts of a whole set of stimuli are particularly important, for these endow the whole with more meaning than the sum of its parts. Most of us are, for example, able to recognize that a tune whistled by a lad in the street is similar to what we have heard played by an orchestra, although none of the particular sounds emitted by the whistler and orchestra is identical. In each case, however, a similar set of *relations* obtains between the various sounds.

Gestalt theory suggests that one tends particularly to organize one's perceptions into 'good' gestalts – to perceive sets of stimuli as wholes in which there is *harmony, closure or symmetry* among the parts. For example, one tends to see figure 1.1 (a) as a circle: as more than twenty-four dots.

One usually sees figure 1.1 (b) as an overlapping circle and square, rather than a combination of figures 1.1 (c) and 1.1 (d) or a combination of 1.1 (e) and 1.1 (f) – because a circle and a square form better, more complete, gestalts than (c) and (d) or (e), and (f) do. And one usually sees figure 1.1 (g) as a set of horizontal lines rather than a set of vertical lines, because there is more *closure* in the horizontal plane.

Wertheimer described a problem as an *incomplete structure or bad gestalt*, which causes intellectual tensions. Such tensions, he said, drive one to find a solution to the problem that brings a sense of harmony between the parts and the whole structure, so that the whole has symmetry and elegance, and the parts have necessity. In essence, Wertheimer's notion of the creative process – as the destruction of an existing gestalt in the service of building a better one – may be expressed as the reorganization or integration of existing items of knowledge and ideas into a new, internally consistent

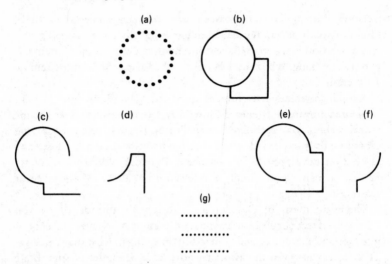

Figure 1.1 *Examples of sets of stimuli perceived as wholes in which there is harmony, closure or symmetry*

form. This is an important concept that can be linked not only to various explanations of the creative process, but also to theories of the general development of intellect and skill. As Gruber (e.g. 1974) and Feldman (e.g. 1988) have explained, one should recognize that creative insight involves *reorganization and transformation*, rather than merely *accumulation* and *combination* of knowledge. These authors contend, moreover, that such qualitative shifts are also characteristic of normal cognitive development.

Early researchers following the Gestalt tradition (e.g. Duncker, 1945; Maier, 1931) focussed on exploring universal tendencies and conducted their research by observing ordinary people (and animals) solving problems in structured situations. If a problem could not be solved by simply applying a familiar strategy it was called a 'productive' or 'creative' problem, as distinct from a 'reproductive' or 'routine' problem. When solving a 'creative problem', subjects might, for example, have to use a common household object for a purpose other than that for which the object was normally intended.

Various 'intellectual process' approaches to creativity are discussed in further detail in chapter 9.

## The legacy of the intellectual-process approach to creativity

The intellectual-process approach to the study of creativity promoted the idea that all people are able to engage in the processes involved in creative thinking. Unless one accepts supernatural explanations of inspiration, or believes that the principles governing the thinking of ordinary people do not also apply to the thinking of geniuses, then one must agree. The thought processes of creative achievers must be governed by universal laws. Indeed facts relating to genius must be explained in terms of universal principles.

Unfortunately, however, followers of the 'process' approach to the study of creativity accepted not only that all people can engage in the processes involved in creative thinking, but also the implications that:

1.  the creative process is more important than the product;
2.  the creative process and capacity to create may be successfully investigated through research on ordinary people or children;
3.  engaging in processes that are called 'creative' necessarily leads to creative production.

These notions have offered researchers a great deal of leeway in describing, operationally defining and measuring creativity, allowing them to conduct 'creative' research on ordinary accessible subjects (like psychology students). Consequently the body of literature on creativity has become enormously swollen with findings of laboratory and classroom studies of behaviours labelled as 'creative'. Correlates of performance on an amazing variety of tests and tasks requiring imagination and artistic effort have been held up as determinants of creativity. Training programmes inspired by the findings have offered unexceptional individuals an opportunity to become creative through engaging in appropriate mental exercises.

Unfortunately, findings and theory derived from laboratory studies of ordinary people are always insufficient and sometimes irrelevant when it comes to investigating the determinants of productive creativity. It may well be true that all people are able to engage in the mental processes underlying creative thinking, but it is certainly not true that all people create something of cultural value by engaging in these processes. There is, moreover, little evidence to support the belief that people who perform well in the laboratory also create something of value in real life.

It therefore seems unlikely that determinants of creative achievement will be discovered by examining facts relating to people who perform well on set tasks. There is, moreover, little reason for believing that environmental or social situations will have an equivalent effect on classroom performance and creative achievements. To understand how and why some people are able to produce something of cultural value, one must look beyond situational variables and discover what determines the development of relevant individual differences.

Although the literature on creativity is apparently still dominated by discussions of research in which test scores or classroom performance are used as criteria of creativity, several related issues have been raised in educational circles: one is the issue of identifying individuals as 'creative' regardless of whether they have created anything; another is the question of fostering 'creativity' as distinct from fostering actual creation (Winchester, 1985). Theorists and educators seem to be increasingly aware that promoting creative activities in the classroom may not be an adequate educational goal. As Bailin (1984, 1985) pointed out, those who advocate the promotion of creativity would not really be satisfied if we somehow succeeded in producing a generation of individuals who possessed a capacity to create but who never actually created anything of cultural value. Creativity is not worthwhile in itself if nothing is ever produced.

## Decline and revival of the interest in giftedness and genius

During the period 1927–1950 relatively little research was conducted on the determinants of genius or intellectual excellence. Oden (1968) pointed to several factors that may account for this neglect. For one there was still some residual belief that genius is too exceptional or too pathological to be explained in terms of laws governing normal behaviour. But perhaps more restrictive were the popular democratic sentiments that inhibited researchers from considering individual differences, particularly differences in intellectual endowment.

Despite the lack of interest in exceptional creators, interest in the creativity of *unexceptional* individuals was boosted by a frequently cited critical event. In Guilford's inaugural address as president of the American Psychological Association in 1950, he drew attention to the importance of recognizing creativity as a distinguishable set of mental abilities, and expressed his regret that (at that time) less than 2 per cent of the psychological literature had to do with creativity. Thereafter, from 1950 to 1965, the earlier interest in genius, eminence and intellectual excellence gave way even further. But there was a seven-fold increase in the proportion of studies on creativity (in unexceptional people) (Albert, 1969). As mentioned in foregoing sections, creativity was described in terms of various types of personality functioning and intellectual processes. Personality traits and test scores became the usually accepted criteria of creativity – and everyone became a potential subject for research.

Whereas Guilford lamented the paucity of work on creativity in 1950, it didn't take long for some to lament the excesses. In 1959 Irving Taylor commented that interest in creativity had become so widespread that a large body of unintegrated theoretic and research material was accumulating (I. A. Taylor, 1959/1972). In addition, interest in superior intellectual ability began to revive. Although democratic sentiments had temporarily forced the notion of giftedness from social consciousness, it had been recognized for thousands of years that gifted children are among a nation's most precious resources, and in 1962 Arnold Toynbee attacked the democratic sentiments that were inhibiting psychologists from considering native differences in intellectual endowment, asserting that

there is at least one current notion about democracy that is wrong-headed to the point of being disastrously perverse. This perverse notion is that to have been born with an exceptionally large endowment of innate ability is tantamount to having committed a large prenatal offense against society. It is looked upon as being an offense because, according to this view of democracy, inequalities of any and every kind are undemocratic. (Toynbee, 1964, p. 5)

An urgent revival of the concern for identification and promotion of the gifted was boosted by the launching of Russia's first artificial satellite 'Sputnik' which, in at least some respects, had a similar effect in scientific circles to that of the atom bomb. Along with the awareness that intellectual superiority was likely to be a deciding factor in the race for world domination and the conquest of outer space came the realization that our quality of life, perhaps our very survival as a species, depends on promoting creativity.

After Sputnik, Soviet scientists wanting a particular piece of equipment had only to say that they needed it to catch up with the Americans to have it supplied, and American scientists found their appeals were met if they warned that their Soviet colleagues were moving ahead. At international conventions playful toasts were offered by the Soviet scientists 'to our American colleagues, for their help in getting us our new proton accelerator!' and by Americans 'to our Soviet friends! without whose aid we could never have talked congress into giving us our new high-flux neutron generator!' (Wilson, 1972, p. 52).

Toynbee (1964) warned that 'to give a fair chance to potential creativity is a matter of life and death for any society. This is all-important, because the outstanding creativity of a fairly small percentage of the population is mankind's ultimate capital asset' (p. 4).

In accordance, gifted children began receiving more systematic attention than ever before. Selection procedures were developed for identifying the gifted, and programmes were designed for satisfying their
intellectual needs, in the hope that their potential might thereby be
actualized and find expression in contributions to the culture. Attention
was drawn to the fact that intellectual ability was not enough – true
giftedness also involved creative ability. Hopes for the future were
invested particularly in actualizing the creative potentials of gifted
children in the faith that from their ranks would come the geniuses or
productive creators of tomorrow.

De Haan and Havighurst (1961) offered the following idealistic
description of the gifted child:

We shall consider any child as 'gifted' who is superior in some ability that can
make him an *outstanding contributor to the welfare of, and quality of living in society.*
(p. 15; my emphasis)

The oft-quoted definition of giftedness by the United States Office
of Education stated that:

Gifted and talented children are those identified by professionally qualified
persons who, by virtue of their outstanding abilities [*sic*], are capable of high
performance. These are children who *require differentiated educational programs in
order to realize their contribution to self and society.* (emphasis mine)

In addition to its syntactical shortcomings, this definition also falls
somewhat short in other respects. Indeed both this and the definition
offered by De Haan and Havighurst, cited above, make predictions
about the possible future achievements of gifted children rather than
defining the nature of their currently observable assets. These definitions
suggest that if (and perhaps *only if*) given the proper opportunity, gifted
children will become the creative adults whose works will enrich society.

There is, however, as yet no real evidence to show that gifted children
who are given special education are likely to 'realize their contribution
to self and society' as suggested in the definition of giftedness provided
by the United States Office of Education. Indeed (as Howe, 1982,
pointed out) we are in no position to judge with any certainty if special
educational programmes, childrearing practices – or even giftedness in
childhood – are sufficient to explain outstanding creative achievement
in adulthood. Although we are able to predict and enhance academic
achievement or success in intelligence and creativity tests, this does not
also predict the kind of performance that endows the culture with
something of original and lasting value. Terman's studies gave good

reason to believe that 'giftedness' and 'genius' should not be regarded as synonymous. Nevertheless it is still taken for granted that gifted children and adult creative achievers represent two layers of the same population. According to N. E. Jackson and Butterfield (1986), most twentieth-century conceptions of giftedness share three related assumptions:

First, to be gifted is to create excellent socially valued products. Second, because children are unlikely to produce creative work that meets absolute standards of excellence and social performance, childhood giftedness is the potential for adult productivity. Third, even though a child's potential for adult productivity cannot be measured well, it is assumed that adult giftedness can be predicted with some accuracy from childhood performance. (p. 151)

As these authors remark, any definition of childhood giftedness that is based on potential for adult productivity is, however, inherently problematic, not only because IQ may not remain stable but also because adult achievements are based on far more than what IQ tests measure. For gifted children to develop into creative achievers, their gifts must become transformed into skills and drives that enable them to produce something of value.

## Conclusion

In this chapter we have taken a brief look at the origin and development of several approaches to 'creativity'. Clearly these various approaches are not merely different ways of looking at the same phenomena. They are based on different conceptualizations of the term 'creativity'.

At present the value of creativity is celebrated with much enthusiasm in the Western world. Though not all agree what one means by 'creative' everyone is in favour of whatever they take it to mean – and most research on creativity is aimed at discovering how to enhance it. Although theories and empirical studies tend to focus on some narrow aspects of creativity, a very eclectic approach is adopted when it comes to applying theoretical suggestions and knowledge gained from empirical studies. Modern psychologists stress that intellectual (cognitive), emotional (affective) and motivational (conative) aspects of human functioning are interdependent, following, for example, Callaway (1969) who suggested that 'socially useful creativity demands the synergistic cooperation of the entire personality, including all physical mechanisms and modes of thought. Affective and conative dimensions are as essential as the cognitive ones' (p. 241). B. Clark (1979) warned 'restrict any one of the functions and you reduce creativity' (p. 244).

In accordance with these sentiments, creativity training programmes typically have several subgoals. They aim, for example, to promote the development of a (healthy, 'authentic') creative personality; to increase the tendency to engage in creative thinking; to upgrade the ability to solve problems, to encourage the imagination to run free; and they strive to make the creative classroom activities intrinsically satisfying. Details relating to the aims and techniques of such programmes may be found in the works of Osborn (e.g. 1953) Parnes (e.g. 1967a, b); Noller and Parnes (1972); Gordon (e.g. 1961); Prince (e.g. 1970); Stein (1974); Torrance (e.g. 1979); and Treffinger, Isaksen and Firestien (e.g. 1982). These programmes do not usually attempt to build knowledge, skill or ability to solve problems in a particular domain such as music or science, in which creativity might be expressed. It is taken for granted that problem-solving skills will transfer from one domain to another.

Although it is indeed valid to suggest that human behaviour is determined by intellectual, emotional, and motivational factors, it is not, however, valid to assume that creativity is determined by the various intellectual, emotional and motivational factors ascribed to it by people who have adopted different concepts of creativity. Conclusions relating to any type of behaviour regarded as creative are no doubt of some value to psychological enterprise. But it is necessary to realize that a person may be creative in one sense of the word but not in another. The various types of behaviour that have been called creative may be determined by different factors – one may not, in fact, be able to promote productive creativity by enhancing personality functioning or by improving ability to solve problems in the laboratory.

As our main concern in this book is with the determinants of *productive creativity*, we turn our attention in following chapters to facts emerging from studies of productively creative people whose works have been recognized by expert opinion as being of exceptional value to the culture. These are the facts that may eventually lead us to conclusions about the intellectual, emotional and motivational determinants of creative excellence.

# 2

## Methods used in research on productive creators

The following chapters discuss a large variety of facts about people who have achieved excellence, and it is interesting, if not necessary, to know a little about the various types of studies from which these facts came. As anyone acquainted with psychological research will realize, it is possible (without much effort) to find shortcomings in every type of psychological study and to challenge the validity of various types of findings. However, if consistent findings emerge from studies in which different methods were employed, one may with some confidence ascribe the correspondence to principles governing natural underlying regularities rather than repeated methodological errors.

Before we examine facts relating to creative achievers, this short chapter explains what sort of people have been the subjects of research on productive creativity, and briefly describes the methods used for investigating their backgrounds, experiences, abilities and personal characteristics. The discussion refers particularly to *sociometric (historiometric) studies, studies of famous historical figures and studies of contemporary creative achievers.*

## Historiometric (sociometric) studies

Historiometric or sociometric studies of creativity involve measuring the creativity of whole societies by assessing the number of notable creative individuals and/or products produced in the societies during certain periods. These studies seek to establish determinants of creativity by examining relations between the incidence of creativity and concurrent events and circumstances. Wide-ranging sociometric studies of creativity have traditionally been conducted by anthropologists or sociologists (e.g. Gray, 1966; Kroeber, 1944; Lehman, 1947; Murphy, 1958; Sorokin, 1951) but for the last decade the field of historiometric studies in psychology has been dominated by Dean Keith Simonton. Numerous references to his published reports are to be found in his monographs on historiometric inquiries into *Genius, creativity and leadership* (Simonton, 1984) and *Scientific creativity* (in press) where various methods for quantifying and analysing data relating to historical events are described in some detail.

Sociometric studies enable one to gain some idea of wide-acting effects of certain circumstances upon the whole society, and suggest how creativity might be promoted and enhanced at a societal level. Although this type of study apparently does little to explain why some individuals in a society would be more creative than others, it does offer one some ideas that could be tested by examining the circumstances surrounding particular individuals. If, for example, it were shown that there is more creativity in a society when a certain commodity is available, one might test the hypothesis that creativity relates to the supply of that commodity, by seeing whether individuals who have ready access to the commodity tend to be more creative than those who do not.

## Studies of historical figures

In contrast to sociometric studies of creativity, studies of famous historical figures focus on the lives and characteristics of highly creative individuals. The subjects of these studies are people who have made their mark on the history of civilization and therefore represent extreme cases of productive creativity. As Darwin suggested, it is legitimate and sometimes advisable in science to look at extreme cases, in which the effects one wishes to study are magnified (Gruber, 1974). Implicit in this approach to the determinants of creativity is the suggestion that *anything essential to the development of creativity will not be absent in the circumstances and characteristics of creative geniuses.* Moreover, by discovering similarities in the life experiences and personal characteristics of such people one may reveal some of the essential determinants of creativity.

### Idiographic studies (case histories) of historical figures

Among various types of studies of historical figures are numerous biographies of famous individuals. (A comprehensive list of references to 3145 works of this nature was drawn up by Rothenberg and Greenberg, 1974.) Many of these idiographic studies adopt a psychoanalytic perspective. A notable exception is Gruber's (1974) study of Darwin, which focusses on the cognitive aspects of the creative process. It was Gruber's (1986) opinion that, to understand the transformation of a gift into a creative achievement, one needs to make an in-depth examination of the lives of individuals who achieved excellence.

In addition to single case histories are collections of 'mini' case histories, or vignettes, providing biographical information on a number of individuals. Notable examples are those compiled by the Goertzel and the Illingworth families (Goertzel & Goertzel, 1962; Goertzel, Goertzel & Goertzel, 1978; Illingworth & Illingworth, 1969) and by Hershman and Lieb (1988).

Idiographic studies present a developmental picture of the whole person. They offer insights into the person's unique qualities in interaction with various aspects of that person's unique environment. Typically they depict the person in various situations and at various stages of life. They not only describe what the person did, but also to some extent help to explain why. Furthermore, case histories not only provide information about the creative person, but also offer the reader some insight into the creative process. For example, as Gruber (1974) explains, by examining the dated jottings in Charles Darwin's notebooks (which are less polished than published works) 'we can, if we look carefully, almost catch his thought on the wing' (p. xv). It is not possible to gain such an intimate, qualitative or comprehensive view of the individual from quantified data relating to large samples of subjects.

The purist may argue that little can be concluded about general influences on genius by examining isolated facts relating to a small selection of individuals. But disregarding biographical facts relating to outstanding individuals because they have not been quantified and statistically analysed may be extremely short-sighted. Full-scale and 'mini' case histories illustrated by excerpts from personal papers present a far clearer picture than coded, quantified data. For example, coded data may indicate that a certain proportion of a group had only three years of formal education. This does not tell one about the quality of that formal education, or about the informal education gained from parents and through systematic self-instruction. Such information is, however, often revealed in biography.

*Nomothetic studies of historical figures (i.e. studies of groups).*

Ideally, of course, one should compare suggestions arising from biographical studies of individuals with facts emerging out of studies of groups. And where possible I have done so in the following chapter, mentioning findings from several systematic studies of large groups of historical figures conducted during the first part of this century. Typically the subjects of these studies were historical figures selected and ranked according to the amount of space allotted to them in biographical dictionaries and encyclopaedias. Galton used this method for selecting his scientific and literary subjects. James McKeen Cattell (1903) adopted it, ranking the top 1000 people mentioned in at least two of six American, English, French and German biographical dictionaries. Havelock Ellis's (1904) 900 subjects were selected from *The dictionary of national biography.*

Subsequently several investigations were based on the same, or parts of the same samples. For example, Cox (1926) used parts of Cattell's (1903) sample; R. K. White (1930) selected subjects from both Cox's and Ellis's samples; later McCurdy (1957) selected from Cox's sample, and (much later) H. S. Walberg, Rasher and Hase (1978) and Simonton (1984) re-evaluated the Cox data. Of course, even when researchers do not draw directly from samples used by others, many of the same individuals are likely to turn up as subjects in various studies of historical geniuses, and at least some of the consistency in various findings relating to geniuses may be attributed to this overlap. This gives good reason for considering findings relating to contemporary creative achievers as well as those relating to historical figures when studying the development of creative genius.

Cox's study entitled *The early mental traits of 300 geniuses* has been widely acclaimed and deserves special mention here, as the findings are referred to repeatedly in following chapters. Albert (1983) maintained that although it is 'a half a century old it remains one of the most fertile pieces of research on the subject [of genius]. Unmatched in the range and depth of their analyses, Cox's results foreshadow many later findings' (p. 45).

For her sample of historical geniuses Cox selected the most eminent of Cattell's list, then eliminated those born before 1450, aristocrats, and any others whose eminence could not unquestionably be attributed entirely to their own achievements. This left 300 subjects, among whom were thirty-nine scientists (including Newton); thirteen artists (including Michelangelo); eleven composers (including Mozart); twenty-two philosophers (including Kant); ninety-five men of letters (including Byron); twenty-seven soldiers (including Cromwell); forty-three statesmen (including Abraham Lincoln); nine revolutionary statesmen (including Robespierre); and twenty-three religious leaders (including Martin Luther). Many biographies were combed for information relating to the early development of these subjects, giving special attention to documentary sources. The material gathered amounted to 6000 typed pages! (Terman, 1947). From this data Cox and her co-workers rated the subjects' intelligence and personality characteristics, and made comparisons between the various groups.

The method used by Cox and her assistants for rating the 'IQ's of their subjects resembled that used by Terman for assessing the IQ of Francis Galton (Terman, 1947). Two IQ indices were calculated for each subject. The first (IQ 1) represented the subjects' intelligence before the age of 17, and the second (IQ 2) represented intelligence between 17 and 26. Each of these indices was arrived at by averaging separate sets of estimates made by Cox and two assistants.

Estimates of IQ 1 were made on the basis of the subjects' mastery of certain universal intellectual tasks such as speaking and reading and performance at school. Any distinctive early achievements were also taken into account. The derivation of the 'IQ' index was based on the principle used for designing IQ tests – the age at which children are usually able to master a task is divided by the age at which the subject mastered the task, and the quotient is multiplied by 100. For example, children usually read at six years, but John Stuart Mill was reading at three. Therefore one estimate of Mill's IQ was $6/3 \times 100 = 200$. Algebra is commonly mastered at 14 and Mill learned it at 8, therefore another estimate of Mill's IQ was $14/8 \times 100 = 175$.

The second set of estimates (IQ 2) was based mainly on the subjects' academic and early professional performance.

For assessing the personality traits Cox and her co-workers working independently, each rated every subject with respect to sixty-seven traits, using a seven-point scale. This allowed them to draw up personality profiles of the various groups of subjects.

There are several notable advantages and disadvantages in using material contained in dictionaries or encyclopaedias for a study of historical figures. Among the advantages are that it is relatively economical for collecting data on a large number of individuals. Samples of living geniuses are far harder to come by. Geniuses are not always identifiable before time has lent some perspective to the value of their work, and those that *are* identifiable are not easily accessible to psychological researchers in sufficient numbers.

A second advantage in using biographical material from dictionaries is that the information in such sources is professionally selected and condensed. Unfortunately however, it is often rather sparse. One is not likely to find equivalent information on all individuals and, when no mention is made of a particular characteristic, one does not know if the individual did not possess it, or if it was unknown to, or regarded as unimportant or irrelevant by, the biographer. This missing data is a nuisance when attempting to quantify information or when making comparisons within and between various groups of people.

A third advantage of using dictionaries is that they provide a means of *ranking* the creativity of famous people, which is not easy unless one knows a great deal about their work. However, the assumption that a person's creativity is commensurate with the space allotted to that person in a biographical dictionary is unfortunately questionable, and the criterion is, moreover, unreliable. Although there may be some truth in the suggestion that people who have produced a greater number or variety of works will be discussed at greater length in dictionaries than those who have produced relatively little, the length of descriptions in dictionaries may also be influenced by other factors. For example, as Raskin (1936) suggested, the amount written by various biographers may be affected by their own particular interests and style. Raskin showed moreover that, in general, items relating to *scientists* emphasize the individual's achievements, whereas those relating to *literary* geniuses devote relatively more space to describing the person. She further demonstrated that there are some large discrepancies in the proportion of space allotted to the same individuals in different sources. Nevertheless, despite these shortcomings, there is little doubt that, in comparison with the general population, people selected for inclusion in dictionaries on the basis of their work are outstanding creators. Fame may not be a perfect index of the relative value of a person's achievements, but it is still one of the best reflections of excellence.

In response to this it may be argued that, although recognized originators are likely to become famous, not all famous people were originators. Some, like royalty, became famous because they were afforded an eminent position by their circumstances and by historical events. This was taken into account in all but the earliest studies of genius, however. For example, Cox eliminated from the list compiled by Cattell all those whose eminence could not rightfully be attributed to their own achievements. In what follows I have further separated data relating to leaders (such as statesmen, soldiers and religious leaders) from that relating to creators. There is no need for any separation in the findings of other researchers such as Raskin, who focussed *only* on intellectual achievements. Moreover, achievements that gain one a place in history are likely to be in some way original. History is little concerned with people who merely learn or repeat what others have done.

In addition to problems mentioned above is another that commonly afflicts studies on historical figures. When studying historical figures one usually lacks a control group. Relatively little information is available on unexceptional individuals who are long since dead, and this makes it difficult to make systematic comparisons between geniuses and their less creative contemporaries. Studies of historical figures are therefore often merely descriptive. Several strategies have, however, been adopted to compensate for lack of control groups. For example, both Cox (1926) and Raskin (1936) compared a subgroup of the most creative subjects in their samples with the samples as a whole. Both found that salient characteristics of their whole group were more marked in the uppermost subgroup, which lent credence to the validity of their criteria and conclusions.

## Studies of contemporary productive creators

In addition to studies of historical figures, biographies and systematic studies of living people provide fertile sources for information on productive creators.

Several notable sets of studies of highly creative living people were conducted around the middle of this century. First, there was a remarkable set of studies conducted by Anne Roe (e.g. 1946, 1951a, 1951b, 1953, 1965, 1970). Although Roe studied creative people in various fields she focussed mainly on the most eminent physical scientists, biologists, anthropologists and psychologists currently living in America. These subjects were far more productive than any of Terman's children of 'genius' ever turned out to be (Terman, 1947). Some were Nobel laureates, and in general they had received a 'staggering number of honorary degrees, prizes and other awards' (Roé, 1970, p. 43). Setting out to discover what contributes to becoming a creative scientist, Roe (1951a, 1951b, 1953) examined each of her subjects exhaustively, conducting personal interviews to gain information on their life-histories, family backgrounds, professional and recreational interests, achievements, personalities and intellectual attributes. In addition, her subjects were given verbal, spatial and mathematical tests, and projective tests (the Rorschach and Thematic Apperception Test for revealing their unconscious motivations).

Another set of studies on outstanding contemporary creators began soon after at the Institute for Personality Assessment and Research (IPAR). This institute had an interesting history. It was founded during the Second World War for selecting men capable of undertaking difficult missions in irregular warfare waged by the US Office of Strategic Services. The candidates of these assessment programmes lived for several days at IPAR (in a house on the Berkeley Campus of the University of California) with six or seven psychologists and one or two psychiatrists, during which they were tested in various ways, and were exposed to real-life problem situations.

After the war similar methods were used at IPAR for conducting research on highly creative people in various fields of work, such as creative architects (MacKinnon e.g. 1962b) writers (Barron, e.g. 1968); research scientists (Gough & Woodworth e.g. 1960); independent inventors (e.g. Gough & Woodworth, 1960; MacKinnon & Hall (see MacKinnon, 1978)); and mathematicians (Helson & Crutchfield, e.g. 1970). During the three-day living-in period, the subjects of these studies interacted freely with the researchers, who gathered information relating to their subjects' life experiences and administered paper-and-pencil tests. Finally the researchers drew up a comprehensive account of each subject on the basis of all ratings and test scores. More recently, Barron (1988) reminisced about this research, and indicated how creative resources are wasted in modern society.

In 1977 Harriet Zuckerman published her study of the winners of a Nobel Prize for science who were currently living in America. This was a sociological study, and not the first or most recent study of Nobel Prize winners (other studies include those by Berry, 1981; R. D. Clark & Rice, 1982; Moulin, 1955) but Zuckerman's thorough reports presented to psychology a most comprehensive view of various objective and subjective experiences in the early lives and education of laureates.

Among the advantages of studying contemporary creators is that this approach allows one to gain first-hand information about one's subjects. It allows one to examine the subjects repeatedly and exhaustively, and to use controls and measuring instruments for which norms are available. However, like other studies of creative genius, studies of contemporary creators also have their shortcomings. Finding enough suitable subjects is a major problem. Large groups of living geniuses are not easily identifiable and readily available. As a result, some researchers compromise by treating *all* artists and *all* scientists as examples of productive creators. But the correlates of this criterion of creativity are not likely to give one a clear idea of the determinants of excellence. Other researchers have compared relatively creative people with less creative peers working in the same institution. This has also proved to be a rather shaky approach. Several researchers, including C. W. Taylor, Smith and Ghiselin (1963), have found that ratings obtained from immediate supervisors, laboratory chiefs, peers, subjective reports and official records bear little relation to one another. Moreover it appears that evaluations by peers and supervisors are not closely or reliably related to the numbers of publications and patents of scientists in industry (R. B. Cattell, 1971; Harmon, 1963). As Cattell pointed out, ratings are personal opinions and depend to some extent on the personality and intelligence of the rater. Creativity tests do little to help. Scores on these tests do not reliably reflect excellent life performance. Indeed scores on creativity tests measure only what the test constructor construes as 'creative' or assumes to account for creativity, and are not even reliably related to one another (see Hocevar, 1981, and Richards *et al.*, 1988, for review and comments). As Hocevar put it, many of the methods that have been 'tagged with the creativity label' do not really measure 'the behaviour that society typically labels creative' (p. 458).

As this book is mainly about genius the following chapters focus on studies of people whose exceptional creativity has been recognized by experts in their fields. In addition, conclusions are illustrated with quotations from the works of notable creators who have revealed their own opinions about their emotions, motives and creative thought-processes. Not all psychologists are likely to regard such subjective opinions as important, but I feel it is time we outgrow the naive belief that quantitative data collected under controlled conditions are more valid than unsolicited testimony from members of the population of interest. Quantitative research may give an impression of exactitude, especially where complicated mathematical strategies are employed to control or correct possible errors of measurement. But insistence on quantification may be dangerous. It may force researchers to measure inappropriate quantifiable artificial substitutes instead of the real variables of interest. In other words, it may engender invalid operational definitions.

There are unfortunately few rules to direct the generation of valid operational definitions. Establishing the validity of operational definitions depends largely on common sense – a poorly valued resource often regarded with some suspicion in psychology because it smacks of being 'unscientific'. Psychological researchers, it seems, prefer to endow their work with an aura of scientific respectability by adopting rules derived from the physical sciences. As Sigmund Koch (1981) put it, they engage in 'scientistic role playing . . . ensconcing inquiry in a spurious systematicity to exorcize their uncertainty' (p. 257). Operationalization of creativity has therefore remained a pitfall for researchers who profess to agree with Toynbee that creative ability is 'mankind's ultimate capital asset' and then measure and investigate behaviours which are of little value to mankind.

# Part II

## The creative person

Having decided to designate people as creative on the basis of the recognized excellence of their works, we turn to the question of what makes them creative.

The following six chapters discuss and interpret what is known about the background, early life, and characteristics of eminent creators. From a systematic examination of this information one may arrive at some answers to the question of 'What determines the development of creative ability?'

# 3

## Social background

Here we consider findings of research on the incidence of creativity in societies, the position of creative achievers within their societies and the position of creative achievers within their families.

### The incidence of creativity in societies

At the time of Christ it had already been noted, by the Roman historian Velleius Paterculus, that clusters of geniuses appeared within relatively short periods (Arieti, 1976). Since then it has repeatedly been recognized that the incidence of genius fluctuates over time and place. Throughout the history of civilization there have been 'golden ages', during which numerous highly creative people lived in one place at the same time, and 'dark ages', when very little progress in thinking occurred. Among golden ages was the extraordinary period known as the age of Pericles in the fifth century BC in Athens where the 'outpouring of art, literature and science surpassed any single period of comparable duration to the present day' (Prentky, 1980, p. 183). Golden ages were also experienced by the ancient Sumerian and Chinese cultures; and more recently European cultures saw a fluorescence of visual arts during the time of the Renaissance, Italian opera in the eighteenth century and German music during the eighteenth and nineteenth centuries. The latter half of the twentieth century will no doubt be seen as the golden age of electronic technology in America and the Far East.

Are regional and temporal clusterings of genius determined purely by chance, as William James (1890) suggested? And, if not, to what may they be attributed? What determines the incidence of creativity in a culture? Do great men make the culture – or does the culture make them? Questions like these have inspired anthropologists and psychologists to conduct research on creativity at a societal level.

Among the early researchers who gave attention to racial factors in genius was Havelock Ellis (1904), who studied British geniuses depicted in the National Portrait Gallery. Ellis showed that blond, blue-eyed Nordic types had produced mathematical and scientific works, whereas dark-haired dark-eyed Celtic types were famous for their verbal-social skills. In line with these findings is R. B. Cattell's (1971) remark that any plot of creativity *per capita* in European areas shows a preponderance of mechanical and scientific invention in the Nordic areas, and artistic or religious work in the Mediterranean areas. In modern times, however, a disproportionate number of highly creative scientists has come from the Jewish race, the members of which are predominantly dark.

Ellis's observations on the physical characteristics of geniuses in the National Portrait Gallery appeared to support Galton's suggestions, that intellectual potentials are genetically transmitted, and fluctuations in the incidence of genius may be attributed to breeding. To Galton, golden ages represented periods during which the gene pools of civilized nations are relatively favourable and pure, but the intellectual foundations of civilizations become undermined when brilliant races interbreed with inferior ones. It was this, he believed, that caused the decline of the ancient Athenian civilization.

Systematic research into the determinants of fluctuations of creativity was initiated by the American anthropologist Alfred Kroeber (1944) who set out to show that Galton was wrong. Kroeber compiled a sample of 5000 creative individuals living between 700BC and AD1900, and traced the incidence of creativity over time and place. Sorokin (1951), Gray (1966) and others subsequently conducted studies of a similar nature. As many of these researches relied on Kroeber's selection of individuals, the findings of these studies were somewhat similar.

First they showed that the answer to the question of whether regional and temporal fluctuations in creativity are determined by chance is 'no'. Geniuses are not scattered randomly through history. They appear in definable clusters at particular places and times, and their occurrence differs significantly from what might be expected in terms of chance (*inter alia* Bullough, Bullough & Mauro, 1981; Gray, 1966; Kroeber, 1944; Simonton, 1984; Sorokin, 1951).

To refute Galton's suggestions, Kroeber (1944) showed moreover that the incidence of genius fluctuates far more rapidly than the biological foundations of a culture do. Kroeber demonstrated that creativity in a society waxes and wanes as a cultural pattern (such as a particular scientific or artistic approach) becomes saturated and its possibilities become exhausted. Similarly Kuhn (1970) later described historical fluctuations in scientific advances in terms of 'scientific revolutions' or 'paradigm shifts'. Kuhn explained that the history of science is not a steady progressive accumulation of knowledge, but is marked by a series of revolutions. 'Normal' science, which has little to do with the introduction of novel approaches, is carried out for a while to test hypotheses in terms of existing theory. While this is happening anomalous facts accumulate and generate questions that cannot be answered in terms of the current approach – and a period of 'revolutionary' science ensues. This revolution brings about a 'paradigm shift' – a new way of explaining and investigating scientific phenomena. But, in time, this new paradigm generates other anomalies and other questions, and another shift begins.

Historical fluctuations in artistic creativity might be explained in similar terms. When a particular artistic style has become overworked and the possibilities for originality are exhausted, artists may be stimulated to find a different form of expression. Highly creative artists may then successfully defy the existing tradition and rules, bring about a change in existing values, and thus provide a new viable direction in which the art may develop. By setting up new standards creative geniuses move the whole culture with them. As Kant (1952) put it, 'genius gives the rule to art'. However, amazing originality may even occur within existing traditions without causing a major shift: the originality of Bach's work, for example, lies in the striking way in which he exploited the complexities of elements in an existing tradition (Bailin, 1985).

Although the Humanists suggest enculturation might be inimical to the spontaneous expression of creativity, it seems a good measure of enculturation is vital to all creative production. Even though eminent creators may introduce original ideas that transcend their culture, the new ideas must always arise from within a traditional discipline. Until the necessary knowledge, techniques and materials have been acquired by the society and are made available to its members, no individuals can equip themselves to be creative: no invention, discovery or artistic work is possible. As L. A. White (1949) put it, it would have been impossible for Pasteur to have made his discoveries at the time of Charlemagne. Newton acknowledged his own debt to his predecessors by conceding,

If I have seen further, it is by standing on sholders [*sic*] of Giants.
(Westfall, 1980, p. 274).

Samuel Butler expressed much the same idea by saying of the theory of evolution that

Buffon planted, Erasmus Darwin and Lamarck watered, but it was Mr Darwin who said 'that fruit is ripe' and shook it into his lap. (Quoted by Koestler 1964, p. 144)

Transmission of knowledge and techniques is not, however, sufficient. To engender creativity in a society, it is also important that the work of individuals is recognized by members of the same and neighbouring disciplines. Cultures vary in their receptiveness to various kinds of talent (Feldman, 1988), and if potentially valuable creative ideas are not recognized and preserved, they will not influence the work of future generations. A work that is totally discontinuous with those that have preceded it is not likely to be appreciated. It may indeed be completely unintelligible (Bailin, 1985). But even original work that continues a tradition may be appreciated by few, and it is important that cultural leaders are sufficiently sophisticated to evaluate and monitor new ideas. If the gate-keepers of the domain are unable to restrict right of entry tastefully – if they allow the proliferation of worthless, pretentious, cultural products while failing to recognize or restricting the production of those that have relatively enduring value – then, as Csikszentmihalyi (1988) suggested, the whole cultural domain may be impoverished.

When the necessary knowledge, materials, social support and incentives are indeed provided by the society, the stimulating effects are often very noticeable. Sometimes, when these conditions are favourable, certain breakthroughs are almost inevitable, and are made by more than one individual. Throughout scientific history similar discoveries have been made almost simultaneously by two or more people working independently. Among the best-known examples are the contemporaneous breakthroughs made by Newton and Leibnitz, who developed the calculus; by Darwin and Wallace, who formulated theories of evolution; by Joule, Helmholz, Thomson and Colding, who formulated the principle of conservation of energy; by Priestley, Cavendish and Rutherford, who discovered nitrogen; by Schodinger, Pauli and Carl Eckart, who discovered the formal connection between wave and matrix mechanics; by Priestley, Scheele, Lavoisier, Spallanzani, and Davy who solved problems relating to respiration; and by Watt and Cavendish, who discovered the composition of water. A further list of multiple simultaneous inventions is presented by J. Rossman (1931, p. 142). Simonton (1979) reported having discovered 449 doublets, 104 triplets, 18 quadruplets, 7 quintuplets, and 1 octuplet in the history of scientific advances. It also happens that many breakthroughs come just too late for the creator to claim priority. Two-thirds of Merton's (1973) sample of about 1400 scientists had been anticipated by others in their work – a good many more than once.

Today, up-to-date information is swiftly available to workers in most scientific fields and they are well aware of the likelihood of being pre-empted in their discoveries. Some of the Nobel Prize winners interviewed by Zuckerman (1977) confessed frankly that someone else was bound to have made their discoveries, had they not made them.

It is frequently claimed that (as Maslow suggested) artistic achievements are more 'original' or 'creative' than scientific achievements are, because an artistic creator is less dependent on the work of others. Had Newton or Einstein not made their breakthroughs someone else would have done so sooner or later; but had Shakespeare not written his *Hamlet* it would never have been written.

Despite the suggestion that art depends less on previous works than science does, there is, however, little doubt that artistic creativity is influenced by previous works – and that it, too, depends greatly on enculturation. Even highly creative art is to some extent a re-assemblage of ideas taken from others: and even the greatest artists have copied parts of other men's work for their own purposes. R. W. Weisberg (1986) reported, for example, that over eighty of Bach's non-vocal works contain material 'borrowed' from the works of others such as Vivaldi, and over 200 of his vocal works were 'borrowed' from Lutheran hymns. Members of the school of Giotto copied some of the figures in their paintings from the compositions of other masters, and although Picasso's work was revolutionary, it was largely inspired by Velasquez and van Gogh (Gedo, 1983). These are only a few simple examples. Indeed, art historians are able to trace various sources of influence upon practically all creative artists.

Creative writing also springs from the works of others. Moreover, as the poet Strindberg explained, creative writers take ideas not only from other writers, but from a variety of other sources as well. 'A poet', said Strindberg,

takes an anecdote told by another man over a glass of wine; he takes an episode out of a stranger's life; he takes the thoughts of philosophers; reports from newspapers; feelings out of his own imagination – and then he writes his little name under all this . . . The poet does as boas do: He covers his prey with slime, and then it belongs to him. Beautiful webs he spins out of his own substance, so they say, yet nobody has seen how many he has sucked out first. (Quoted by Hock, 1960, p. 77)

Goethe also confessed to appropriating the ideas of others: 'The greatest genius will never amount to anything if he wants to limit himself to his own resources . . . What would I be, what would remain of me if this kind of appropriation were to endanger the quality of genius?' he asked (Hock, 1960, p. 79). 'Who can say that he has discovered this or that? After all it's pure idiocy to bring about priority; for it's simply unconscious conceit not to admit frankly that one is a plagiarist' (quoted by Whyte, 1978, frontispiece).

Like Strindberg, Goethe also acknowledged that his ideas had sprung from a variety of sources.

I have collected and used everything that I have seen, heard, observed. I have drawn upon the works of nature and of man. Every one of my writings has come to me through a thousand different things. The scholar and the ignoramus, the wise man and the fool, childhood and old age have contributed their share. Without suspecting it, most of the time, they offered me the gift of their thought, their abilities, their experiences. My work is a combination of beings taken from the march of nature: the whole carries the name of Goethe. (Quoted by Hock, 1960, pp. 79–80)

The suggestion that creators depend on the works of those who have gone before them leads one to recognize that golden ages reflect the advent and effect of great men, who not only create something of value but also act as role models and inspire others to greatness.

Kroeber (1944) agreed with the suggestion originally set forth by the Roman historian, Velleius Paterculus, that historical clusterings of creativity might be attributed to the availability of exceptional role-models – great masters who not only impart knowledge, set examples for emulation, but also act as 'pace setters' and help to maintain standards. As Kroeber explained, each generation emulates, learns from and then tries to outdo its masters. Offering empirical support for this suggestion, Simonton (1978) showed that the amount of creative works produced by specific generations is significantly related to the amount of creative production in *only two* preceding generations. According to Simonton, this indicates that the development of creative ability in a rising gener-ation is affected by the number of contemporary creators and patriarchs in their late fifties and sixties who might act as role-models. He further supported this argument by pointing out that a specific type of creativity occurs at certain times and places. Sometimes there are advances in science or philosophy, at others there are novel developments in the arts.

It seems people not only tend to emulate someone they admire, but also to emulate what is generally admired in their society. This is reminiscent of Plato's remark 'what is honoured in a country will be cultivated there', which has been endorsed by many, including Arieti (1976) and Torrance (1967), who subscribe to the idea that talents most likely to develop in a society are those that are imbued with an heroic character. The suggestion that a society that honours and rewards creativity is most likely to bring it about has received (somewhat indirect) support from various types of studies. For example, Torrance (1967) found (contrary to the popular suggestion that most boys aspire to being firemen or engine drivers) the preliminary choice of occupations by children from various cultures in fact corresponded with those occupations that were most esteemed by the cultures at large. McClelland (1961) studied a wide range of cultures, showing that attitudes toward achievement are not only transmitted by living role-models but may also be instilled early in life, through achievement themes in fiction.

One would think that historical events and circumstances affecting the general lifestyle within the society would have a marked effect on the incidence of creativity in a society. Findings in this area are, however, far from clear. For example, it has *not* been consistently shown that creativity varies with the affluence of the society (R. B. Cattell, 1950; Simonton, 1984). Creativity *does*, however, appear to increase with an increase of urbanization in the society (Bullough, Bullough & Mauro, 1981; Cattell, 1950) and also with civil disturbances or other indications of internal diversity and irritability (Cattell, 1950; Simonton, 1984).

It has been suggested that internal diversity, lack of unification, or lack of strong nationalistic tendencies and authoritarian attitudes foster a divergent outlook that is favourable to creativity (e.g. Simonton, 1984). Although this might apply in some cases, it is not invariably true. As MacKinnon (1978) reminded us, it is as well to remember that German scientists created rocket bombs under Hitler and that Russian scientists were the first to put a satellite into orbit.

All this leaves one to wonder whether creative production in a particular field is at all affected by historical events that have no direct effect on creators' ability to continue with their work. On the whole the literature seems to indicate that, although creativity is affected by circumstances within the discipline, or by circumstances that have a direct effect on the discipline, the influence of historical events is generally slight. Simonton's (1984) findings led him to conclude that the development of creative potential in the young may be sensitive to various influences, but once initiated, productivity is relatively immune from all but severely disrupting events. Whatever the circumstances, once a person has experienced creative achievement, creativity seems to provide its own impetus. Only physical illness, age and disrupting events which actually prevent creators from going about their work appear to interfere with creative production.

Gray (1966) described historical trends as a series of overlapping economic, social and political cycles, each of which go through formative, developed, fluorescent and degenerate stages. When there is a coincidence of the developed and the fluorescent stages of the three cycles, creativity abounds. Considered from these points of view, golden ages may be seen as the fruitful seasons in the natural economic, political and social growth of a culture. This view would lead one to conclude that, although societal fluctuations in creativity are not random, *any specific individual's* chances of becoming a celebrated creator depend on whether that person is in the right place at the right time.

Although this may to some extent be true it is certainly far from being the whole truth. There are many individuals at the same place and time, but few who create anything of notable value, even when the social climate is highly favourable. The distribution of creative products over the individuals in a society is in fact always very 'skewed'. Dennis (1955) found for example that 11 per cent of all compositions produced by the 200 famous composers in his sample had come from one man, and 64 per cent of all the compositions had been composed by only 20 people. Moles (1968) found that although there have been thousands of composers of classical music, the compositions still regularly performed were composed by only 250 of them. Examining the distribution of the total number of works produced by these 250 composers, Moles estimated that

36    composers had produced 75 per cent
16    composers had produced 50 per cent
10    composers had produced 40 per cent
 3    composers had produced 20 per cent (Mozart, Beethoven, Bach)

In fields other than music the proportion of contributions by individuals is much the same (Dennis, 1955; Simonton, 1984). Simonton suggested the highly skewed distribution of creative productivity appears to be an undeniable law of historiometry. What this amounts to is that *however favourable the cultural climate, only a few people are likely to account for most of the creative products of the society*. Therefore one cannot account for the creativity of individuals entirely in terms of cycles in their culture. As Arieti (1976) so nicely put it 'culture does not make great men. It only offers, to those who meet other conditions, the *possibility* of *becoming* great' (p. 310; italics in the original).

The bounties of chance do not relieve creators of the necessity for meeting the 'other conditions' to which Arieti refers. Creators must equip themselves to make good use of any gift of fortune that might come their way: 'Chance favours the prepared mind', said Pasteur. Although creators may in some way revolutionize their culture, they must always place themselves in a position to do so by assimilating something from the culture before becoming originators. To prepare themselves for producing something new, they must first become knowledgeable about the old (R. W. Weisberg, 1988).

## Conclusions arising from studies of the incidence of creativity in societies

Taken as a whole, sociometric research has suggested that even if intellectual potentials are genetically transmitted, historical fluctuations of creativity cannot be attributed to genetic influences. Nor can such fluctuations be merely attributed to chance. Creative advances must also rest on accumulation of knowledge in the culture; role models to set the standards; social transmission of relevant knowledge and skills, and cultural values that hold out rewards for those who apply knowledge and skill effectively. Further, it seems cultural influences act particularly strongly on the development of certain people. But, once their creative ability has developed, their output is relatively unaffected by events other than those that prevent them from going about their work.

The question remains as to which people are most likely to develop creative ability and why. If knowledge, materials and models do indeed play a major role, then one might expect that children who have the most access to such benefits are the most likely to become creative. Another suggestion is that certain children may be more receptive than others to such influences. The validity of these suggestions will be considered in the following sections, where research on creative individuals is reviewed and some light is shed on what sort of people they are likely to be.

## The position of creative achievers within the society

### Socio-economic class

Over the ages and in modern times, in different societies and in various disciplines, creators have always come from what is generally referred to as the middle to upper-middle classes (e.g. Albert, 1975; J. McK. Cattell & Brimhall, 1921; Chambers, 1964; Cox, 1926; Moulin, 1955; Raskin, 1936; Roe, 1951a, 1951b; 1953; Simonton, 1984; Zuckerman, 1977). They tend moreover to come from a particular segment of that socio-economic level – from professional-class homes.

The occupational status of the fathers of samples of historical geniuses, contemporary Nobel laureates and other creative men in various scientific fields is indicated in tables 3.1, 3.2 and 3.3.

As table 3.1 shows, the fathers of more than half of Cox's (1926) sample of historically eminent individuals were noblemen or professional men. Cox's data relating to the maternal grandfathers of the subjects suggested that they too had occupations which placed them mainly in the upper social strata.

Raskin's (1936) sample consisted of creative men of letters and scientists of the eighteenth century. Table 3.2 shows that professional fathers were over-represented in both groups. Much the same applied to the occupations of the maternal grandfathers of these subjects.

The occupations of the fathers of Roe's (1953) total sample of contemporary creative scientists are shown in table 3.3.

Table 3.1. *Occupational status of fathers: Cox's 282 eminent men*

| Father's profession | Percentage of subjects |
|---|---|
| Professional and nobility | 52.5 |
| Semi-professional, gentry and higher business | 28.7 |
| Skilled workmen and lower business | 13.1 |
| Semi-skilled | 3.9 |
| Unskilled | 1.1 |
| No record | 0.7 |

Adapted from Cox (1926, p. 37)

Table 3.2. *Occupational status of fathers: Raskin's samples of eminent writers and scientists of the eighteenth century*

| Father's occupational status | Percentage of scientists N = 112 | Percentage of writers N = 122 |
|---|---|---|
| Nobility and gentry | 8 | 13 |
| Professional | 47 | 41 |
| Semi-professional | 14 | 29 |
| Skilled and clerical workers | 14 | 11 |
| Farmers and artisans | 15 | 4 |
| Unknown | 2 | 2 |

Adapted from Raskin (1936, p. 27)

Table 3.3. Occupational status of fathers: Roe's total sample of contemporary creative scientists

| Father's occupation | Percentage of scientists N = 64 |
|---|---|
| Professional | 53 |
| Business | 31 |
| Farmers | 8 |
| Skilled labourers | 2 |
| Other | 6 |

Adapted from Roe (1951a, 1951b, 1953)

Table 3.4 allows comparison of the socio-economic origin of the scientists in various fields, and shows that theoretical physical scientists are more likely than scientists whose work is more practical to come from professional homes.

In keeping with the findings so far reported, Zuckerman (1977) found that most Nobel Prize winners in science were the sons of professional men. Table 3.5 shows the occupations of the fathers of American-reared Nobel laureates (1901–1972) in comparison with the occupation of fathers of scientists of about the same age who had received a doctorate, and fathers of employed males in the general American population of 1910. From this table one may see that, in comparison with men in

Table 3.4. Roe's findings relating to the proportion of men from professional homes in various fields of science

| Field of science | N 64 | Percentage of subjects with professional fathers |
|---|---|---|
| Theoretical physical scientists | 12 | 84 |
| Experimental physical scientists | 10 | 50 |
| Psychologists | 14 | 50 |
| Biologists | 20 | 45 |
| Anthropologists | 8 | 43 |

Adapted from Roe (1951a, 1951b, 1953)

Table 3.5. Zuckerman's findings relating to the occupations of fathers of American-reared laureates, scientists with doctorates and employed males

| Father's occupation | Percentage science laureates N=71 | Percentage science doctorates N=2,695 | Percentage employed males N=29,847,000 |
|---|---|---|---|
| Professional | 53.5 | 29.1 | 3.5 |
| Managers and proprietors | 28.2 | 18.7 | 7.7 |
| Farmers | 2.8 | 19.5 | 34.7 |
| Sales, service and clerical workers | 7.0 | 13.1 | 12.8 |
| Skilled or unskilled workers | 8.5 | 18.0 | 41.3 |
| No information | — | 1.5 | — |

From Zuckerman (1977, p. 66)

the general working population, a very high proportion of highly qualified men of science come from professional homes. But it is also noticeable that *the percentage of Noble Prize winners coming from professional homes is almost double that of other scientists with doctorates coming from professional-class homes.*

The foregoing examples, which refer to eminent creators in various periods and cultures, indicate convincingly that there is something about a professional-class home that enhances the probability of a child becoming a creator.

One is reminded of the sociometric studies discussed in the previous section, which suggested that the development of creative ability might be influenced by role models, appropriate values, encouragement and access to information and materials. These suggestions fit well with the fact that creators come largely from professional homes, for it is in such homes that children would be especially likely to enjoy those benefits.

One is also bound to wonder whether financial status plays a major role in the relation between social class and creativity. As Bertrand Russell pointed out, some creators like Shelley and Darwin wouldn't have been able to create if they'd had to work for their living (R. W. Clark, 1975). Although findings relating to the socio-economic origins of creators do not accord with the stereotype of the impoverished creator starving in a garret, they do *not*, however, suggest that creativity is related to wealth. A professional-class background does not necessarily mean financial opulence. Indeed, Visher (1948) found that only 9 per cent of 883 American Starred Men of Science had been 'well off' in childhood; 34 per cent had been 'comparatively financially poor', and 87.5 per cent had been aided by scholarships, fellowships or assistantships during their tertiary education – 68 per cent had been 'significantly aided'. Similarly, Roe (1951b) mentioned that some of the physical scientists she studied had suffered poverty in childhood, and most of her subjects were able to attend college only because they had been financed by fellowships. It seems, therefore, that other influences of a professional-class home are more important than the financial status it may offer. The prayer of Agar – 'give me neither poverty nor wealth' – may be appropriate for would-be creators.

Further support for the suggestion that the development of creative ability depends on professional rather than financial status of the home comes from records relating to Nobel Prize winners. Although bursaries and fellowships had become increasingly available to able students with limited means, and there had been an upward trend in the proportion of scientists coming from families of skilled and unskilled workers in America when Zuckerman conducted her study, *there had been no such trend in the social origins of Nobel laureates.* Moreover (as one can see from table 3.5), laureates are almost twice as likely as scientists with doctoral degrees to come from professional homes. In this respect Nobel laureates have in fact more in common with American supreme-court judges, admirals and leaders of the armed forces than with other scientists living during roughly corresponding periods. Figures show that 54 per cent of the laureates, 56 per cent of the judges, and 45 per cent of the admirals and generals came from professional-class homes (Zuckerman, 1977).

It is not easy to decide with any certainty why this should be, if the figures are reliable and not the product of some artifact. But it seems reasonable to suggest that a professional background not only encourages a child to follow a profession but also generates the ambition to get to the top – whether or not the chosen profession allows much scope for creative production. Getting to the top in some professions such as science does, however, challenge, indeed demand, one to be creative.

In contrast to most findings relating to the background of creative achievers are a few exceptions which give further reason to believe that intellectual ambition is the operative factor underlying the relation between professional-class home and incidence of creativity. Helson and Crutchfield (1970) found that only 27 per cent of their sample of sixty creative mathematicians came from professional homes, and Mac-Kinnon and Hall (MacKinnon, 1978) found that only two of fourteen inventors came from professional or semi-professional homes. Most subjects in these two studies were from the lower socio-economic strata. Furthermore Zuckerman (1977) found that, in contrast to other Nobel laureates, 75 per cent of those of Jewish origin were from the lower socio-economic strata.

One might suggest that becoming an inventor involves less intellectual aspiration than becoming a scientist does, as invention involves practical rather than theoretical skills. As shown in table 3.4, practical creativity (e.g. the creativity of experimental scientists) is less dependent on a professional-class background than is theoretical creativity. But why is it that so few of Helson and Crutchfield's sample of creative mathematicians and so few Jewish Nobelists come from professional homes? Mathematics is hardly a practical profession. A lead to the explanation may be found in Helson and Crutchfield's description of their sample of mathematicians: about half of the parents of the mathematicians were Jewish!

It seems professional and Jewish homes have something in common that favours the development of creative ability. And this leads us to consider the effect of religious denomination on creative achievement.

*Religious denomination*

It has consistently been shown that Catholics are under-represented and Jews are over-represented in samples of highly creative achievers (e.g. Arieti, 1976; R. B. Cattell & Butcher, 1972; Chambers, 1964; McClelland, 1963; Roe, 1951a, 1951b, 1953; Zuckerman, 1977). Although 4 per cent of Americans are Catholic, only 1 per cent of Nobel Prize winners have been Catholic. None of Roe's (1953) sample of sixty-four leading scientists was Catholic. On the other hand there have been disproportionately many Jews among the Nobel laureates. Although only 3 per cent of the American population is Jewish, 27 per cent of the American laureates have been Jews (Zuckerman, 1977).

Further it has been noted that the proportion of Jews among eminently creative scientists has increased during the present century (Visher, 1948; Zuckerman, 1977). Starred Men of Science studied by Visher in 1948 differed conspicuously from those studied by J. McK. Cattell in 1903. As Visher explained, his sample included fewer scientists of 'Puritan' stock (as distinct from, for example, 'other English', Irish and German), and more of German and Jewish origin. Particularly noticeable is the disproportionately higher number of creative Jewish mathematicians in Visher's sample. This complements Helson and Crutchfield's later finding that about half of the parents of their sample of creative mathematicians were Jewish.

The shift of proportion may of course be at least partly attributed to the influx of Jews from Germany – but the fact remains that creativity has repeatedly been shown to be unequally distributed among people of various religious denominations. This may seem to indicate a hereditary determinant – but it may also have something to say about the effects of cultural values. It does not seem to have anything to do with religion per se, as it has been repeatedly shown that very few creative scientists (including Jews) have any interest in religion (e.g. Chambers, 1964; Helson & Crutchfield, 1970; Lehman & Witty, 1931; MacKinnon, 1962b; Roe, 1951a, 1951b, 1953). Therefore the operative factor underlying the tendency to creativity in Jewish people seems not to be religion but culture.

One might imagine that, for the Jews as a minority group which has been continually subjected to persecution and prejudice, there is little complacency. Their social status is insecure; but this may be overcome to a certain extent through developing intellectual skills. Zuckerman (1977) explained the over-representation of Jews among Nobel Prize winners in terms of self-selection, showing that the first selective process stems from the Jewish tradition which sets a great value on learning. Whereas 40 per cent of American Gentiles go to college, 80 per cent of Jewish youths do so. The proportion of Jews among laureates is nine times higher than that in the general population. But the proportion of Jewish laureates is only three times higher than that of Jewish university professors. In other words it seems that, in comparison with Gentiles, a greater proportion of Jews acquire intellectual skills.

The question remains as to whether the acquisition of these skills depends on native intelligence, or on social transmission of a sense of values that inspires the young to develop their intellect. An answer is to be found in Terman's longitudinal studies of gifted children. Terman found that gifted people who were eventually most successful in their tertiary-educational and professional achievements in adulthood were not distinguishable from the less successful on the basis on scores on intelligence tests or academic achievements at school (Terman, 1947) – but their family backgrounds were markedly different. For example, the educational tradition was much stronger in the groups of successful subjects. In line with this was the fact that there were proportionately three times as many Jewish subjects in the successful group as in the less successful group. Terman's explanation was that the Jewish child is under pressure to succeed, with the result that, at the same level of intelligence, Jewish children accomplish more than do children of any other racial stock.

### Conclusions arising from studies of socio-economic status

Taken together, findings of studies relating to socio-economic status and religious denomination suggest that creators come from social subgroups in which children are most likely to be exposed to intellectual models and given access to educational materials. The question remains as to why people who come from professional homes tend not only to become learned but also creative. The findings in this section suggest that families in which learning is highly valued not only motivate children to acquire intellectual skills but also stimulate ambition *to excel* – by going beyond what others have produced. It may be argued that is what 'creative achievement' implies.

McClelland (1961) suggested that eminence may be a function of acquiring the motives of an aspiring middle class, rather than the despair of poverty or the complacence of wealth. It seems, indeed, that the probability of eminence may also be positively affected by lack of complacence not only of wealth but also of entrenched social stability. Today it is apparent that many children of Asian immigrants into America are excelling intellectually. If a disproportionate number of them become creative achievers in the future, we may have further confirmation of the importance for creativity of intellectual values and lack of complacence in the cultural subgroup and home.

### Position within the family (birth order)

Creators typically come not only from certain positions within their society but also from a certain position within their family. Studies of historical geniuses and contemporary creative achievers have consistently shown that highly creative individuals tend to be only or first-born children. A list of studies that have presented strong supporting evidence of a sizable significant relation between birth order and eminence is given by Schachter (1963, p. 757). To this list one might add the studies conducted by Albert (1980), Altus (1966); Helson and Crutchfield (1970), Sutton-Smith and Rosenberg (1970) and Visher (1948), which also support the hypothesis that the only or first-born child is more likely than others to attain eminence.

Although it is consistently found that being first-born is particularly favourable to high levels of scientific creativity, this does not apply to eminence in general. In their sample of 314 eminent personalities of the twentieth century Goertzel, Goertzel and Goertzel (1978) found that, in comparison with eminent people in other fields, there were fewer politicians among the first-born. A disproportionate number of politicians were middle children. Somewhat in keeping with this is Albert's (1980) finding that whereas 36 per cent of Nobel laureates were either an only child or only son, only 3 per cent and 14 per cent of two groups of eminent politicians were in this position. It has further been shown that revolutionaries are less often first-born than are other eminent figures (H. J. Walberg, Rasher & Parkerson, 1979). Focussing on the differences between winners of various kinds of Nobel Prize, R. D. Clark and Rice (1982) showed Nobel Prize winners for science are more likely to be first-born than winners of either peace or literature prizes. They also found, however, that recent science laureates are not as likely to be first-born as those at the beginning of the century.

What sense can one make of all this? First of all, why should it be that creators tend to come from the ranks of the first-born, whereas political achievers do not? The findings of a systematic earlier study by Schachter (1963) may lead to a possible explanation. As would be expected, Schachter found no birth-order effect when taking samples at random from the general population, and the same applied to samples of high-school pupils (where attendance is compulsory). However, a marked effect was noticed in samples of undergraduate college-students, and a still greater effect was found in graduate students. (The percentages of first-born in the high-school, undergraduate and postgraduate samples were 35.2, 50.2 and 57 respectively.) This shows a systematic selection of first-born children as education increases, which made Schachter suspect that the relation between genius and family position is 'simply a reflection of the fact that scholars, eminent or not, derive from a college population in which first-borns are in a marked surplus' (Schachter, 1963, p. 768).

As birth rate had been negatively related to socio-economic status prior to Schachter's study, he wondered whether these findings could mean that a large proportion of college students come from smaller than average families with higher economic status, who can afford tertiary education for their children. This was not the case. There was a marked over-representation of first-borns in college and graduate students in families of all sizes. Moreover, average academic achievements were higher for the first-born than for others. In other words, first-borns tend to do better in their school work. This is consistent with the findings of many investigations that have shown that birth order is inversely related to intelligence. First-born children are more likely to be intelligent than others (e.g. Nichols, 1967; Terman, 1925; Thurstone & Jenkins, 1929). Schachter suggested that it would be unreasonable to accept that innate intelligence varies with birth order, and therefore the inverse relation between academic achievement and birth order should be attributed to motivation.

The above fits well with R. D. Clark and Rice's (1982) finding that birth order has a more notable effect on *scientific* laureates than on winners of peace and literary prizes. As these authors mentioned, the kind of 'achievement orientation' required of scientific creativity is most likely to be acquired by early-born children, who are more likely to go to college and have a relatively high level of achievement motivation. Clark and Rice also found, however, that birth order has relatively little effect in *small, modern* families. These findings point to the importance of stimulation by parents, as parents of small families would be better able than parents of larger families to give their later-born children relatively undivided attention.

A somewhat different explanation of the relation between creativity and birth order came from Eisenman (1987), who suggested that both are related to a tendency to take risks. Eisenman showed that first-born males are inclined to take more risks than others (in classroom activities). As later explained, this tendency is also reflected in the test performance of eminent inventors.

## Conclusions

Studies relating to the social background of genius suggest that creative achievers come from societies in which relevant knowledge and materials are available, and creativity is recognized and valued. There is also reason for suggesting that the knowledge, skills and values necessary to creativity are socially transmitted within these societies by good role models who provide information, act as good examples and set the pace.

Studies relating to the socio-economic positions of creators show they come from social subgroups in which children tend to be intellectually stimulated, encouraged to learn and achieve, but are not necessarily financially and socially secure.

Birth-order studies show that creative achievers tend to come from positions within the family in which they are likely to have the undivided attention of adults, at least for a while. As adults are usually more intellectually stimulating than peers, first-born children are likely to be given more intellectual stimulation. First-born children are moreover the only focus of their parents' aspirations for a while and are likely to be the main recipients of encouragement, and perhaps pressure to excel.

The findings of the various types of nomothetic studies mentioned in this chapter seem to suggest consistently that intellectual stimulation and values upheld in the home play an important role in the development of the potential to create. It is nevertheless advisable to see whether these suggestions are borne out in idiographic studies and autobiographical accounts of various aspects of the home backgrounds of creative achievers. Thence come most of the facts discussed in the following chapters.

# 4

## The home environment

Although much of the information about the home backgrounds of creative achievers is difficult to quantify and measure objectively, several striking recurrent themes are noticeable in the biographical data pertaining to creative achievers. As explained in this chapter, these themes relate to intellectual stimulation, values upheld in the home, the emotional climate in the home, bereavement, isolation from peers, and parental style of control.

### Intellectual stimulation in the home

There is ample evidence from studies of both historical and contemporary creative achievers to suggest that they typically enjoy a good deal of intellectual stimulation in their childhood homes – not only from parents and other adults, but also through independent intellectual pursuits.

Researchers have noted that historical creators typically occupied special positions in their families that accorded them an unusual amount of attention from adults (Albert, 1978; McCurdy, 1957). One of the recurrent themes in the literature is that of a future creator being formally tutored at home, by a parent (or other adult or older child) who devoted a great deal of energy to the task. For example, John Stuart Mill, Pascal, Goethe, William Hamilton, Lord Kelvin, Edison, Leibnitz, Norbert Wiener, Tennyson and Karl Witte were educated by parents. After the death of his wife, Pascal's father gave up his own work so that he might be able to tutor his children. Mozart's father devoted himself almost entirely to his son's education (and his expectations of the young Mozart were enormous). In some cases a parent set out deliberately to make a genius. The British philosopher, John Stuart Mill, was the product of such an exercise. Before Mill was three years old his father began to drill him in the basic intellectual skills, and he was protected from all contact with other children except his siblings throughout his childhood.

When he was three his father began to teach him Greek, by presenting him cards inscribed with common Greek words together with the objects they represent. The following illuminating description of Mill's early development is quoted by Goertzel and Goertzel (1962).

John Mill had been brought up on a definite plan, based on a psychological theory, intended to make him not merely a reasoning machine but a machine that reasoned in a radical way. To that end he had been subjected to certain influence both intellectual and personal, and to that end he had been protected from all others. Up to his eighteenth birthday the experiment was a complete success. His mental activity was enormous, and he delighted in it; his corporal pleasures had been severely limited to what was necessary for life. Any display of emotion had been ruthlessly stamped out. Like a machine, he had no ideas of his own, and his intellect was all the stronger for being narrow. (p. 68)

Mill did eventually develop many creative ideas of his own – but these ideas reflected a sound *intellectual discipline*, which might well be an important factor that was ignored by Freud, by those who have focussed narrowly on the creative process and by theorists of a Humanistic persuasion who proposed that freedom from evaluation and lack of standards are necessary for the development of creative potential.

Norman Wiener, creative mathematician and writer, asserted that some fine minds had come to nothing precisely because they lacked the type of training and discipline he had received 'in rather excessive proportions' from his father. From his father, he said,

I learned the standards of scholarship which belong to the real scholar, and the degree of manliness, devotion and honesty which a scholarship career requires. I learned that scholarship is a calling and a consecration, not a job. I learned a fierce hatred of all bluff and intellectual pretense, as well as a pride in not being baffled by a problem which I could possibly solve. (Wiener, 1953, p. 292)

Although it is no longer an accepted practice to keep children out of school and educate them at home, studies of contemporary creative achievers reveal that they too usually received a high degree of intellectual stimulation in their childhood homes (e.g. MacKinnon, 1962b, 1978). Moreover, there are indications that creative achievers typically acquire a very particular type of intellectual skill from their parents. Roe (1951b) found that scientists who scored highest on verbal imagery tests had fathers in 'verbal' professions, such as law, the clergy or college teaching. Almost without exception the parents of MacKinnon's (1962b) architects had artistic interests. Case histories of creative achievers, including Mozart and Picasso, indicate that many creators-to-be acquired the basic skills necessary to their profession from their fathers or other members of their family.

Parents need not give a child lessons in order to stimulate it intellectually. H. J. Walberg (1988) referred to the 'curriculum of the home' in terms of informed conversations about school and everyday events, encouragement and discussion of leisure reading, joint analysis of television and peer activities. A child may also be intellectually stimulated in the home through participating in intellectual and creative activities with adults, and through casual exposure to adult conversation. This type of exposure and participation is likely to account for several members of the same family becoming creative in a particular field. We have already seen how one of Pierre and Marie Curie's descendants became infected with enthusiasm through exposure to the work of his parents. Feldman (1988) noted that musical prodigies may also be thus affected, remarking that it is to the advantage of musical prodigies to come from musical families, where 'music is all around them from their earliest days' and is played and enjoyed 'as if it is the most important and central thing a person can do, and for such families it often is' (p. 280).

Galileo, one of the eminent scientists who became fired by enthusiasm through contact with models in his parental home, was first attracted to mathematics by listening through a half-open door to a friend of his father explaining Euclid (Gibson, 1913/1970). Indeed many youthful geniuses seem to have been inspired through discovering the works of Euclid (though mostly by more direct methods than listening through doors). Einstein (1949/1979b) described two events in his childhood that made a lasting impression on him. One was being shown a compass (at the age of four or five). The other was being given a book dealing with Euclidian plane geometry which came into his hands at the age of twelve. Bertrand Russell, the famous mathematician and philosopher, thus described his own thrilling introduction to Euclid:

At the age of eleven, I began Euclid, with my brother as my tutor. This was one of the great events of my life, as dazzling as first love. I had not imagined there was anything so delicious in the world. (Storr, 1983, p. 829)

Although the literature reveals that some creators were given intensive tuition in their childhood homes, and that many acquired elements of their discipline through interacting with parents and other models, this does not apply to all creative achievers. It is important to note that, in childhood and youth, creators also characteristically provide their own intellectual stimulation through *independent intellectual pursuits*. Some of the highest scores assigned by Cox (1926) to creators as children were on items relating to the extent of *mental work* given to special interests, hobbies, and extracurricular studies. Her findings underline the impression gained from other research and from biographies, that creators dedicated themselves conscientiously, persistently and tenaciously to intellectual or constructive extracurricular activities in childhood.

One of the most consistent findings in the literature relating to the childhood and youth of creators is that they tended to read omnivorously and voraciously (e.g. MacKinnon, 1978; McCurdy, 1957; Roe, 1953; Simonton, 1984). Edison (1948/1968) claimed to have read every book in the Detroit library in his youth. Pablo Neruda (1977) confessed to having gobbled up everything indiscriminately like an ostrich. McCurdy (1957) showed that creators tended to read advanced books in childhood – books that were written for adults. Lillian Hellman (1969) described how she began to read:

filled with the passion that only comes to the bookish, grasping, very young . . . bewildered by almost all of what I read, sweating in the attempt to understand a world of adults I fled from in real life but desperately wanted to join in books. (p. 11)

## Values upheld in the home

It is clear that creative achievers are not only given intellectual stimulation in their childhood homes, but are also encouraged to value intellectual achievement.

We have seen that creative achievers tend to cluster in the types of societies and in subgroups of those societies that instil the value of intellectual achievement in their children. The notion that such values affect the development of genius is indeed supported by biographical information relating to individuals. For example, MacKinnon's (1978) subjects reported that their families valued intellectual and cultural endeavour, success and ambition. They also had a plentiful supply of role models in the form of family acquaintances who occupied prominent or responsible positions in the community. Roe (1953) found that learning was valued and pursued for its own sake in the homes of practically all her highly creative subjects, and in the transcripts of interviews conducted by Roe and by Zuckerman (1977) one almost invariably finds mention of models who had inspired their subjects with positive attitudes toward learning. This is noticeable in biographies too. Not all the models who influenced creators were personally known to them. Authors or heroes of books, or famous people in the discipline of interest also played important roles. Michael Faraday, one of the relatively few scientists who came from a humble home, saw scientists as heroes, and aspired to become one after reading books in the possession of his employer. Among these was the book that Faraday later declared had led him to science. It was *Mrs Marcet's conversations in chemistry*, a volume of little importance, except that it gave the initial impetus to a boy who became one of the world's scientific geniuses.

Graham Greene (1969), the famous novelist thus described a turning point in his life when he was about fourteen years old,

[when] I took Miss Marjorie Bowen's *The Viper of Milan* from the library shelf, the future for better or worse really struck. From that moment I began to write as the other possible futures slid away: the potential civil servant, the don, the clerk had to look for other incarnations. Imitation after imitation of Miss Bowen's magnificent novel went into exercise books. (p. 16)

Walters and Gardner (1986) described and listed exciting 'crystallizing experiences' that set outstanding creators on their life's course. It seems many of these experiences come through contact with masters in a particular creative field. But often (even in humble homes) the influential people in the early lives of creative achievers were members of their own family. One of the clear examples of the transmission of cultural values by humble parents is to be found in a lecture given by Louis Pasteur many years after the death of his parents:

Oh! my father, my mother . . . If I have always associated the greatness of Science with the greatness of France, it is because I was impregnated with the feeling that thou hadst inspired . . . Not only hadst thou the qualities that go to make a useful life, but also the admiration for great men and great things. To look upwards, learn to the utmost, to seek to rise ever higher, such was thy teaching. (Vallery-Radot, 1937, p. 377)

## Emotional climate in the home

Although creators typically seem to be richly endowed with intellectual values and stimulation in their homes (or are at least given opportunity and materials in which they might find stimulation for themselves), it seems they are often deprived of emotional comfort.

In line with the theories put forward by Adler, Rank, Rogers, Fromm and other theorists of a Humanistic persuasion, it is still somewhat widely assumed that to become a creative person one must have loving supportive parents and a happy home environment. The investigations instigated at IPAR during the Second World War cast some doubt on this assumption, however. The IPAR researchers found that a healthy stable home background, affection from parents, and satisfactory interaction with peers is characteristic of well-adjusted individuals, but – to their surprise – they found that some of their extraordinarily creative subjects had suffered traumatic experiences, brutality, frustrations and deprivations in childhood. MacKinnon (1960/1983), who was one of the investigators admitted that 'Those of us who were members of the OSS assignment had it vividly impressed upon us how little we know about the development of personality' (1983, p. 376).

Other investigators have also found that creative achievers do not typically enjoy the benefits of a secure and happy home environment in childhood. For example, Goertzel and Goertzel (1962) noted that 75 per cent of a group of 400 eminent historical figures had been troubled – by broken homes, rejecting, over-possessive, estranged or dominating parents; almost 50 per cent by financial ups and downs; over 25 per cent by physical handicaps; and some by parental dissatisfaction with the child's progress or vocational choice. Later, Goertzel, Goertzel and Goertzel (1978) found that 85 per cent of 400 eminent people of the twentieth century had come from markedly troubled homes. This applied to 89 per cent of the novelists and playwrights, 83 per cent of the poets, 70 per cent of the artists, and 56 per cent of the scientists. Berry (1981) noted that, in comparison to scientific laureates, those who win a Nobel Prize for literature more often originate from disturbed or declining backgrounds and suffered physical disabilities.

Among further indications that there may be relatively little affection, attachment, warmth, or closeness between creative achievers and their parents are findings relating to scientists (Chambers, 1964; Roe, 1951a; Stein, 1962), psychologists (Drevdahl, 1964; Roe, 1953), and architects (MacKinnon, 1962b). Both Roe and Chambers found that creative psychologists had experienced more open hostility and rejection than other scientists, who typically felt distant from their parents. (Strangely, this applied to Maslow, who insisted that the motivation to actualize the self depends on the satisfaction of needs for security and love.)

Koestler (1959/1986) tells us that Johannes Kepler described his father as 'A man vicious, inflexible, quarrelsome, and doomed to a bad end . . . [who] treated my mother extremely ill, went finally into exile and died'; and his mother as 'small, thin, swarthy, gossiping, and quarrelsome, of a bad disposition' (p. 231).

Gore Vidal (1977) concluded from his own experience of creative writers that 'hatred of one parent or the other can make an Ivan the

Terrible or a Hemingway; the protective love, however, of two devoted parents can absolutely destroy an artist' (p. 34).

Among other troubles that afflicted the emotional well-being of creators-to-be in childhood were ugliness, deformity and disease. Over 20 per cent of the Goertzel and Goertzel (1962) sample were troubled by physical handicaps. To a child physical deformity is hard to bear. Alexander Pope had to bear repulsive deformity, and later referred to his life as 'that long disease'. At the age of twelve years he wrote these sad lines, which reveal his strong need to hide himself from the world:

> Thus let me live unseen, unknown.
> Thus unlamented let me die.
> Steal from the world, and not a stone
> Tell where I lie. ('Ode on solitude')

## Bereavement

A surprising consistent finding in studies of the early life-experiences of eminent people is that a disproportionate number of both creators and eminent politicians were bereaved of at least one parent in childhood. Among those who have given particular attention to this phenomenon are Albert (1971) and Eisenstadt (1978).

Eisenstadt found that 25 per cent of a sample of 699 famous historical figures had lost at least one parent before the age of ten years, 34.5 per cent before fifteen years, and 45 per cent before twenty years. Unfortunately, not even the most rudimentary census-statistics are available for the times during which many of these historical subjects lived, and it is difficult to judge the life expectancy of a heterogeneous sample of individuals from different periods in history. However, parental loss in Eisenstadt's subjects is certainly markedly greater than would be expected in modern Western populations. The percentages for death of mother and for death of both parents by fifteen years of age in his sample were found to be more than three times greater than in the general population at the beginning of the twentieth century (for which census data are available).

Albert (1980) extracted figures relating to childhood bereavement from various studies of historical and contemporary eminent people, psychologically disturbed patients and general populations. He too found that the rate of parental loss in historical figures was more than three times as high as it is in twentieth-century populations. This applied to achievers in general: artistic and scientific creators as well as politicians and eminent individuals in military fields.

The only other subgroups with approximately the same proportion of childhood bereavement are delinquents and suicidal depressives. Table 4.1, which is adapted from Albert (1980), shows the percentage of individuals in various groups who lost a parent before the age of sixteen. In that table it may be seen that 26 per cent of Roe's eminently creative scientists of the twentieth century lost a parent before sixteen years of age. This is three times greater than the parental loss in the general population of America (8 per cent) only ten years later. Furthermore one can see that the proportion of individuals who have suffered early bereavement is higher in the groups that deviate further from the norm – in both achieving and maladjusted directions. In the creative direction there is an increase from the general population to gifted youth, to competent scientists, to creative scientists. On the negative side there is also an increase in the proportion of individuals who suffered early bereavement – from the general population to delinquents, to those with severe problems. The implications are that the death of a parent may have some influence on either adaptive or maladaptive development.

This suggestion is reflected in the quotation from Thomas De Quincey on the frontispiece of Eileen Simpson's (1987) poignant work *Orphans*:

It is, or it is not, according to the nature of men, an advantage to be orphaned at an early age.

Another recurrent theme noted in the early lives of creators (for which I have no exact statistics) is death of a sibling. This was a fairly common event in the lives of children in previous centuries, which does not of course mean that the event had little effect; and it is clear that it made an indelible scar on some creators, including De Quincey, who was unable to remember the moment but unable to forget the pain he suffered as a result of the death of his beloved sister, aged nine, when he was six years old. Here is one of the many passages he wrote on the subject:

O! moment of darkness and delirium . . . Rightly it is said of utter, utter, misery, that 'it cannot be remembered'. Itself as a rememberable thing is swallowed up in its own chaos. Blank anarchy and confusion of mind fell on me. Deaf and blind I was, as I reeled under the revelation. I wish not to recall the circumstances of that time, when my agony was at its height. (De Quincey, 1785–1803/1950, p. 21)

As many creators do not, of course, suffer bereavement in childhood, bereavement is certainly not essential for the development of creative ability. Nevertheless, there is little doubt that bereavement is

Table 4.1. Percentage of subjects who lost a parent before sixteen years of age – adapted from Albert (1980)

| Group | N | Percentage of subjects bereaved |
|---|---|---|
| *Politicians* | | |
| American presidents | 39 | 34 |
| British prime ministers | 48 | 35 |
| *Creative* | | |
| Cox's historical geniuses | 135 | 30 |
| Eminent scientists (Roe, 1953) | 64 | 26 |
| Competent scientists (Eiduson, 1962) | 40 | 20 |
| Eminent French and English poets [lost father] (Martindale*) | 33 | 24 |
| Eminent English poets and writers (Brown, 1968) | 57 | 55 |
| *Gifted* | | |
| Terman's gifted | 1000 | 16 |
| *Psychologically disturbed* | | |
| Highly depressed | 100 | 27 |
| Medium depressed | 97 | 15.5 |
| Non-depressed (Beck, Sethi & Tuthill, 1963) | 100 | 12 |
| Outpatient depressives | 216 | 49 |
| Outpatient controls | 267 | 21 |
| *Controls* | | |
| College students (Gregory, 1965) | 1696 | 6 |
| Adolescents, general population (Hathaway & Monachesi, 1963) | 11329 | 8 |
| General British population (Ferri, 1976) | 17000 | 9 |

* personal communication to Albert (1980).

commonly seen in the childhood of creators. And this leads one to ask what mechanism may be held to account for a positive relation between bereavement and creative achievement.

Various suggestions have been put forward to explain how the trauma of losing a parent in early life might affect development. Eisenstadt (1978) suggested that creative achievement, delinquency and suicide are all expressions of dissatisfaction with society. Creative achievement, which to some extent involves destruction of current beliefs and practices, may be seen as an attack on society. In somewhat softer vein, it may be construed as becoming independent of social demands, and controlling one's own destiny. Others have suggested that creativity may be the outcome of establishing a certain style of coping (Eisenstadt, 1978; Roe, 1953). Bereavement is likely to threaten the child with feelings of isolation, sadness, guilt and unworthiness (Berrington, 1983; Eisenstadt, 1978). Some children may try to allay or compensate for these feelings by proving they are able to cope with their emotions and the environment. Further it has been proposed that parental loss may engender a need for power (Albert, 1980; Berrington, 1983; Eisenstadt, 1978; Horney, 1937), and a nationwide survey by Veroff *et al.* (1960) showed that, in comparison with controls, males who had been bereaved of a parent before the age of sixteen had significantly higher levels of power motivation.

Horney's (1937) views on anxiety and neurosis are bound to evoke suggestions as to why parental bereavement is relatively common in leaders and creators as well as in psychologically distressed people. Horney expressed the opinion that anything that disturbs the security of the child in relation to its parents may cause a basic anxiety – a feeling of being small, helpless, deserted, endangered in a world that is out to humiliate, cheat, attack and betray one. There are three ways in which the child with such feelings may react, said Horney. One way is by *turning toward people*, soliciting their love, approval, admiration, and protection. Another way is by *turning away from people*, withdrawing and seeking independence and self-sufficiency, perfection and unassaila-bility. And the third way is by *turning against people*, seeking power, prestige and domination, or exploiting them. Although these orienta-tions are found in normal people, they are especially marked in the neurotic, who has been affected by rejection, neglect, overprotection or other forms of harmful experiences in early life.

As we will see, there is some reason for explaining a lifestyle marked by creative endeavour in terms of *turning away from people* – seeking independence and perfection. But it might also involve *turning toward people* – seeking admiration as well *turning against people* – seeking prestige.

## Isolation

Another recurrent theme in the literature on the childhood of creative achievers is social isolation and loneliness. Many creative achievers were isolated from other children because of restrictions placed upon them by parents; illness; constant movement of the family from one com-munity to another; lack of siblings, or natural shyness. For whatever reason, it seems that creators typically engaged in solitary activities in childhood (Goertzel & Goertzel, 1962; Illingworth & Illingworth, 1969; MacKinnon, 1962b; McCurdy, 1957; Roe, 1951b).

Winston Churchill seems to have noticed this. His biographer William Manchester (1983) remarked that

In Winston's books one may trace a steady theme: Great men are frequently products of boyhood loneliness. He wrote 'Solitary trees, if they grow at all grow strong; and a boy deprived of a father's care often develops, if he escapes the perils of youth, an independence and vigour of thought which may restore in after life the heavy loss of early days'. (p. 188)

Some case histories of eminent creators indicate that, as children, they suffered intensely from loneliness. For example Joseph Conrad thus described his feelings during the time when he had already been bereaved of a mother and his father lay ill:

I don't know what would have become of me if I had not been a reading boy. My prep finished, I would have nothing to do but sit and watch the awful stillness of the sickroom flow through the closed door and coldly enfold my scared heart. I suppose that in a futile childish way I would have gone crazy. Often, not always, I cried myself into a good sound sleep. (Quoted by Illingworth & Illingworth, 1969, p. 31)

In other cases there are signs of resignation to loneliness. English poet, Sir Edmund Gosse, explained that

The mere fact that I had young companions, no story books, no outdoor amusements, none of the thousand and one employments provided for other children in more conventional surroundings, did not make me discomforted or fretful, because I did not know of the existence of such entertainments. I have no recollection about any curiosity about other children, nor of any desire to speak to them or play with them. They did not enter into my dreams, which were occupied entirely with grown up people and animals. I am unable to recollect exchanging two words with another child till after my mother's death. (Quoted by Illingworth & Illingworth, 1969, p. 7)

But there are also indications that in some cases the child's distance from others may have been at least partly determined by the nature and inclinations of the child. This seems to have applied to Einstein. Abraham Pais (1979), who knew Einstein well, began his tribute to the great man by saying 'if I had to characterise Einstein by one single word I would choose apartness. This was forever one of his deepest emotional needs' (p. 35). And Einstein confessed

I . . . have never belonged to my country, my friends, or even my immediate family with my whole heart; in the face of all these ties, I have never lost a sense of distance and a need for solitude – feelings which increase with the years. (Moszkowski, 1970, p. xvii)

Some indication of the reason for Einstein's apartness is seen in a little quatrain which his secretary, Helen Ducas, discovered among his notes after his death:

> That little word 'WE' I mistrust, and here's why,
> No man of another can say 'He is I'
> Behind all agreement lies something amiss.
> All seeming accord cloaks an abyss
> (Ducas & Hoffman, 1979, p. 100)

In terms of Erikson's (1950) theory of personality development one might ascribe Einstein's lack of a sense of intimacy to a negative resolution of the 'crisis of trust'. But whatever the initial reason for isolation, it seems to have become a style of life for many creators. As shown in chapter 8, a number of them in fact testified to the importance of loneliness for the development of their own creative skills.

## Parental style of control

Popular assumptions relating to the rearing of children hold that authoritarian control, criticism and rigid discipline are bound to inhibit the development of creativity, and some research on this topic has shown that 'potentially creative' children generally have non-authoritarian parents (e.g. C. C. Anderson & Cropley, 1966; Getzels & Jackson, 1963; Nichols, 1964; Nichols & Holland, 1963; P. S. Weisberg & Springer, 1961). It seems, however, that these conclusions relate to ingenuity in the classroom rather than to creative life-performance. Although children who score well on creativity tests may come from democratic or even permissive homes, historical geniuses and contemporary creative achievers were not always permissively or democratically reared. In fact many were strictly, sternly, unfairly, or even cruelly disciplined.

Among the many who described the cruelty they suffered in childhood is the Russian novelist, Ivan Turgenev, who wrote:

I have not a single happy memory of my childhood. I used to be birched almost daily for all sorts of trifles. One day one of my mother's companions, an old woman, seemed to have caught me doing something, what it was I do not know to this day, and told my mother about it. She thrashed me herself with her own hands, and in reply to my entreaty to tell me why I was being punished, kept saying 'you know very well why I am thrashing you'. (Quoted by Illingworth & Illingworth, 1969, p. 17)

The following morning the punishment was repeated by the mother who threatened to continue doing so until the boy confessed, although he was still at a loss to know what had been his crime.

In similar vein the Russian playwright, Anton Chekhov, wrote that

Despotism and lies so disfigured our childhood that it makes me sick and horrified to think of it . . . I remember father began to teach me, or to put it more plainly, whip me, when I was only five years old. He whipped me, boxed my ears, hit me over the head, and the first question I asked myself on awakening every morning was 'Will I be whipped today?' I was forbidden to play games or romp. (Quoted by Illingworth & Illingworth, 1969, p. 18)

Among numerous other victims of parental cruelty was Beethoven, who might be described today as a battered child. His father would drag him out of bed in the middle of the night and make him practise till morning, beating him if he flagged (see Ehrenwald, 1984).

Whether or not the parents of these men were as tyrannical as sometimes depicted, one cannot tell with any certainty. But it is important that parents were *perceived and remembered* as tyrannical by many highly creative offspring (Goertzel & Goertzel, 1962; Illingworth & Illingworth, 1969; MacKinnon, 1978; Roe, 1951a, 1953).

It is also difficult to say if historical geniuses were typically more strictly disciplined than other children of their times. The overall view of childhood in past centuries indicates that the childrearing styles were far less permissive or democratic than they are today (e.g. Schorsch, 1979). However, it is clear that authoritarian discipline in the home does not preclude the possibility of a child becoming a creative achiever of the highest rank. As Roe (1953) suggested, it may even engender a sense of rebellion which leads to creative behaviour. Some of her subjects said they had been firmly controlled, and others felt they had been overprotected by their parents, which engendered strong rebellious feelings. They resented the restrictions placed upon them, and when freedom was not given, they took it.

It is often considered important to foster a child's sense of autonomy for enhancing the development of creativity (e.g. Cropley, 1967; Getzels & Jackson, 1961; P. S. Weisberg & Springer, 1961). But findings relating to the childhood of creative achievers do not consistently support the idea that their autonomy was deliberately fostered by parents. Among those who were strictly discouraged from becoming autonomous was John Ruskin, the famous British man of letters, who explained:

I obeyed word or lifted finger, of father or mother, simply as a ship her helm: not only without idea of resistance, but receiving the direction as a part of my own life and force, a helpful law, as necessary to me in every moral action as the law of gravity in leaping. (Quoted by Illingworth & Illingworth, 1969, pp. 4, 5)

Even when Ruskin went to University at Oxford he was not released from parental control. His mother took rooms there to watch over him.

Although MacKinnon's (1962b) subjects were allowed a great deal of freedom and were expected to exercise their autonomy in childhood, few other authors have shown that highly creative subjects were deliberately encouraged to engage in autonomous behaviour. Roe (1951a) reported overprotection of creative biologists in their childhood. And isolated case histories of geniuses are inconclusive. It seems one cannot conclude that encouragement of independence is a prerequisite for creative achievement even if creative achievers do eventually become independent. Some were simply left to their own devices, or neglected. Others rebelled against over-control and went their own way.

## Conclusions

Having reviewed various studies relating to the early development of potential achievers, Albert (1978) concluded that

The consensus of these studies is that the creative person-to-be comes from a family that is anything but harmonious – one which has built into its relationships, its organisation of roles, and its levels of communication a good deal of tension if not disturbance at times, what I term a 'wobble'. But along with these characteristics, there is a commitment to achievement as opposed to just 'having fun', a special focus of interest and aspirations upon the indexed child, and a great deal of family effort to see that these aspirations are met. (pp. 203–204).

There is much evidence to support these suggestions and further to indicate that the childhood homes of creative achievers, both past and present, were typically rich in opportunity and encouragement to achieve intellectually, but poor in emotional comforts.

From the evidence, one may indeed go so far as to suggest that creators typically suffered some deprivation and distress in childhood. Not all suffered the same form of discomfort. Some were bereaved of parents, some were rejected, some were sternly disciplined. Some were exposed to emotional tensions, financial insecurities or physical hardships. Some were overprotected, lonely or insecure, and some were ugly, deformed or physically disabled. Many suffered several of these hardships in combination.

There is little, if indeed anything at all, in this picture that corresponds with the Humanistic views discussed in chapter 1. There is little to suggest that creative achievers enjoyed lack of conditions of worth or unconditional positive regard, which Rogers believed to be essential to the development of creative attitudes and productivity. There is little to suggest that their lower needs were satisfied on a regular basis, which Maslow suggested to be necessary for the development of a need for self-actualization. Fromm's views of loving interaction between parent and creative child also fail to fit this picture.

There are, however, indications that, as Adler suggested, feelings of imperfection or inferiority may stimulate a tendency to improve the self. And there are also indications that, as Freud suggested, creative endeavour may take sustenance from energy diverted from unrequited emotional needs. The correspondence between Freud's and Adler's theories and research findings relating to creative achievers is understandable in the light of the fact that they based their theories (at least partly) on their observations of eminently creative people, whereas most of the Humanists denied or distorted information relating to outstanding creators and based their conclusions simply on their rather rosy conceptions of a 'self-actualizing personality'.

As we have seen, historiometric studies of cultural fluctuations of creativity and nomothetic studies of the socio-economic background and birth order of creative people also suggest that creativity is promoted by intellectual stimulation and intellectual values in the childhood home.

Clearly, however, creative achievement does not depend on coming from an intact family. Although it has been suggested that a one-parent home provides an inferior intellectual environment and that early loss of a parent is likely to result in intellectual deficits (e.g. Zajonc, 1976), the figures relating to creative achievers show this is not invariably the case.

It is also clear that there must be some mediating link between the fact that creative achievers tend to suffer distress in childhood and are creative at a later stage. It would, however, be advisable to consider some other theory and facts that have emerged from research before coming to firm conclusions as to the nature of this link.

# 5

# *Education and career*

We have seen that creative achievers typically receive a considerable amount of intellectual stimulation in their childhood homes – from parents, from other role models and through independent intellectual activities, such as reading. It is at home that some also gain their basic education, develop career aspirations and begin to practise some professional skills. In this chapter the focus moves from the home to other aspects of their intellectual development – their formal education and career.

## Education

Although it might seem relatively easy to quantify education (in terms of number of years spent at educational institutions, or levels attained), it is in fact not that simple to measure education meaningfully. In the first place, neither the number of years of attendance at an accredited institution nor the level attained faithfully reflect the *quantity* of instruction received. Instruction may regularly occupy the greater part of the day, or it might be spasmodic. In the second place, numerical indices give little indication of the *quality* of instruction. Therefore, in addition to quantitative data, the following section considers qualitative effects of education, such as creators' feelings about the value of their education.

### Academic levels attained

Among the most eminent geniuses in history are some who received little or no education from formal institutions. Michael Faraday, whose name is high in the ranks of science, left school at fourteen. He described his education as most ordinary: 'consisting of little more than the rudiments of reading, writing and arithmetic at a common day school. My hours out of school were passed at home and in the streets' (quoted by MacDonald, 1964, p. 11).

On leaving school, Faraday became employed by a bookbinder, and the inspiring part of his education began. He began to instruct himself by reading all he could lay his hands on and attended a few public lectures given by scientists of the day. The enthusiasm engendered by this rather limited experience led him to seek employment in a scientific setting (as a menial assistant to Sir Humphry Davy), which enabled him to further his knowledge.

Edison, the most prolific inventor of all times, left school before the age of fourteen, but his mother tutored him at home, where he also read avidly and conducted experiments. Even when employed on the railways, Edison continued with his experiments – in baggage vans. Evariste Galois (1811–1832) was also tutored at home by his mother. When he eventually attended school he remained independent, studying and developing mathematical principles on his own, until the day of his early death at the age of twenty-one. During his studies he came across a textbook that enabled him to master the whole structure of geometry. At the end of them his posthumous papers served as the basis for a new field of mathematics (Bell, 1937).

As I have noted, there were also some remarkable geniuses who never attended school at all. Blaise Pascal stands out among them. After the death of Pascal's mother (when he was three years old), his father devoted his time entirely to the education of his children – and it may say something for the dedicated tuition of Pascal senior that before dying at the age of thirty-nine years, his son Blaise invented and constructed the first calculating machine, gave Pascal's laws to physics, proved the existence of the vacuum, helped to establish the science of hydrodynamics and (with Fermat) formulated the theory of probability. Blaise Pascal's prose style is, moreover, said to have influenced the French literary language, and his philosophies to have 'affected the mental cast of three centuries' (quoted by Illingworth & Illingworth, 1969, p. 51).

Not all creators receive so little formal education outside the home however, and although education, in the broader sense, includes all forms of acquisition of knowledge, it is unfortunately most reliably measured in terms of levels attained at formal institutions. Research based on such quantitative information has presented a fairly clear picture of the relation between level of formal education and historical eminence. Much of this research has been conducted by Dean Keith Simonton, who separated the creative subjects from the leaders in Cox's sample, applying multivariate analyses to the data (controlling for factors such as economical status, intelligence and life span). Simonton found the relation between the education and eminence of historical figures could be represented by an inverted U curve, the peak of which falls on a point representing some tertiary education as shown in figure 5.1.

As figure 5.1 suggests, in historical times, level of education was positively related to the probability of creative achievement – up to a point. But at the uppermost levels the relation is negative. Interesting to note, there is apparently a linear, but negative, relation between education and leadership in historical times (also shown in fig. 5.1). Stating it simply and bluntly, Simonton (1976) concluded that, 'though creativity is first encouraged and then discouraged with increases of formal education, leadership is strictly discouraged' (p. 224).

As the sample used by Simonton included subjects from a wide range of historical periods, nationalities and fields of creative endeavour, he presumed that the findings would generalize widely. On the other hand, one might expect that they would *not* apply to science in modern times. It seems improbable that a person as unschooled as Faraday could attain the highest ranks of scientific eminence today, because knowledge accumulates over the centuries and an increasing amount of education

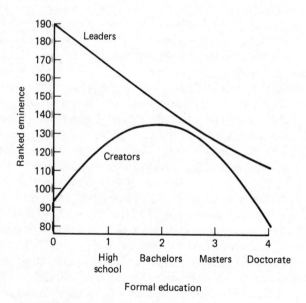

Figure 5.1  *Simonton's findings on the relation between level of formal education and ranked eminence of leaders and creative achievers (from Simonton 1984, p. 65).*

is likely to be needed for lifting the potential creator onto the shoulders of those who have gone before him. Today, one would therefore expect a linear relation between education and scientific creativity, or at the very least an upward shift of the optimal level of education for scientific achievement.

Nevertheless, as Simonton's trend analysis of historical data had shown no general tendency for the optimal level of education to increase over the five centuries represented by Cox's sample, he supposed his conclusions might hold for contemporary achievers, and tested a modern sample. For this purpose he classified the twentieth-century achievers selected by Goertzel, Goertzel and Goertzel (1978) into four groups. In the first group were leaders (*inter alia* politicians and military men), in the second were celebrities (including athletes, performers, businessmen, editors), in the third were scientists and inventors, and the fourth group consisted of artistic creators (e.g. painters, composers, writers and film producers).

An analysis of the relation between eminence and education in each of these categories revealed that the only group in which there was a linear positive relation between education and eminence was the group of celebrities. *For each of the other groups the relation between education and eminence was a curvilinear function, the distribution of which could be represented by an inverted U curve.* For the leaders the peak fell just above a bachelor's degree, and for artists the peak fell below a bachelor's degree. For scientists the peak was the highest, falling between a bachelor's and doctoral degree. These findings indicate that education is more conducive to becoming a leader in modern times than it was in past centuries, that a bachelor's degree is still unnecessary for attaining eminence in artistic fields (although it is preferable to having no secondary education) and that one still does not need a doctoral degree to make a notable contribution to science. Simonton (1984) concluded that the inverted U form of the curvilinear relation between creativity and education is probably a universal and enduring phenomenon, likely to vary only with respect to the optimal level of education in various disciplines.

If the curvilinear relation is indeed reliable, how may it be explained? Why does creativity seem not to increase steadily with higher levels of education? Simonton (1984) suggested two alternatives. One suggestion is that the development of creative potential may be stifled by excessive training. Students who concentrate their energies on becoming academically proficient may subordinate their creative abilities to learning. Several other authors (e.g. Gordon, 1961; Kuhn, 1970) have made similar suggestions, expressing the opinion that education may inhibit creativity by causing the person to become over-committed to the traditional manner of approaching the problems inherent in the discipline. Simonton's second suggestion was that creative achievers tend to discontinue their education when they feel they have learned enough to continue on their own – they may simply become bored with formal instruction, or disenchanted with what formal institutions have to offer. In other words it may not be a case of 'increases of formal education discourage creativity', but 'creativity discourages increases of formal education'. This attitude is clearly expressed by Einstein in a letter to a friend 'I shall not become a Ph D . . . the whole matter has become a bore to me' (Hoffman, 1972, p. 55).

Nevertheless Einstein did become a Ph.D – by submitting one of his publications for consideration, while working for the patent office in Switzerland. His highest academic attainment may therefore be attributed to independent activity rather than to formal education.

## Academic performance

Some eminent creators excelled at school and in their university careers. For example, scientists Robert Oppenheimer, Marie Curie and Max Planck had brilliant academic careers. It is nevertheless obvious that creative achievements are not reliably foreshadowed by academic performance. Not all eminently creative people were good scholars. Charles Darwin confessed that he was rather below average and considerably slower to learn than his sister (F. Darwin, 1929). Pasteur worked extremely hard at school but had difficulty in passing examinations (Vallery-Radot, 1937). Although it is often noted that Einstein was a poor scholar, this is not quite true (Hoffman, 1972). When writing in later life of his unhappiness and mediocre performance at school, he focussed on his weaknesses which included a poor memory for words and texts. The fact is that he was always far beyond the school curriculum in mathematics and physics. At the age of sixteen he taught himself calculus and had acquired some extraordinary scientific insights (Hoffman, 1972).

The IPAR researchers found their highly creative subjects in various fields were not distinguished by the grades they had received at school and there was an (insignificant) negative correlation between performance at college and later creativity. Only in the case of architects were college grades significantly correlated ( +0.27) with subsequent creativity. MacKinnon (1978) suggested this might have something to do with the fact that the work done by architectural students at college to some extent resembles the work they perform later in their occupation. The most creative architects were, however, generally not 'A' students. Nor were they poor students, or lazy students. On average they gained a 'B'. But they were extraordinarily independent, producing very good work in courses that caught their interest, and doing little or no work at all in courses that failed to interest them (MacKinnon, 1978).

Although there is little consistent evidence to suggest that scholastic success is a reliable predictor of creative achievement, it appears that creativity in science or philosophy is more likely than other forms of creativity to be foreshadowed by some academic success. H. J. Walberg, Rasher and Parkerson (1979) found that, in comparison with other groups, the philosophers in Cox's and Cattell's samples had been more academically successful. All Roe's (1951b) physical scientists and Visher's (1948) Starred American Men of Science had done well at school, and Chambers (1964) found that creative scientists had done better at school than control scientists, excelling in mathematics and showing strong intellectual drives. Bloom (1963) found an unusually high level of academic achievement predicted future scientific creativity, but at lower levels academic performance was not related to subsequent creative achievement.

On the whole it seems that if one wishes to predict creativity, achievements at school or college are not a reliable basis on which to do so – except that *scientific creativity might be expected in very outstanding students who are particularly interested in science.* This cannot, however, lead one to the conclusion that other creative achievers are stupid or ignorant in their childhood and youth. It may merely reflect their lack of interest in the courses offered at school.

## Attitudes towards education

Dislike of school is a universal phenomenon. One is more likely to find critical than favourable comments about school in biographies, whether or not the subjects of the biographies are creative. And most collections of case histories of eminent creators are replete with examples of sad and amusing antagonistic remarks about school and teachers. Einstein's feelings towards education are legend. Reminiscing about school, he declared it had demotivated him, and complained that

One had to cram all this stuff into one's mind for the examinations, whether one liked it or not. This coercion had such a deterring effect on me that, after

I passed the final examination, I found the consideration of any scientific problem distasteful to me for an entire year. (Einstein, 1949/1979b, pp. 16–17)

And yet it is often possible to discern, under the unfavourable attitudes to *school*, a favourable attitude to *learning*. Einstein (1949/1979b) further remarked that

It is, in fact, nothing short of a miracle that the modern methods of instruction have not yet strangled the holy curiosity of inquiry; for this delicate little plant, aside from stimulation, stands mostly in need of freedom; without this it goes to ruin without fail. It is a very grave mistake to think that the enjoyment of seeing and searching can be promoted by means of coercion and a sense of duty. (1949/1979b, p. 17)

A favourable attitude to learning is also seen in the writings of Jean Sibelius the Finnish composer, who was, however, somewhat indecisive about the joys of school:

If I am asked what interested me most at school, I can say with a clear conscience 'Nothing'. I must, however, make an exception in favour of natural science, which coincided with my love of nature. History was able to engross me at times, if it dealt with periods that appealed to the imagination; then I read the dry school book as if it were a novel. I must not forget the classical languages, that opened up a new exalted world of beauty. Homer and Horace had a significance in my development that I cannot value highly enough. (Quoted by Illingworth & Illingworth, 1969, p. 253)

Bernard Shaw replied sternly to his biographer, Buffin, who had described him as unteachable,

You say I was an unschoolable boy at a bad school. But what is an unschoolable boy? I was greedy for knowledge, and interested in everything, and if school taught me nothing except that school is a prison and not a place of teaching, the conclusion is that pedagogy is not yet a science. (Quoted by Illingworth & Illingworth, 1969, p. 253)

Nor does it seem that contemporary achievers have a particularly positive attitude to school. Sixty per cent of Goertzel, Goertzel and Goertzel's twentieth century sample disliked school, and only 30 per cent were favourably disposed.

Nevertheless, even though creative achievers may have been unfavourably disposed to school, they did, after all, reach standards of excellence in their subsequent works. And it seems unreasonable to arrive at conclusions about the negative effects of schooling on creativity from facts relating to people whose intellectual development reflected little negative influence. One may only hope to gain some indication of the *positive* effects from their self-reports.

*Evaluation of education*

On examining the self-reports of creators one is likely to find that they value most highly those aspects of education that helped them in some way to pursue their careers. Accordingly, scientists have more positive attitudes towards higher levels of education than towards school. Nearly a third of Visher's (1948) Starred Men of Science felt their high-school training had contributed much to their later achievement. Nearly two-thirds considered their college training had been valuable, but almost all considered their postgraduate training had been considerably valuable.

Favourable attitudes to higher levels of education may at least partly be attributed to the fact that at higher levels students are able to work relatively independently, and to focus on their subject of interest. And there is much to suggest in the foregoing discussion that creators take an interest in, and do well in, subjects that are closely related to their field of interest. As academic training is more necessary to science than to most other forms of creative achievement, this may also explain why creative scientists are more interested in academic training than other creators are. One gains a similar impression from the way in which creators evaluate their teachers.

*Valued qualities of teachers*

Although some creative achievers may have been negatively disposed toward school, one finds they were usually positively influenced by someone who taught them – either an adult member of the family or a teacher. Even Einstein acknowledged his debt to some of his teachers. In childhood he was encouraged by an uncle and by an older friend who gave him books on algebra, mathematics, physical science and philosophy, which he greatly enjoyed discussing. One of his teachers at the detested Luipold Gymnasium (from which he was eventually expelled for being disruptive), was a man named Reuss, who was less rigid and conforming than others and encouraged students to think for themselves. In adulthood, when his work had already begun to be recognized, Einstein visited Munich to call on Reuss, now retired. Unfortunately Einstein's appearance was so unkempt that the old man, who did not recognize him, presumed him to be on a begging errand and the meeting was rather abrupt. Another teacher remembered by Einstein with gratitude was August Tuchschmind, who taught him in his final years at a Swiss school. Einstein remembered this school as 'remaining for me the most pleasing example of such an institution' where teacher and student were joined in 'responsible and happy work such as cannot be achieved by regimentation, however subtle' (R. W. Clark, 1971, p. 25).

Among those who have made systematic enquiries into the contributions of teachers to the development of creators are Roe (1951a, 1951b, 1953); Visher (1948); H. J. Walberg, Rasher and Parkerson (1979) and Zuckerman (1977), whose studies reveal that teachers apparently promote the development of creators through encouraging them to pursue their interests. Examining facts relating to the lives of Cox's and Cattell's subjects, Walberg, Rasher and Parkerson found that creative achievers typically receive slightly more encouragement to pursue their particular interests from teachers than from parents. (A number were encouraged by both.) Visher's (1948) Starred Men of Science reported that their academic years had contributed to their ultimate success mainly by establishing their ideals and ambitions. They had received more encouragement to become scientists from teachers than from parents.

Teachers apparently also contributed to the development of future creators by encouraging independent activity. Roe's (1953) highly creative scientific subjects reported that somewhere in the course of academic training they had a teacher who encouraged them to find out things for themselves, or who let them do so, or who made them do so because he did not wish to be bothered by them. And 'once intellectual independence was really tasted, nothing else mattered much pedagogically; bad teaching was only an irritation' (Roe, 1953, p. 53).

Goertzel and Goertzel (1962) found that their subjects valued exchange of ideas, intelligent appreciation of their special interests and 'best liked' teachers who let them proceed at their own pace and allowed them to work unimpeded in their area of interest. They remembered affectionately all adults and classmates who had challenged their thinking, introduced them to exciting books, or supplied them with materials for their work.

A third way in which teachers seem to influence the development of creative ability is by providing good models for emulation. It appears that, particularly at higher levels, creators value and gain most from teachers who are especially able in their own sphere of interest – in other words, teachers who are good models. There is considerable evidence to indicate the effectiveness of such models for enhancing the development of first-rate creative ability. The history of art is replete with examples, and the power of such models in science is well demonstrated by the following astounding figures. Six of Enrico Fermi's students won the Nobel Prize. Ernst Lawrence and Niels Bohr each had four students who won the prize and Nernst and Meyerhoff each had three. But these figures still pale before the record set by J. J. Thompson and Ernest Rutherford, who between them trained seventeen Nobel laureates (Zuckerman, 1977). There is little question of these figures being attributed to chance! One cannot, of course, say that these men could have taught anyone to win a Nobel Prize. However, it is obvious that these teachers (all of whom won a Nobel Prize themselves) were not only creative in their own work, but also able to identify outstanding creative potential in others, and to shape it effectively.

It seems that chance plays a relatively minor role in the success attained by Nobel laureates. Zuckerman (1977) found that laureates, like other members of the scientific elite, had attended a comparatively small number of institutions for tertiary education, and attributed this to selectivity on the part of both students and institutions. As students, future laureates were well informed about important events and people in the scientific world. They were discriminating in their choice of universities, departments and mentors. It turned out that more than half the American Nobel laureates in science had been apprenticed to men who won the Nobel Prize themselves (69 per cent of these apprentice-ships were completed before the prize was awarded to the master). Moreover the prestigious institutions and masters recruited their students selectively, so it is likely that the high standard of work at these superior institutions would be maintained. The implications are that *those who are highly creative themselves are the most fit to judge a high level of creative potential and train people to be creative.*

It remains to consider how highly effective masters influence their senior students. Zuckerman refers to the importance of 'socialization' – the process whereby people are inducted into a culture or subculture which includes more than education or training. Her subjects agreed that the acquisition of knowledge is the least important consideration when one is apprenticed to an eminent master. Many students had more knowledge of their subject than their masters did. What they had gained from their masters was a style of thinking, a method of working, standards, values and attitudes, rather than knowledge. One of her subjects explained that good mentors taught their students not only 'the words' but also 'the music' of science.

Creative scientists, although they may at times exhibit a careless disregard for rules, have a passionate regard for exacting *standards*. Zuckerman's Nobelists agreed that a good master evoked such standards by his own excellent performance; by demanding excellence from his students – and by being a severe critic. Nobelists felt that working with exacting masters had taught them to measure up to the best standards, and they had gained self-confidence by learning to meet those standards. In other words their self-concepts were based not on believing or hoping, but on *knowing* they were capable of producing good original work. At the highest levels of creativity it is probable that few besides the creators themselves are able to assess a new creation, and it is necessary that they should learn to adopt an objective critical attitude towards their own work. Such an attitude may be adopted from critical masters. It is not, of course, enough for masters to be critical. To be effective, their criticism must be based on sound insight and aesthetic appreciation – what one would call 'taste'.

Zuckerman's Nobelists also reported they had tried to live up to their masters. They felt obliged to reciprocate for the time, effort and expertise spent on them, by producing excellent work and acquiring 'scientific taste'. As Zuckerman explained, scientific taste involves the development of the ability to identify important problems, to identify gaps and decide which problems are ripe for solution at the time and, of course, also to provide elegant solutions. And it is now recognized that the ability to distinguish between consequential and trivial questions is an important characteristic of creative achievers (e.g. Perkins, 1988; Sternberg, 1988; Walberg, 1988).

## Conclusions arising from studies relating to the education of creative achievers

The foregoing discussion leads to the conclusion that learning is necessary to the development of creativity of the highest order, although attendance at an academic institution is not essential. Those who lacked formal education acquired a good deal of education in their homes. Contemporary artistic creators typically acquire some tertiary education, and scientific creators usually acquire a considerable amount of it.

Although a few creators excel at school, not all are good pupils or academically successful. In general they appear to be somewhat unfavourably disposed to school, and tend to focus on their subject of interest, engaging in a considerable amount of self-instruction rather than merely adhering to a school curriculum. They read a lot, and instruct themselves with the aid of books and practical experimentation. At lower levels of schooling they appreciate teachers who allow them to pursue their particular interests, let them work independently, and encourage them to pursue careers in line with their interests and abilities. It seems that positive attitudes towards learning initially established in the home are then often directed into the *particular direction* of the future career by teachers who are able to recognize the nature and degree of the child's potential, and provide good examples to emulate.

From Zuckerman's interviews with Noble laureates in science one gathers that, at the highest level of tertiary education, grooming by good teachers is important for placing a student in a favourable position to attain eminence. Effective teachers establish high standards for themselves and encourage their protégés to be self-critical and aim high. But it is also apparent that by the time potential achievers reach the higher levels of tertiary education, their sights are already set on achievement. There are strong indications that *relevant interests, motivation, and skills are usually to some extent already operative before creators reach the highest levels of their academic careers.*

All this provides considerable support for the suggestions put forward in earlier sections – that the development of creativity begins early and is promoted by stimulation and by emulation of exemplary models, who set the pace and direction. It is also clear that the development of the future creator's basic skills is promoted by independent activity.

## The career

Several consistent themes may be seen in findings relating to the careers of highly creative people. First, creators typically decide on and start their careers at an early age; second, the quality of their work is positively related to the quantity they produce, and third, they typically produce their first and their best works at more or less equivalent ages. Each of these themes is discussed in the following section.

### Early beginnings

When he was ten or eleven years old Jean Piaget published his first article and was offered the position of curator of the Geneva Museum of Natural History by the director – who was unaware that the writer of the article was a school boy. Gauss derived important mathematical principles at the age of fifteen years. Wiener had a Ph. D at eighteen, and Henri Poincaré received public recognition for his work before entering college.

As intimated in foregoing sections, eminent creators typically crystallize their interests, and become in some way involved in their future careers in childhood or early adolescence (Albert, 1971, 1975; Cox, 1926; Lehman, 1953; Raskin, 1936; Roe, 1951a; Simonton, 1984). Even those who make an uncharacteristic late start to the career, often show some interest in their discipline in childhood. For example, although Darwin started comparatively late on his career as a naturalist (having first made abortive attempts to become a medical doctor or a clergyman) he devoted a considerable amount of his time to collecting insects and other natural materials as a child (F. Darwin, 1929). This again gives the impression that creative achievers are typically very interested in learning about something in childhood, though not necessarily about what they were taught at school.

Albert (1975) suggested that the early career decisions of eminent creators are no doubt related to intellectual precocity, and he proved his point by showing that the age at which the eminent individuals in Cox's (1926) sample had begun their careers varied inversely with their IQ. In other words the more intelligent they were the sooner they became interested in their professions. It should, however, be remembered that Cox's estimates of IQ were partly based on the age at which the subjects mastered certain intellectual tasks in childhood and youth, including those relating to their future professions. For example evidence of superior literary or musical compositions or scientific writings at an early age would signify an early interest in the profession and also raise the estimate of that person's IQ. Consequently there is bound to be some overlap between Cox's estimates of IQs and the age at which subjects became actively engaged in tasks relating to their careers. Indeed any IQ index for children embodies a comparison with norms for children of the same age. It is an index of precocity, and is bound to be associated with 'early beginnings'.

These methodological shortcomings do not, however, detract from the fact that the particular interests and abilities of creative achievers in youth were typically related to their future careers. Moreover, Torrance (1987) showed that creativity in adulthood can be predicted by a child's future career image. Children who know what they are 'in love with' and are relatively sure what they will be when they are adults, are more likely than others to be creative in adulthood.

There does, however, appear to be some difference with respect to the ages at which career-related interests developed in creative achievers in different fields. Roe (1953) found that, in general, physical scientists displayed their interests at an earlier age than others. Biologists made their decisions somewhat later and psychologists later still. These findings are supported by those of Chambers (1964) who found that creative psychologists made their career decisions later than other creative scientists. This may be explained by the fact that children generally show an interest in physical phenomena before they become interested in biological or psychological phenomena. A young child is indeed better able to master relatively concrete, reliable, predictable facts than less tangible, less reliable, less manageable biological or psychological phenomena. As Einstein put it, in a letter to Max Born, 'living matter and clarity are opposites – they run away from one another' (in French, 1979, p. 275).

One cannot help but notice the parallel here between ontogenetic and cultural development. In the history of science one finds that creative advances were made in the physical sciences before the biological sciences – and psychology arrived rather late.

## *The relation between precocity and productivity*

Highly creative people do not seem to 'run out of steam'. They typically start early, are extremely prolific, and continue to work in old age (Albert, 1975; Dennis, 1956; Simonton, 1984). An example of a highly creative psychologist to whom this applies is Jean Piaget. Piaget published his first paper at eleven years of age, had about 300 publications to his credit, and was still active in his profession more than sixty years later. (He began his career as a biologist and focussed on epistemology only after obtaining a doctorate.)

The relation between precocity and extended productivity may be explained in various ways. Firstly, it might be explained in terms of what Merton (1968) called 'the Matthew effect' – a term derived from the phrase 'unto every one that hath shall be given', which comes from the Gospel according to St Matthew. The 'Matthew effect' refers to the fact that the contributions of someone who has already gained recognition will be more highly regarded and more readily accepted than equivalent contributions from a relatively unknown person. A similar notion is expressed in a well-known saying among artists that the signature is the most valuable part of a painting.

Simonton (1984) suggests the Matthew effect may partly explain the vast productivity of those who were successful beginners, because those who are initially successful and receive a relatively high degree of credit for whatever they do may thereby be encouraged to continue producing. This might account for quantity, but it cannot account for quality that stands the test of time. Moreover, not all highly creative geniuses were successful from the start. It is well known that many persisted in the same direction despite lack of public recognition – and even against considerable opposition.

Galton would no doubt have explained the relation between precocity and productivity in terms of natural endowment of superior intellectual ability and energy. Facts discussed in the foregoing pages offer the alternative (but not exclusive) suggestion that precocity and productivity tend to occur together because they both result from a tendency that arises early in life – to concentrate efforts in one area rather than distribute them across a variety of pursuits. This tendency might result in the early development of knowledge and ability in a particular area, and eventually a large quantity of creative works. Although it is questionable whether relevant knowledge and professional skill are *sufficient* to creative achievement, they *are* clearly necessary.

## *The ages at which the first, best and last works are produced*

As knowledge accumulates in a society there is more to learn and one would imagine that it would take longer to acquire the basic knowledge and skills inherent in a discipline. Nevertheless, even in science, the age at which highly creative people make their first notable contributions has not been delayed much beyond the twenties. More than a century ago George Beard (1874) found that 70 per cent of the greatest contributions had been made by men under forty years of age, and that 80 per cent of the world's best works had been produced by people under the age of fifty. Beard concluded that there is a rapid incline in creativity up to the peak of an eminent career at about forty, and then a slow decline to almost nothing by eighty years. Later Raskin (1936) found that eminent men of letters and scientists of the nineteenth century had produced their first works in the twenties, flowered into full maturity ten years later, and then remained active until about ten years before death. (This refers to creative achievers who live for longer than sixty years, which Raskin found to be usually the case.)

Findings of research conducted around the middle of this century showed that the productivity of highly creative people does not decline to a very great extent in later adulthood, indicating that Raskin was closer to the mark than Beard was (see Davis, 1954; Dennis, 1954, 1966; Lehman, 1953). More recently it has been shown that the relation between age and productivity is a single-peak curvilinear function (Simonton, e.g. 1985). Musicians and dramatists usually reach their peak in the thirties or forties, after which their production drops rather sharply; poets and mathematicians usually produce their best work at a relatively young age, before forty; on average, prose writers are at their best at about forty-three; both the quantity and quality of the work of first-rate scientific creators reach a peak at forty and then hardly decline at all, and the creative productions of historians and philosophers may gradually peak up to the age of sixty (Cole, 1979; Simonton, 1984; Zuckerman, 1977).

The upper age-limit for creative work seems to be set only by physical decline that causes dementia, or inability to go about one's work. Milton finished his great work *Paradise lost* at the age of sixty-six. In Lehman's sample there were six mathematicians who had made their *only* contributions after the age of seventy. Goethe wrote his *Faust* at eighty-two. Michelangelo was the chief architect of St Peter's from the age of seventy-two until his death at eighty-nine. Thomas Hobbes continued his controversial writing until he died at ninety-one years of age. Thomas Mann wrote what he called his 'wildest' book at seventy while physically ill – and Fontenelle published his final defence of the Cartesian vortices (in 1752) at the age of ninety-five!

Various, but not entirely incompatible, suggestions have been offered to explain the rise and fall of creativity over the life-span. Simonton (1983, 1984) suggested that a creator begins with a certain supply of creative potential, which becomes, so to speak, 'used up', and he constructed a mathematical model to show that the rate at which potential is consumed is proportional to the amount of potential still available. Most suggestions as to the reason for the rise and fall of creativity over the life-span refer, however, to motivation or energy, and to intellectual growth or decline.

Beard (1874) suggested that creativity is a function of enthusiasm and experience – enthusiasm providing the motivational impetus, and experience the skill to discriminate between good and bad ideas. He explained that the declining enthusiasm of youth and the increasing experience of age reach an equilibrium between thirty-eight and forty years of age, at which stage inspiration is balanced with wisdom. In other words, decline in motivation or energy is balanced by intellectual growth. One way of construing Beard's notion of enthusiasm is in terms of instinctual energy. It is likely that Freud would have explained decline in creative production in terms of declining sexual energy. And it is notable that creativity involving a relatively high degree of *emotional expression*, such as poetry, usually declines relatively early.

R. B. Cattell (1971) proposed that changes in creative output may at least partly be explained by the rise and fall of biologically determined 'fluid intelligence'. As fluid intelligence underlies abstract thinking its decline would have a particularly notable effect in areas such as mathematics.

Lehman (1953) suggested that the curve of productive creativity reflects a natural rise and fall of physical vigour. This is difficult to reconcile with the fact that many highly creative people were extremely productive in spite of ill health. For example, Darwin constantly suffered ill health, and Blaise Pascal before dying at the age of thirty-nine told his sister that after the age of eighteen years he had never passed a day without pain (Cox, 1926; Illingworth & Illingworth, 1969). It therefore seems more appropriate to suggest that rise and fall of creativity relates to growth and decline of *intellectual* rather than physical vigour.

Intellectual vigour may be construed in terms of biological resources, but it is obviously not simple to explain in practical terms exactly what those resources are. Perhaps one might construe it in terms of *speed of intellectual processing*. It has been shown that there is generally some decline in the speed of mental operations in adulthood which may be attributed to biological changes (e.g. Horn & Donaldson, 1977; Whitbourne & Weinstock, 1979). Decline in productivity might therefore (at least partly) be attributed to reduction in speed of intellectual processing. However reduction in speed may be compensated for by experience of how to employ energy most economically, and by development of automatic skills. This suggests that, as one grows older, learning may compensate for biological decline (but there comes a point where such compensation is inadequate.)

Furthermore, as several researchers, including R. B. Cattell (1971), Cox (1926) and Roe (1953) have suggested, the use of available energy and intelligence is determined by personality and motivation. Overall deficits in intellectual vigour may be compensated for by directing as much energy as possible in a single direction. All the energy available to a creator may be mustered and directed into work. Therefore creative production would depend not only on biological and intellectual resources but also on singularity of interests and motivation.

*Quality versus quantity of creative production*

It is interesting to note how extremely productive some highly creative people are. To mention but a few examples, Edison held 1093 patents, lodging on average one patent every two weeks of his adult life (R. W. Clark, 1977); Bach composed on average twenty pages of finished music per day – enough to keep a copyist busy for a life-time of standard working hours writing out the parts by hand; Picasso produced more than 20 000 works; Poincaré published 500 papers and thirty books;

Albert Einstein had 248 publications; Freud had 330 (Simonton, 1984). These figures lead one to realize a very important fact – *these people must have spent the major part of their waking hours and their energy on their work.*

The question arises as to whether quality is sacrificed to quantity when a creator is so prolific, and the answer appears to be 'no'. Findings of research in the area have indicated that, although even the most eminent creators sometimes produce somewhat inferior work, quality generally varies with quantity (Albert, 1975; Barron, 1963; Dennis, 1954; Simonton, 1984). This is nicely exemplified by the quality of Edison's contributions. Although there is usually some difficulty in establishing to what extent a new invention represents an addition to what has already been patented, there was often little such difficulty where Edison's inventions were concerned. When Edison presented his plans for a sound-recording machine, the patent office could find no record of anything of that kind (J. Rossman, 1931).

Dennis (1954) calculated the correlation coefficient representing the relation between quantity and quality of works produced by eminent scientists to be 0.46. Zuckerman (1977) found that Nobel Prize winners for science published about twice as many papers as a control group of American Men of Science, and Simonton (1984) found that the best predictor of enduring eminence in a sample of 696 composers was their melodic productivity. There is not, however, a perfect relationship between quality and quantity, and there are some notable exceptions to the rule in the history of major contributions to the culture – especially where quantity refers to number of published works. At one extreme is the biologist John Edward Gray, an English naturalist who published 883 papers but is not mentioned in any history of biology (Dennis, 1954). At the other is Gregor Mendel, who is mentioned in all histories of biological science for making some of the most important contributions to biology through publishing only seven papers. And then of course there was Copernicus who published only one scientific work – which he knew to be unsound.

The usual relation between quality and quantity could be explained in terms of (a) quality resulting from quantity; (b) quantity resulting from quality, and (c) both being a function of the same determinants.

Campbell (1960) favoured view (a). He proposed that creativity, like learning, results from trial and error and selective retention of ideas that are generated by chance. In this respect cultural evolution somewhat resembles biological evolution. The more ideas generated, the more likely it is that some of them are adaptive and survive the test of evaluation. As Simonton (1988) put it, those who buy the most lottery tickets stand the best chance of winning. This is obviously the principle applied in creativity training-programmes. However, the use of this model to explain high levels of creativity must rest on the assumption that creative people are capable of producing at least some exceptionally good ideas, and have the ability to evaluate the worth of the ideas. View (b), which holds that quantity results from quality, suggests that creators are encouraged to continue creating when they produce something worthwhile. This too implies that they must be able to generate something of worth in the first place. In fact both (a) and (b) must also imply (c), which suggests that the tendency to produce something valuable must depend on relatively enduring ability and interest.

Finally one should consider whether perhaps there is typically some variation in the *quality* of creators' products during the course of their careers. Although Dennis and Lehman suggested that quality may decline, Simonton (1985) showed that, in the case of psychologists, the proportion of important works to total output remains constant. As Simonton pointed out, this supports Campbell's suggestion that the degree of success *per unit* of work does not relate to age – which implies that the secret of success is to be productive.

## Conclusions

Findings relating to the careers of creators lead one to conclude that, although there is some variation among disciplines, creative achievers typically crystallize their interests early, and that their early interests persist and decide their careers. A fit between special abilities and choice of career seems indeed to be an important factor in the development of creative ability.

Although a future creator's special abilities are not always well developed or discernible in childhood, and their niche not always clearly recognized by themselves or by teachers (as happened in the case of Darwin, Freud and William James), most creators know what they want to do, and develop the necessary skills. They do not appear to need what Erikson called a moratorium – time free from commitment for discovering a match between their own proclivities and expectations. They acquire the necessary skill and knowledge for producing their first notable works in the twenties and their best works in the thirties and forties. And they keep going. This brings us back to Simonton's suggestion that once creative achievement has been experienced, little seems to side-track achievers and deter them from producing. There is indeed little support for the old wives' tales about the self-destructive nature of precocity. In the case of creative achievers, early ripe does not cause early rot: precocity does not foretell of premature decay. Although there may be fluctuations in the quantity or quality of work produced over their life-spans, in general they keep working. They obviously spend a major part of their waking hours working – and decline caused by aging may be compensated by experience.

# 6

## Characteristics of creative achievers

Apart from being extremely productive, what sort of people are creative achievers? Are they generally intelligent? Are they mad, as the ancients would have it? Have they any distinctive personality characteristics? Are there any connections between their early experience, characteristics and creative ability?

With good reason, several authors (e.g. R. W. Weisberg, 1986) have asserted that there is no difference between creative geniuses and other people. This is of course true in most respects – but not in all. If one wishes to explore the determinants of genius, it is necessary to discover how geniuses differ from ordinary people while resembling other geniuses – not only with regard to their life experiences but also with regard to their personal characteristics. In this chapter, we look at some of the facts relating to their intelligence, pathology and personality.

### Intelligence of creative achievers

Research into the relation between creativity and intelligence is beleaguered not only by the problem of quantifying creativity but also by the problem of quantifying intelligence. 'Intelligence' has been construed and measured in various ways. Already in 1927 Spearman remarked that it had become a mere vocal sound with so many meanings that it was left with none. As 'intelligence' is not an absolute reality that exists independently of the constructions placed upon it, we alter the focus in this section, allowing it to rest briefly on one or other of several constructions of intelligence.

Intelligence is now frequently described as the *ability to adapt to the environment and to adapt the environment to oneself* (e.g. Albert & Runco, 1986; Charlesworth, 1976; Sternberg, 1986, 1988). Sternberg, for example, explains that intelligence is expressed in purposively adapting to the environment; shaping the existing environment into a new one, or selecting real-world environments that are relevant to one's culture and circumstances. If one considers intelligence in these terms, there is no question of considering its relation to creativity – especially scientific creativity. If intelligence means selecting and shaping environments, it *is* creativity. The human species adapts to the environment through selectively shaping the environment rather than through physical mutation. As Mayr (1970) pointed out, it is not the development of superior biological visual apparatus that allows people to see better, but the construction of microscopes and telescopes; it is not the development of superior leg muscles that allows them to move faster but the construction of cars and aeroplanes. Survival of the human species does not depend on the biological production of a great number of expendable progeny, but on scientific means for controlling the self-defeating effects of overpopulation. Therefore when one looks at intelligence as adaptation, scientific creativity is indeed the highest level of intellectual functioning: and (as Toynbee put it) man's ultimate capital asset. It represents capacity for developing new and better ways of mastering the environment.

The adaptation-to-the-environment view of intelligence does not however allow one to explain the extent to which intelligence overlaps or subsumes creativity, or to make direct comparisons between a person's intelligence and creativity. One way of making such comparisons is to arrive at some numerical scores of intelligence and compare them with scores representing creativity. Most research on the relation between creativity and intelligence has involved comparisons of scores on tests of general intelligence and tests of creative problem-solving ability (in unexceptional children or youths). Frequently cited studies of this nature were conducted by Getzels and Jackson (1962), who published a monograph on the subject. As we are presently concerned with the intelligence of productive creators ·rather than school children, these ·studies are, however, irrelevant in the present context, and we turn instead to assessments of the intelligence of productive creators.

### Research on the relation between intelligence and creative achievement

Two main strategies have been used for assessing the intelligence of productive creators. The first, which was used by Cox (1926) for assessing the intelligence of historical figures, involves deriving an IQ index from biographical data as described in chapter 2. The second, which was used for research on contemporary achievers, involves the administration of intellectual tests.

*Facts emerging from Cox's* (1926) *research on historical geniuses.* The IQs of all Cox's historical geniuses were assessed as being all above normal, ranging from 120 to 200 with a mean of 158.9. The average IQs for various subgroups of the creators and leaders in her sample are shown in table 6.1. As these IQs are based on comparison between the age at which subjects mastered certain tasks and the age at which such tasks are usually mastered, the overall impression gained is that Cox's subjects were *intellectually precocious.*

Table 6.1. Average IQs of subgroups in Cox's sample of geniuses

| Group | N | Average IQ |
|-------|---|-----------|
| Philosophers | 22 | 173 |
| Scientists | 39 | 164 |
| Revolutionaries | 9 | 163 |
| Fiction writers | 53 | 163 |
| Non-fiction writers | 42 | 162 |
| Religious leaders | 23 | 159 |
| Statesmen | 43 | 159 |
| Musicians | 11 | 153 |
| Artists | 13 | 150 |
| Soldiers | 27 | 133 |

Adapted from Cox (1926)

In stating her conclusion as to the intelligence of geniuses in childhood, Cox suggested that

Youths who achieve eminence are distinguished in childhood by behavior which indicates an unusually high IQ. (p. 216)

and

the extraordinary genius who achieves the highest eminence is also the gifted individual whom intelligence tests may discover in childhood. The converse of this proposition is yet to be proved. (p. 218)

As Cox's estimates of IQ and of eminence were both to some extent based on performance in youth, one would expect her to find positive correlations between eminence and intelligence. Finding, however, that IQ did not differentiate between *high* and *exceptionally high* levels of creative achievement, Cox suggested that superior performance in adulthood may be expected when the childhood IQ is above 150, but it cannot be guaranteed even if the childhood IQ is 200, as the achievement of *greatness is determined by factors other than intelligence.*

Several researchers have re-examined the Cox data in an attempt to gain greater clarity on the IQ/eminence relation. H. S. Walberg, Rasher and Hase (1978) drew attention to the fact that eminence is likely to vary over time if it is rated on the basis of space allotted to the individual in encyclopaedias, as encyclopaedias are periodically updated. On re-evaluating the eminence of Cox's subjects in terms of modern encyc-lopaedias, these authors found that, although IQ was positively related to eminence, it accounted for only about 5 per cent of the variance in eminence.

As it is difficult to show a valid and reliable correlation between creative achievement and intelligence in historical geniuses, one may only suggest that they were, on average, highly intelligent, in the sense that they were precocious in mastering intellectual tasks. However, as Cox and others (e.g. R. B. Cattell, 1971; Simonton, 1984; H. S. Walberg, Rasher & Hase, 1978) suggest, intelligence is necessary, but not sufficient, for genius. Other factors may decide whether or not a person's intelligence is used to highly creative ends. As Cox's most highly eminent subjects were notably persistent, it was her conclusion that

high but not the highest intelligence, combined with the greatest degree of persistence, will achieve greater eminence than the highest degree of intelligence with somewhat less persistence. (1926, p. 187)

*Research on contemporary creative achievers.* On a few occasions the intel-ligence of highly creative contemporary individuals has been assessed by administering tests – a practice that may lead one to discover more about the test than about the intelligence of the creative achiever. A frequently mentioned example of such a case refers to the illustrious French mathematician Henri Poincaré , who obtained such a poor score on the Binet intelligence test that 'had he been judged as a child instead of the famous mathematician he was, he would have been rated by the test as a imbecile' (Bell, 1937, p. 532). In terms of his life performance it is out of the question that Poincaré was an imbecile. Apart from being creative, he was a skilled mathematician and writer. So, if Poincaré was not fooling, his score merely shows that the Binet test was unsuitable for assessing an intellect of that calibre. As Hudson (1970) remarked 'mental tests are, after all, primitive affairs, and the skills they test are exceedingly simple. When we ask a scientist to complete a verbal analogy for us, or a numerical series, we are asking him to perform a skill insultingly trivial compared with those he uses in his research' (p. 226). One must also face the strong possibility that creative achievers are in some respects brighter than test constructors, and that their answers take certain factors into account that test constructors fail to consider.

However, not all studies of the test performance of creative achievers have backfired to the same extent. For example, researchers at IPAR (e.g. Barron, 1968; MacKinnon, 1978) found the average scores of various groups of contemporary creative achievers to be generally above normal on the Terman Concept Mastery Test (which is essentially a test of word knowledge, general information and reasoning ability). The scores of the various groups of creative and control subjects are shown in table 6.2.

Table 6.2. Mean scores and standard deviations of various groups on the Terman Concept Mastery Test

| Group | N | Mean score | Standard deviation |
|-------|---|-----------|---------|
| Creative writers | 20 | 156.4 | 21.9 |
| Creative female mathematicians | 41 | 131.7 | 33.8 |
| Creative research scientists (inventors) | 27 | 118.9 | 28.2 |
| Research scientists (non-inventors) | 18 | 117.3 | 30.9 |
| Creative architects | 40 | 113.2 | 37.7 |
| Undergraduate students | 201 | 101.7 | 33.0 |
| Air Force captains | 344 | 60.1 | 31.7 |
| Independent inventors | 14 | 50.8 | 34.7 |

Adapted from MacKinnon (1978, p. 93)

On the whole researchers have found that creative subjects are indeed above average in intelligence (as measured by tests) but, above a basic level, intelligence does not vary with creative production (Barron, 1968; Bloom, 1963; Cox, 1926; Drevdahl, 1956; MacKinnon, 1978; Roe, 1953; Helson & Crutchfield, 1970; Hudson, 1970; D. W. Taylor, 1963). MacKinnon (1978) suggested that there is probably a correlation between intelligence and creativity of about 0.40 over the total range of these variables, but beyond the IQ of about 120 the relation is negligible (the only group to whom this does not apply is mathematicians, as a correlation of 0.31 was found between their creative life performance and intelligence scores).

These conclusions are essentially in agreement with Cox's findings, which suggested that the intelligence of historical geniuses was generally above average but, above a certain level, their intelligence was not reliably related to creativity. It implies that intelligence is necessary but not sufficient to creative achievement. Even this is an oversimplification, however, for intellectual abilities seem more important than others for creativity in various domains.

## The specific mental abilities of creators.

People tend to agree that 'creativity', 'intelligence' and 'wisdom' have something in common, and that creativity is closer to intelligence than to wisdom (Sternberg e.g. 1988). Some take it for granted that a genius is intellectually 'brilliant' in most respects. It seems in fact that many geniuses, though outstandingly able in some respects were rather unwise, inept, or even rather stupid in others. Darwin has been described as virtually innumerate (Hudson, 1970). Mozart had difficulty in expressing himself clearly in words, his sentences tended to follow a rhythmic rather than meaningful pattern. In many of Mozart's writings there are reversals and repetitions of words, phrases, and sounds. The following extract, quoted by Ehrenwald (1984), comes from one of Mozart's least offensive letters to his female cousin:

I have received reprieved your letter telling selling me that my uncle carbuncle, my aunt, can't and you too are very well hell. Thank God, we too are in excellent health. Today the letter setter from my papa Ha! Ha! dropped safely into my claws paws. I hope that you too have got shot the note dote which I wrote to you from Mannheim. If so, so much the better, better than much so. (p. 108)

One can, with a little imagination, 'hear' the effects of Mozart's characteristic style of musical composition on the structure of the above phrases, which give the impression that some automatic habit, developed through composing, also dominated his verbal constructions. Ehrenwald points out that the structure of the phrase 'if so, so much the better, better than much so' is strikingly similar to the structure of the celebrated finale in act 2 of *Figaro*.

Feldman (1986) pointed out that some geniuses, like Mozart, are perhaps best described as prodigies – children who express an enormous amount of talent through a narrow channel. This is not to say that any were 'idiot savants' (who have tremendous talent in some area but are subnormal in other respects), for that would prevent them from organizing their talent and using it effectively in accordance with cultural and situational demands. Neither does it imply that prodigies are always geniuses, as Feldman explained, for genius requires that one leave some original mark on one's field.

The 'prodigy' notion of genius fits with Howard Gardner's (1983) view of intelligence as a collection of separate intelligences, which implies that one may, for example, be extremely intelligent with regard to music but not with language. One might well expect a creator to have a high level of the particular intellectual abilities that relate directly to his work. To give ability tests their due, this is in fact reflected by test scores. One may see in table 6.2, for example, that creative writers gained on average higher scores than other groups of creative subjects on the Concept Mastery Test (which is largely a test of verbal ability). Roe (1951b) found that the mathematical section of the verbal-spatial-mathematical test compiled by the College Educational Testing Service for her study of biological scientists was too easy for her sample of physical scientists (which at least suggests that the physical scientists were mathematically as able as the test constructors). Moreover, Roe found differences between different types of physicists where other intellectual abilities were concerned. On the verbal test the average score of the experimental physicists was significantly lower ($p < 0.05$) than that of the theoretical physicists (whose occupation involves more verbal activity). One can also see from table 6.3, which shows the scores obtained by Roe's (1951a, 1951b, 1953) subjects on verbal, spatial and mathematical ability tests, that there were notable differences between the scores of physical scientists, biologists and psychologists.

Table 6.3. *Scores obtained by scientists in various disciplines on various ability tests (Roe, 1953)*

| Type of ability test | Type of scientist | | |
| --- | --- | --- | --- |
| | Physicists | Biologists | Social scientists |
| Verbal | 57.6 | 56.6 | 59.0 |
| Spatial | 13.0 | 9.4 | 10.0 |
| Mathematical | too easy | 16.8 | 13.7 |

It seems reasonable to conclude that different levels of various intellectual abilities are necessary for creativity in specific fields. Creative advances in the physical sciences would demand a higher level of mathematical ability than is needed for producing artistic works. But scientific creativity would require a lower level of verbal ability than is necessary for creating a philosophical or literary work.

In addition, it seems, various types of creators have different styles of thinking and working. A particularly interesting study that cast some light on the varying styles of inventors was reported by MacKinnon (1978), who compared the test performance of (a) relatively non-inventive scientific researchers; (b) inventive scientific researchers (academically trained and employed in occupations demanding inventive activity); and (c) independent, spare-time inventors (with little academic education, and non-inventive employment). The average scores of these three groups on the Terman Concept Mastery Test are shown in table 6.2, where it can be seen that the independent inventors gained far lower scores than research scientists and a control group of undergraduate students. Most surprising was the fact that the most inventive subject of all – a man who held the most patents and whose inventions were also qualitatively superior – was an independent inventor who obtained a score of only 6 on the Concept Mastery Test. The lowest score obtained by a research scientist was 72. Low scores might, of course, reflect lack of formal education, but on closer inspection of the test paper of the most inventive subject it was found that his extremely poor score reflected something more than a low level of verbal and reasoning ability. It could be partly explained by the fact that marks are subtracted for incorrect answers on the Concept Mastery Test. Had this man left blanks instead of guessing when he did not know an answer, he would have gained a score of 87 instead of 6. In addition, it was found that, on the whole, research scientists were cautious and gave relatively few incorrect answers, whereas independent inventors did not hesitate to take chances.

On analysing the work styles of the three groups of researchers and inventors mentioned in the foregoing paragraph, Gough and Wood-worth (1960) found, *inter alia*, that both scientific and independent inventors were less likely than non-inventive researchers to be interested in academic methodological problems and elegant solutions. It seems that inventive people, particularly independent inventors, are happy to involve themselves directly with the practical aspects of a problem, take chances or find ways to the solutions they seek through using insights gained through practical experience, rather than concerning themselves with methodological niceties. This is not to say that such individuals would be incapable of acquiring academic skills, or that the products of independent inventors are generally inferior to the products that come out of research institutions. MacKinnon (1978, p. 106) quotes a list of inventions of the first part of the twentieth century which were conceived by inventors working alone without the backing of a research institution. On this list, which was originally compiled by Jewkes, Sawers, and Stillerman (1958) are air conditioning; automatic transmission; Bakelite; ball-point pen; catalytic cracking of petroleum; cellophane; chromium plating; cinerama; cotton picker; cyclotron; domestic gas refrigeration; electric precipitation; electron microscope; gyrocompass; hardening of liquid fats; helicopter; insulin; jet engine; Kodachrome; magnetic recording; Penicillin; Polaroid camera; power steering; quick freezing; radio; safety razor; self-winding wrist watch; Streptomycin; Sulzer loom; synthetic light polarizer; Xerography; zip fastener.

## Conclusions relating to the intelligence of creative achievers

In general the findings of research discussed in this section lead to the conclusions that

1. eminently creative achievement is often foreshadowed by precocity in childhood and this precocity is sometimes concentrated in certain areas;
2. creativity requires a minimal level of general skill that allows one to manage one's particular ability effectively; but above a certain level of intelligence there is no firm relation between creative achievement and general intelligence as measured by tests, or as assessed in terms of general ability to master the physical and social environment;
3. creators do, however, have a high level of the specific ability that relates to their particular field of achievement;
4. creative skills are expressed in various modes (intellectual or practical) according to the creators' education and experience.

Precocity may reflect superior innate biological potential, based on sound neurological functioning – which R. B. Cattell (e.g. 1971) called 'fluid intelligence' – considered to be the main determinant of creative achievement. However, although one may accept in principle that underlying potential may be inferred and assessed from current behaviour, the fact of the matter is that one cannot separate the potential from the actual. Fluid (innate) intelligence may be *conceptually* distinguished from crystallized (acquired) intelligence at an abstract level, but these cannot be expressed (or assessed) in isolation. In both life performance and test performance *the expression* of fluid intelligence depends on crystallized intelligence – and fluid intelligence can only (hypothetically) be compared in individuals who have had identical experience.

It is often held that no test is culture-free. As Charlesworth (1976) put it: 'If a person performs poorly on a test it is reasonable to ask how much that test actually represents the common every day environmental tests the individual has been put to and to which he or she has become adapted' (p. 159). But neither is life performance culture-free. From the beginning of life, behaviour is shaped by example and experience. Even in early life, childrens' intellectual performance, for example their ability to acquire language and literacy, can only be expressed when they have been exposed to relevant examples, material and/or instruction. Therefore, although precocious mastery of intellectual skills may indeed depend on superior fluid intelligence (which one cannot hope to measure through intelligence tests), it must also be determined by early experience. It may reflect early demands made on the child, and/or voluntary dedication of energies to intellectual pursuits.

Let us return to the case of John Stuart Mill for an example. Mill's father, James, began to drill him methodically in the basic intellectual skills before he was three and protected him throughout his childhood from all contact with other children except his siblings. Given the same biological potential (fluid intelligence) a child who plays all day with other children and is never exposed to books would simply not have the opportunity to master reading and algebra as early as Mill did.

It is indeed questionable whether, even conceptually, one may separate biological from acquired intelligence. There is an enormous body of physiological and psychological research to show neurological functioning changes as experience leaves its impact on neuronal and synaptic structures. This means the neurological substrate of intellectual behaviour changes continually, and it is likely to develop most in those areas where experience has had its greatest effects. This is not to say that genetic potential plays no part in determining the efficacy of intellectual functioning. It says that the genetically determined neurological structures underlying intellectual functioning *are constantly being reshaped*. The brain is not only the processor but also the product of experience.

We have noted that creative achievers usually gain relatively high scores on tests that measure *the type of ability that is basic to the area of their creative achievement*. This specialization may account for the fact that ratings of creative achievement do not bear a simple relation to scores on tests of general intelligence. The abilities measured by tests of general intelligence may not vary with the specialized abilities of the creators. As Sternberg (1988) put it, creativity depends as much on the direction as on the level of one's intelligence.

Much of the foregoing discussion points to the suggestion that creative ability develops through learning. One should not, however, take this to mean 'learning to be creative', or 'learning to think creatively' as construed in creativity programmes. It refers to acquiring knowledge and skill (in the area of the creator's speciality). When considering how to promote creativity, designers of creativity programmes and psychological theorists have tended to overlook the importance of learning. Understandably so – as creativity is considered to be antithetical to reproducing learned material. There is, nevertheless, much to suggest in the findings relating to the intelligence of eminent creators that creativity depends on acquired (crystallized) intelligence in some specific area. And it is likely that the development of the necessary crystallized intelligence is initiated by intellectual stimulation and independent intellectual activity in the home. Further developments may be attributed to emulation of appropriate models, self-instruction and education.

Of course skill and creativity are not synonymous, but facts (and common sense) strongly suggest that skill, even if not sufficient for creativity, is an important vehicle for it. It is, however, unfortunately fashionable in some circles to divorce creativity from skill entirely, and to preclude the use of skill when measuring creativity in controlled situations (e.g. Hennessey & Amabile, 1988). One should not generalize conclusions from such research to productive creativity, nor should one discuss them in conjunction with facts about 'people like Einstein' (as many researchers tend to do). Productive creativity cannot be divorced from skill.

## The relation between creative achievement and psychopathology

We come now to the age-old suggestion that genius is related to madness.

The question of if, and how, creativity is related to psychopathology has intrigued students of human nature over the ages, and still brings forth argument. As I have already mentioned, the ancients generally believed there to be a positive relation between creativity and madness, attributing both to the invasion of external forces. Nowadays there are three main views on the subject: one alleging creativity and pathology are positively related; another suggesting they are negatively related, and a third denying there is any relation at all.

In support of the first view are biographical studies of geniuses abounding with vivid and convincing examples of mental distress and bizarre behaviour – and also with some rather bizarre explanations for it. Among such explanations are those proffered by early researchers such as Lombroso (1895), who concluded that genius could be attributed to a mental degeneration associated with physical deformity, sterility and tuberculosis (among others). Nisbet (1912) related genius to no less than forty moral and physical afflictions, including vanity and gout. In the light of more recent studies it appears that the observations made by these researchers were not entirely unfounded, but their interpretations clearly reflect the danger of neglecting to identify, or of misidentifying, intervening variables. For example, the variable intervening between physical deformity and creative production need not be mental degeneration. It might have something to do with restriction of physical activities and diversion of energy into intellectual pursuits.

There is little doubt that many highly creative individuals suffer mental distress and exhibit bizarre behaviour. Many are considered mad – and admit they consider themselves to be so. Specific cases are described in, for example, Goertzel and Goertzel (1962), Illingworth and Illingworth (1969), Prentky (1980), and Storr (1983). Prentky (1980, p. 4) presented a table showing how the disorders of some historically eminent writers, artists, scientists and composers would probably be diagnosed in terms of contemporary nosology – quoting various examples of the symptoms these eminent people displayed. Prentky concluded that, although biographers and researchers may have been inexact in classifying the maladies of some individuals, in most cases they had ample reason for considering the behaviour abnormal.

As both mental health and creativity are positively valued in modern society, unwelcome findings that suggest a positive relation between creativity and pathology are often ignored. Those who espouse the idealistic suggestion that creativity inheres in mental health dismiss such evidence as 'anecdotal'. Haensley, Reynolds and Nash (1986), for example, asserted that findings linking genius and psychopathology are contrary to contemporary knowledge, pointing out that 'despite popular conceptions [that genius is allied to madness] gifted individuals are more likely to be taller, more attractive, and physically and emotionally healthier than their peers, and to have fewer behaviour problems as children and adolescents' (p. 129). This type of criticism is based on findings relating to gifted school children and clearly reflects a typical (uncritical) acceptance of the notion that giftedness and creative achievement are naturally and reliably related.

Among systematic empirical studies that have indicated that the incidence of mental disorder is higher among productive creative achievers than in the general population are those by Andreasen and Canter (1974); Juda (1949); Karlsson (1970, 1978); and McNeil (1971). Several researchers have attempted to discover what particular type of pathology is most commonly manifest in highly creative individuals in various fields. A particularly extensive study by Juda (1949) (which took twenty-six years to complete) involved about 5000 interviews and collection of data from about 19 000 people, including 131 creative artists, 181 creative scientists and members of their families. Juda's findings revealed that the incidence of psychic disturbance was significantly higher in creative achievers and their families than in the general population. He further concluded that the patterns of pathology typically differed in artists and scientists – the incidence of schizophrenia being three times as high in artists as in the general population, and the incidence of manic depressive disorders being ten times higher in scientists than in the general population. Non-psychotic disorders were twice as frequent among artists as in scientists. It was also shown that manic depressive disorders were more prevalent in the families of both artists and scientists than in the general population.

Later Karlsson (1978) showed that psychopathology (especially manic depressive disorders) was significantly more prevalent among the highly creative achievers listed in Iceland's 'Who's who' than among those whose eminence could be attributed to factors other than creativity (for example social position). On the basis of biographical material Karlsson claimed to have found the rate of psychosis to be 30 per cent for great novelists; 35 per cent for great poets; 35 per cent for great painters; 25 per cent for great mathematicians and 40 per cent for great philosophers. Other nomothetic studies supporting the suggestion of a positive relation between creativity and psychopathology are described by Richards (e.g. 1981) and by Holden (e.g. 1987). Among recent idiographic case histories of manic depression in creative achievers are those by Hershman and Lieb (1988).

It may be argued that such studies do not conclusively prove that genius is reliably related to psychopathology. Firstly, it is impossible to make accurate comparisons, as one cannot say with any certainty exactly how many of the general population are, or have been, mentally disordered. Secondly, even if eminent people are more inclined than others to exhibit bizarre behaviour and to report that they suffer mental distress, there is some argument as to whether this really reflects pathology. Those who deny that psychopathology and creativity are related suggest that creators are considered to be insane merely because they apparently have mental experiences that ordinary people are unable to share or understand (Storr, 1983). It has also been suggested that the behaviour of eminent people is no different from that of others but it comes under the limelight and is more closely scrutinized than the behaviour of their less famous contemporaries. In addition, creative individuals may be more inclined than conventional people to admit or exaggerate their aberrations (Nicolson, 1947). Other suggestions are that creative people feign madness, that their behaviour is eccentric rather than pathological (Becker, 1983; Hankoff, 1975; Nicolson, 1947), or that they deliberately induce altered states of consciousness to invite inspiration (Kubie, 1958; McKellar, 1957; Storr, 1983). Further, specific suggestions have been put forward to explain particular cases. For example, it was suggested that Faraday's malady might be attributed to poisoning from the mercury which he used in large quantities for his electrical connections.

Even though the above arguments may all be to some extent valid, on balance the literature relating to creative achievers seems to indicate that creativity is indeed positively related to psychopathology. It certainly refutes the suggestion that creative achievement depends on mental health. Authors (e.g. Prentky, 1980; Richards, 1981) who have extensively and critically reviewed relevant biographical data and research findings (relating to creative achievers, not school children) have concluded that there is indeed a higher degree of psychopathology among creators than in the general population. It seems that the age-old notion that genius is related to madness was not entirely unfounded, even if some invalid *explanations* have been offered.

If one accepts that mental illness and creativity can, and do tend to, co-exist in the same individual, the question remains as to whether they have common origins or whether one leads to the other.

Among those who believe there is a common origin – that creative behaviour and psychopathology have a *common genetic basis* – were Hammer and Zubin (1968) and Jarvik and Chadwick (1973). Empirical support for this suggestion was provided, for example, by Juda (1949), Karlsson (1978) and McNeil (1971), all of whom reported a high incidence of mental disorder not only in creative people but also in their families. These authors suggest that the genotype may tend to produce highly unusual behaviour which might be advantageous under certain conditions, as a modifier of other behaviour. Karlsson explained the relation in terms of a mutant gene that determines over-arousal, which might lead to creativity but also to psychopathological symptoms in those who cannot tolerate excessive levels of arousal. A somewhat similar explanation was offered by Prentky (1980), who suggests that the same neuro-chemical aberration that impairs the fragile filtering mechanism in thought-disordered patients also provides an advantage for creative thinking. These explanations converge on the suggestion that neuronal structures that function unreliably may generate not only bizarre ideas, but also unusual ideas that contribute to creative production.

Among those who believed *pathology results from creativity* were Galton, Tsanoff and Cattell. Although Galton (1869) did not accept that genius was a form of madness, he admitted that there was a large body of evidence to suggest that they were somehow related, and proposed that pathology may result from an over-excited creative mind. Tsanoff (1949) suggested that creative behaviour involves excessive tension that may imbalance the highly strung individual. R. B. Cattell (1971) suggested the prolonged concentration necessary for profoundly creative work could account for the type of 'neuraesthenia' which he considered to be the only type of nervous breakdown likely to be more frequent in geniuses than others.

On the other hand, some have suggested that *creativity results from psychopathology*. Among these is Holden (1987), who concluded that a tendency towards manic depression allows a richness and intensity of experience not shared by ordinary people. This conclusion was based on medical reports, which indicate that children showing early signs of manic depression have extremely vivid imaginations and surprising ability to concentrate on a task. Hershman and Lieb (1988) noted that hypo-mania fosters lively attention to everything, and that hypo-manics see connections between ideas and circumstances that others do not notice. These authors also pointed out that hypo-manic people tend to think and act at great speed, radiate vitality, enjoy the challenge of difficult projects and are willing to take chances – all of which are useful to creative enterprise.

From a slightly different point of view, Lichtenstein (1971) saw the combination of anxiety and ability as a 'productive neurosis', and argued persuasively that neurosis motivates the creator to reduce anxiety through productive effort. Among others who suggested that *creativity is a way of coping with psychopathology* are Roe (1953), Richards (1981) and Storr (1983). These authors explain that creative individuals may be less likely than others to be negatively affected by their pathology, because they are able to find an outlet for their inner tensions in creative activity. To Storr (1983) creative activity protects a person against mental breakdown: 'inspiration and madness have in common only the fact that the ego is influenced by something emanating from a source beyond its ken' (p. 263). Neurosis or psychosis implies that the ego is overwhelmed by such influences, but the ego of the creative person is not overwhelmed. It takes control. The work of the creative person is adaptive. Neurotic symptoms are not.

Support for such suggestions has come from the results of tests on creative individuals, which indicate that creative achievers are characterized by both high levels of psychopathology and ego strength (self-control). Even in the absence of psychopathology, the responses of highly creative subjects on diagnostic tests resemble those of disturbed individuals (see, e.g. Barron, 1968; R. B. Cattell, 1971; Götz & Götz, 1979; MacKinnon, 1962b, 1978; Mohan & Tiwana, 1987; Roe, 1953). Among the Rorschach protocols for her highly creative scientists Roe (1953) found some 'which would occasion no surprise in a clinic for the maladjusted' (p. 52). But she also discovered that the subjects seemed to have brought their problems and anxieties under control, encapsulating them, and diverting their energies into their work. Götz and Götz found that successful artists gained higher scores than less successful artists on psychoticism on the *Eysenck Personality Questionnaire.* Mohan and Tiwana found that creative Indian writers gained high scores on psychoticism, neuroticism and alienation. MacKinnon and Barron found that highly creative individuals obtained relatively high scores relating to psychopathology of various types on the *Minnesota Multiphasic Personality Inventory* (MMPI). Creative writers were more deviant than less creative writers on every scale (depression, hypomania, schizophrenia, paranoia, psychopathic deviation, hysteria, hypochondriasis, and psychaesthenia), and creative architects were more deviant than their less creative colleagues on some of these scales. However, it was notable that the creative subjects not only scored abnormally high on the scales relating to psychopathology, but also on scales measuring ego strength. R. B. Cattell and co-workers (e.g. R. B. Cattell, 1971; Cattell & Butcher, 1972; Cattell & Drevdahl, 1955; Cross, Cattell & Butcher, 1967; Drevdahl & Cattell, 1958) have shown combinations of emotional instability and ego strength in creative achievers (scientists having stronger egos than artists and writers). And there has been some consensus of opinion that the highly creative achiever is characterized by the co-existence of mental weaknesses and strengths (Hershman & Lieb, 1988; Richards, 1981).

Prentky (1980) maintained that the ideal combination for creativity would be a high degree of intelligence paired with an optimum degree of deviation. Woody and Claridge (1983) were essentially in agreement with this idea, suggesting that intelligence influences the threshold for psychotic breakdown, a high intelligence insulating against insanity. This is much in accordance with Freud's (1908/1973b) suggestion that the creative person is able to bring unrealistic material generated by the id under the control of the ego.

When considering why madness may be related to genius, it is important also to remember that both mental depressives and genius come from a population in which the incidence of bereavement in childhood is relatively high. This gives reason to suggest that certain anxiety-provoking experiences in childhood might predispose the individual to be creative and/or mentally disturbed. It also implies that, in certain families, the common factor underlying creativity and psychopathology may not be genetic – difficult circumstances in family life might lead to both creativity and psychopathology. This suggestion is supported by the high incidence of insecurity, rejection, loneliness and other factors leading to lack of emotional satisfaction in the childhood of eminent creators.

*Conclusions relating to psychopathology*

One cannot conclude that psychopathology is a prerequisite for creative achievement, as some highly creative achievers are *not* disordered. On the other hand one cannot accept that mental health is necessary for creative achievement, as some creative achievers are indeed blatantly disordered.

In the light of research findings it would be reasonable to accept that the incidence of psychopathology is higher among creative achievers than in the general population, and that there might be a common genetic basis underlying a predisposition toward psychopathology and original thinking. It would, however, be unwise to presume that productive creativity results simply from an unusual style of thinking. Without knowledge and skill, and without motivation to employ them in the service of producing something meaningful, there would be no useful product of an unusual style of thinking – or merely a bizarre one.

I have suggested in the foregoing discussion that the thin line between madness and genius may not lie where it has traditionally been drawn – between abnormal and supra-normal intellectual functioning. There is reason to believe that the mediating link between creativity and pathology may be a *motivational thrust* (resulting from emotional insecurity) *leading to two possible outcomes – intellectual gains and emotional disorder.*

## Personality characteristics

It has for some time been recognized that creative achievement is closely related to certain personality characteristics (e.g. Barron, 1968; Bloom,

1963; R. B. Cattell, 1971; Cattell & Drevdahl, 1955; Chambers, 1964; Cox, 1926; Dellas & Gaier, 1970; Freeman, Butcher & Christie, 1971; MacKinnon, 1978; Roe, 1953; Stein, 1974). Moreover, there is relatively little argument as to which characteristics these are. The findings have been fairly consistent, showing a fair degree of overlap, despite the fact that many researchers have been involved in the enterprise, different approaches and measuring instruments have been used, and a variety of productively creative individuals have served as subjects. Dellas and Gaier (1970) suggest that the similarity of the various findings indicates that the traits in question may have some bearing on creativity 'in the abstract' regardless of field.

R. W. Weisberg (1986) and others have made the point that one cannot predict creativity on the basis of personality traits, nor can one engender creativity by instilling the traits in uncreative subjects. The traits that are typical of productive creators are of course not necessarily the determiners of their creativity. As Barron and Harrington (1981) mentioned, it remains to discover which of them relate to all effective behaviour, which are non-causal correlates of creativity, and which are the outcomes of creative achievement.

The ideal method of distinguishing determinants from effects of creative achievement would be to conduct longitudinal research on creative achievers, beginning in their childhood and assessing them from time to time as they develop into and through adulthood. This method is, however, fraught with difficulties. Besides spending a great deal of time and money on such an enterprise, one has the problem of ensuring that a fair number of one's original sample of children will eventually turn out to be productively creative. Even if one were to start with a very large sample, one is likely to end up with very few (if any) who excel – as Terman experienced.

A less exact, but more manageable, way of gaining insights into the relation between personality and creativity is to compare information relating to creators in their childhood and youth with findings relating to the personalities of adult creators. For this purpose the data compiled by Cox (1926) and her associates are particularly useful.

As mentioned, the Cox data were extracted from an enormous amount of biographical material relating to the early lives of historical geniuses. Cox and co-workers rated the hundred most eminent of their subjects for whom sufficient information was available on sixty-seven 'character traits'. Their sample consisted of artists (including Michelangelo), musicians (including Mozart), poets (including Byron), philosophers (including Kant), scientists (including Newton), historians (including

Gibbon), statesmen (including Lincoln), combatant soldiers (including Nelson) and religious leaders (including Luther).

Although it might be argued that all the subjects were in some sense creative, for the present purposes statesmen, soldiers and leaders will *not* be regarded as creative achievers here, and will be collectively referred to as 'leaders'. By separating leaders from creators in Cox's sample, one is not only able to compare the characteristics of creators in youth and adulthood, but also to compare the early characteristics of creators with the early characteristics of leaders. Such comparisons might help one to distinguish the antecedents of creative achievement from the antecedents of achievement in general.

It is unfortunately impossible to perform precise statistical analyses on these data. For one, Cox did not publish (and probably did not determine) the statistical significance of the differences between creators and leaders on the various traits. As she published average scores for various groups rather than raw data, no tests of the significance between the scores of creators and leaders can be conducted at this stage. It must therefore be admitted at the outset of the following discussion that the differences and likenesses discussed have not been conclusively shown to be significant in precise probabilistic terms. Nevertheless, it would be shortsighted to ignore the noticeable correspondence and differences between Cox's findings and more recent findings relating to adult creators.

In the following discussion, adult creative achievers are compared with Cox's geniuses in youth, where possible, with special regard to emotional, intellectual, social and motivational traits.

*Emotional traits*

Not surprising in the light of conclusions relating to psychopathology, are the findings that contemporary adult achievers are characteristically emotionally unstable, impulsive and labile (Barron, 1968; Gough, 1964; Helson & Crutchfield, 1970). Although this applies to various types of creators, artistic creators (including men of letters) are usually found to be more emotional and unstable than scientific creators (Barron, 1968; R. B. Cattell, 1963; Drevdahl & Cattell, 1958; Raskin, 1936) – this fits well with Berry's (1981) finding that Nobel Prize winners for literature seem to suffer more distress in childhood than scientific laureates do.

The creator's emotional instability appears to be already apparent in youth. Cox and her co-workers found depression and anger were to be characteristic of most groups of *creators and leaders*. Young creators-to-be were especially liable to depression, but tended to oscillate between cheerfulness and depression (musicians tended to be somewhat more cheerful than others). They were also markedly prone to anger – flaming up at the slightest provocation (as is characteristic of mania).

This seems to indicate that creators who manifest clear signs of psychopathology represent extreme cases of a common tendency toward emotional instability. Moreover as emotional instability was noticeable in youth, it is probably not simply the outcome of the tensions induced by highly demanding creative work, but may arise from natural predispositions and early experience, and may play some role in the development of creative achievement.

It is important to note however that Cox's *leaders* were also characteristically unstable in youth. This suggests that emotional instability might contribute to *achievement in general* rather than to creative achievement in particular. It is therefore reasonable to conclude that people who are easily and intensely aroused might have a relatively high degree of energy, that could be directed into either creative work or leadership. However, not all people who are easily aroused use their energy to these ends. Something must harness and steer emotional energy in one or other direction.

In accordance with this suggestion is the suggestion that despite their emotional instability, creators have a high degree of ego strength or self-control (Barron, 1968; R. B. Cattell, 1963; Cattell & Drevdahl, 1955; Cross, Cattell & Butcher, 1967; Drevdahl & Cattell, 1958; MacKinnon, 1962a, 1978; Stein & Heinze, 1960). The implications are that they are capable of controlling their labile emotions and using them effectively. Moreover, it seems that even if creators are not able to control their emotional reactions completely, they are adjusted in the sense of being effective and happy in their work (Cattell & Drevdahl, 1955; Roe, 1953).

*Intellectual attitudes*

I have mentioned that creative achievers generally have a high degree of the specific kind of intellectual ability that is basic to their field of work. Further it has been shown that adult creators are well informed, set high value on intellectual matters, and are flexible and open to new ideas (Barron, 1968; Chambers, 1964; Helson & Crutchfield, 1970; MacKinnon, 1978; Roe, 1951a, 1951b, 1953). They are also open to intuitive feelings and are guided by aesthetic values and judgments (e.g. Barron, 1968; Blatt & Stein, 1957; Clifford, 1958; Gough, 1964; MacKinnon, 1962a, 1978; Roe, 1946, 1953; Zuckerman, 1977).

Although aesthetic values are usually associated with artists, the references above relate to scientific as well as artistic creators. All groups, scientific and artistic, studied by the researchers at IPAR gained higher scores on theoretical and aesthetic values than on other values measured by the Allport-Lindzey scales (MacKinnon, 1978). Furthermore, biographical material reveals that scientists as well as artists find deep satisfaction in the beauty of their creations (Haefele, 1962). Max Born hailed the advent of relativity as making the universe of science not only grander but also more beautiful. Jacques Hadamard suggested that mathematical invention is choice guided by aesthetic sense, and that the decisions of mathematicians are informed by their sense of beauty. Beauty is the first test, agreed the creative mathematician G. H. Hardy (1969). For Hardy there was no permanent place in the world for ugly mathematics.

Poincaré explained that scientists delight in nature because they find it beautiful. He did not, however, speak of sensual beauty which strikes the senses, but of the profounder beauty which comes from harmonious order of the parts of a system. Among others who have spoken of beauty in science are Paul Dirac (1963), who on receiving the Nobel Prize for physics, remarked:

It seems that if one is working from the point of view of getting beauty in one's equations and if one has really sound insight, one is on a sure line of progress. (p. 47)

In even stronger terms, Michael Polanyi, chemist and philosopher, spoke of science in terms of an 'intellectual passion'. To Polanyi (1964) the appraisal of what is profound rather than trivial depends on

a sense of intellectual beauty; that is an emotional response which can never be dispassionately defined any more than we can dispassionately define the beauty of a work of art. (p. 135)

Einstein also judged scientific works in terms of beauty, and Max Planck suggested that the new ideas of the creative scientist are not generated by deduction but by 'artistically creative imagination' (quoted by Koestler, 1964). Kuhn (1970) explained that application of aesthetic sensitivity was indeed essential to the progress of science.

Something must make at least a few scientists feel they are on the right track, and sometimes it is only personal and inarticulate aesthetic considerations that can do that. Men have been converted by them at times when most of the articulate technical arguments pointed the other way . . . even today Einstein's general theory attracts men principally on aesthetic grounds, an appeal that few people outside of mathematics have been able to feel. (p. 158)

Inherent in all these remarks is the suggestion that underlying scientific creativity is an intellectual motivation that is fuelled by a positive evaluation of learning and achievement, and guided by aesthetic sensitivity – which may relate to a need for emotional satisfaction. This idea will be pursued in the following chapter, but for the moment we note that the creator's sense of beauty is characteristically perceptible in youth. The artists, musicians and writers in Cox's sample gained high scores on aesthetic feeling. On the other hand, the scores obtained by future scientific creators and leaders were not extraordinary (although above average). It is therefore likely that aesthetic sensitivity may *contribute* to the development of artistic creators' ability to produce emotionally satisfying sensual effects.

## Androgyny and sexual orientation

Various researchers have noted that creative achievers tend to be androgynous (e.g. Barron, 1963; Blatt & Stein, 1957; Bloom, 1963; E. F. Hammer, 1964; Helson, 1967; MacKinnon, 1978; Roe, 1946, 1953). Briefly, this means that creative men and women tend to have both masculine and feminine interests. On reviewing research in this area Dellas and Gaier (1970) concluded that the integration of the necessary 'feminine' sensitivity and intuition with 'masculine' purposive action and determination is conducive to creativity.

It is important to realize, however, that the conception of 'feminine' and 'masculine' is largely culturally determined. In most Western cultures aesthetic sensitivity is regarded as feminine. A male creator will therefore be classified as androgynous because he is interested and is involved in aesthetic enterprise. As aesthetic sensitivity and androgyny in males are conceptually related in Western society, they may therefore be seen to vary together.

There is less clarity with regard to the sexual orientation of creators. Various biographers have suggested that many eminently creative historical figures, including Leonardo da Vinci, Michelangelo, Nobel, Tchaikowsky, Walt Whitman, Proust, were obviously homosexually inclined, and others, including Newton, possibly so. It has been shown that creative achievers are less likely than others to be happily married – or to be married at all (Ellis, 1904; Herzberg, 1929; McCurdy, 1957), and that they are relatively low in heterosexual interests (e.g. MacKinnon, 1978). But it is difficult to state with any certainty whether creators differ significantly from others as regards sexual orientation, largely because there is insufficient information about the intimate habits of most historical figures and the norms for their times. Even in modern times it is possible to keep some facts relating to sexuality private – though impossible to prevent speculation. T. S. Eliot, who was an unhappy boy and miserable adult, requested in his will that his literary executor try to prevent any biography being written about him. There have nevertheless been many such volumes – in which Eliot has been variously described as homosexual or impotent. Indeed this applies to many modern authors of note (see examples mentioned in Goertzel, Goertzel and Goertzel, 1978).

Although no reliable relation between homosexuality and creativity has been demonstrated, several authors have expressed a belief that they are indeed related (e.g. Ehrenwald, 1984; Gedo, 1983). Cox's findings on the characteristics of creative achievers in youth offer little help in this regard; and we are left with the suggestion that there is some support for Freud's contention that creativity results from the diversion of sexual energy from socially censured outlets into socially valued endeavours. More about that in the following chapter.

*Independence*

Creators are 'independent' in various respects. For example, it has frequently been shown that, as adults, they tend to be *emotionally independent of others*: reserved, withdrawn and introverted, preferring solitary to group activities, and having difficulty or little interest in establishing warm interpersonal relationships (e.g. Barron, 1968; Blatt & Stein, 1957; Bloom, 1963; R. B. Cattell, 1971; Cattell & Drevdahl, 1955; Cross, Cattell & Butcher, 1967; Drevdahl & Cattell, 1958; MacKinnon, 1962a, 1978; McClelland, 1963; Mohan & Tiwana, 1987; Roe, 1951a, 1951b, 1953).

When it comes to their work they are also characteristically *intellectually* independent. Although they are interested in the work of others and may be influenced by admired models (particularly significant workers in their field), they are typically autonomous and self-sufficient. They tend to be dominant: showing a need for personal mastery, displaying initiative, and rejecting external regulation. Although they tend to be reserved, they are not likely to wait for someone else to tell them what to do or to fall in with the plans of others without question (Barron, 1968; Blatt & Stein, 1957; Cattell & Drevdahl, 1955; Chambers, 1964; Cross, Cattell & Butcher, 1967; Drevdahl, 1964; Drevdahl & Cattell,

1958; Helson & Crutchfield, 1970; MacKinnon, 1961, 1965, 1978; McClelland, 1963; Peck, 1958; Roe, 1951a, 1951b, 1953; Stein, 1974; Van Zelst & Kerr, 1951; Ypma, 1968). Cattell (1971) explained that the characteristics of being withdrawn and introverted as well as being dominant, bold and assertive are not as incompatible as one would think. He showed these traits to represent two independent personality factors.

In addition to being emotionally and intellectually independent, creators are also characteristically independent in the sense of being *non-conforming, unconventional and radical* (Barron, 1968; Blatt & Stein, 1957; Cattell & Drevdahl, 1955; Drevdahl, 1956; MacKinnon, 1978; Van Zelst & Kerr, 1951). Along with their rebelliousness may go some disorderliness and a tendency to be exhibitionistic (Barron, 1963). Among those in whom this tendency was especially marked was Salvador Dali, whose attention-seeking behaviour persisted from childhood to old age. As a child Dali waited one day until his classmates (with whom he had no satisfactory relationships) were watching and then leapt from the top of a staircase. In his old age he attended an exhibition of his works in a scuba diver's wetsuit.

Cox's reports give reason to believe that, in youth, achievers have a strong need to be recognized. Among the lowest scores obtained, especially by musicians, were those on the item 'absence of eagerness for the admiration of the crowd. Absence of enjoyment of the limelight and applause. Not playing to the gallery'. Apparently at least some creators enjoy public recognition, although they eschew social influence.

Not all creative individuals are disorderly or exhibitionistic, however, and there have been minor differences among the findings of various researchers in this regard. For example, some researchers found creative achievers to be 'bohemian' (e.g. Cattell, 1971), whereas others (e.g. MacKinnon, 1978) did not. MacKinnon found the highly creative person more likely to be deliberate, responsible and industrious – a 'man with a briefcase' rather than a sloppy, loose-jointed bohemian (who, MacKinnon suggests, is more likely to be only moderately creative or have pretensions of being creative). However, MacKinnon's subjects were architects, whose work involves conforming to certain professional practices, and it is likely that the non-conformity of certain creators might be tempered by the demands of their occupation, clients, and the situation in which they find themselves. For some types of creators it is necessary to develop social presence and poise.

Cox found that artistic creators and writers were unconventional in youth. What is more, all her subjects tended to devote a fair amount of their time in youth to *independent, self-directed extracurricular studies or special interests.*

As I have mentioned, there is little to indicate that the parents of creators typically make a deliberate attempt to foster independence. Their independence in youth therefore either reflects some innate tendency, or a reaction to something other than parental encouragement. As Roe (1953) suggested, it may reflect a rebellion against unwelcome parental control or overprotection. But it may also be that independent behaviour is reinforced by some reward system inherent in that behaviour, as discussed later.

*Self-image*

Questionnaires reveal that contemporary creators appear to be self-confident and have good insight into their own capabilities. They typically describe themselves explicitly as creative, or in terms that investigators have found to be related to creativity: using adjectives such as independent, inventive, determined, industrious, enthusiastic. In contrast, less creative control groups are more likely to describe themselves as responsible, sincere, reliable, tolerant, sympathetic or understanding (e.g. MacKinnon, 1962a, 1978; Stein, 1974; C.W. Taylor, 1963).

One finds too that creators identify themselves with their work (see, e.g., Roe, 1953). And, although they appear to be little concerned about their social image, the image of their work is obviously very important to them. This is well illustrated in Einstein's (1949/1979b) autobiographical notes, most of which are devoted to a discussion of his theories. While discussing the development of his scientific ideas, Einstein suddenly interrupts himself:

'Is this supposed to be an obituary?' the astonished reader will ask. I would like to reply: essentially yes. For the essence of being a man of my type lies precisely in what he thinks and how he thinks, not in what he does or suffers. (p. 31)

Geniuses typically recognize the value of their work – and have little hesitation in admitting it. Before writing *The divine comedy* Dante assessed himself as the sixth greatest poet of the world (quoted by Hayward, 1974, p. 135). 'I cannot write with a modesty I do not feel' wrote Ruskin. Referring to his letters to *The Times*, he confessed 'twenty years hence, if I live, I should like to be able to refer to these and say "I told you so, and now you are beginning to find it out"' (quoted by Hayward, 1974, p. 221).

The inability of others to recognize the value of creative work immediately has been a continual and powerful source of frustration to creators throughout history. But their faith in themselves seems to help them overcome the frustration, to maintain high levels of aspiration, and keep going. Sometimes, however, the obstacles cannot be overcome, and creators have as their only comfort their hope that sometime in the future understanding might grow and endow their memory with the rewards that were lacking to their person.

The sufferings inflicted on scientific martyrs such as Copernicus, Galileo and Semmelweiss are legend. Recently we have been reminded of the less physical troubles experienced by two people who lacked the means whereby to bring their ideas to fruition. Over 150 years ago Charles Babbage had a dream which he shared with Ada, the Countess of Lovelace, who was Lord Byron's daughter. Babbage and Ada believed they could create a machine that would not only be able to perform the basic mathematical functions, but also do advanced mathematical and logical operations. This machine would, moreover, have a memory – which would enable it to store data, and it would not be restricted to particular types of operation: it would be programmable. It would even be able to play games like chess.

In those days machines had to be mechanically driven. Little was known of the practical uses of electricity (and micro-chips were, of course, unheard of). The embodiment of Babbage's principles would have needed the power of about a dozen locomotives to drive it and would have had to be the size of a football field. Besides the fact that Babbage and Lady Lovelace had insufficient money to build anything of this magnitude, it would have been impossible to construct the thousands of necessary mechanical parts with sufficient precision.

Charles and Ada died without seeing their dream come true. They never glimpsed the faintest sign of the revolution that the computer was to bring about a hundred years later. But Charles did manage to construct some simplified mechanical forerunners of the modern computer. And with these he left to posterity the trust that the future would bring the appreciation that had been lacking during his life. The latter part of his autobiographical writings includes the following statements and predictions:

The great principles on which the Analytical Engine rests have been examined, admitted, recorded, and demonstrated: The mechanism itself has now been reduced to unexpected simplicity. Half a century may probably elapse before anyone without those aids which I leave behind me, will attempt so unpromising a task. If unwarned by my example, any man shall undertake and shall succeed in really constructing an engine embodying in itself the whole of the executive department of mathematical analysis upon different principles or by simple mathematical means, I have no fear of leaving my reputation in his charge, for he alone will be fully able to appreciate the nature of my efforts and the value of their results. (Babbage 1864/1969, p. 450)

Ada is remembered as the first ever 'programmer', and a computer soft-ware environment used by the United States armed forces bears her name.

The creative subjects and leaders in Cox's sample seemed already in youth to believe in their own powers, and were characteristically self-confident. As Cox (1926) put it: 'They esteemed their special talents' and tended to rate themselves correctly as a whole, but especially with regard to their specific talents. The correspondence between these findings and those relating to adult creators suggests that self-confidence, especially where specific abilities are concerned, is a determinant or a catalyst rather than an outcome of creative achievement. Moreover Cox's findings show that this is characteristic of leaders as well, which suggests that *appreciation of one's own particular talents may contribute to achievement in general.*

## Differences between creators and leaders

So far, most of the characteristics shown to be typical of creative achievers appear to have been already notable in childhood, and may therefore be regarded as antecedents rather than outcomes of creative achievement. But many of the characteristics of creative achievers are also typical of future leaders in youth. It is therefore likely that they contribute to achievement in general rather than only creative ability. To gain some idea of where the main differences lie between creators and leaders (and therefore of factors contributing especially to creativity) one must examine Cox's findings a little more closely. Noticeable differences are then to be seen in (a) the degree of their corporate involvements, and (b) the particular nature of their interests and activities.

Cox's leaders gained very much higher scores than the creators did on items worded 'Degree of corporate spirit (in whatever body interest is taken, e.g. college, school, country, native place). Working or playing for the group rather than for his own advantage' (p. 173), and 'Sense of corporate responsibility (whether to family, school, moral or religious superior, or ideal). Tendency to do his duty rather than to follow personal inclination; opposite of individualism' (p. 175). Leaders also gained higher scores than creators on items concerning desire to impose their will on people; 'forcefulness, or strength of character', and 'wideness of influence' (Cox, 1926, between p. 212 & p. 213).

What this suggests is that creative achievers in youth are less interested than leaders in community affairs or political concerns; are also less 'group orientated' but more individualistic and independent.

It is also clear from Cox's findings that in youth creators are less inclined than leaders to engage in physical activities. Cox's findings reveal that leaders spent almost as much time and effort on special interests, hobbies, extracurricular studies as creators did, but it is apparent that *the type of extracurricular activities* in which they engaged differed considerably: leaders gained high scores on items relating to 'Degree of bodily activity in pursuit of pleasures (games, sports, etc.). Physical energy displayed' and 'Tendency to self-expression in action rather than in thought'. They were also more inclined to be 'Hyperkinetic vs Hypokinetic' and to 'doing something, rather than thinking something about it' (p. 174). Moreover, leaders (excepting religious leaders and statesmen) obtained high scores on the item 'Skill in and devotion to athletics, sports, or physical feats'. Creators had low scores on these items relating to physical activity. The implications are supported by findings of studies of contemporary creators, which also show creative achievers typically do not enjoy team games or sport (e.g. Chambers, 1964; Roe, 1953).

Comparisons of the characteristics of creators and leaders as a whole, lead to the conclusion that creativity, as distinct from other types of achievement, relates to withdrawal from social involvements into some form of intellectual (rather than physical) activity.

## Motivational traits

Most of what has been mentioned is based on average scores and refers to general rather than universal tendencies. Obviously not all creators are likely to have exactly the same personal characteristics, nor are they likely to have any particular characteristic to exactly the same degree. There may be some variation across samples and individuals (and even within individuals at different stages of life). However certain characteristics are particularly consistent and especially marked. In particular it is noticeable that *the most salient and most consistent characteristic of creative achievers is persistent enthusiastic devotion to work*. Creators are energetic, persevering, dedicated, productive and thorough (e.g. Barron, 1968;

Blatt & Stein, 1957; Bloom, 1963; Cattell & Drevdahl, 1955; Chambers, 1964; Cross, Cattell & Butcher, 1967; Drevdahl & Cattell, 1958; Gough, 1964; Helson, 1971; MacKinnon, 1978; Peck, 1958; Raskin, 1936; Roe, 1951a, 1951b, 1953; J. Rossman, 1931; Van Zelst & Kerr, 1951; Ypma, 1968; Zuckerman, 1977). Even Galton, who saw genius as genetically determined, recognized the necessity of an 'inherent stimulus' that urges geniuses to attain and maintain excellence.

Not only every sample, but every individual within each sample appears to be characterized by persistent dedication to work. In discussing her research on scientists Roe (1970) commented that 'the one thing that all of these sixty-four scientists have in common is their driving absorption in their work. They have worked long hours for many years, frequently with no vacations to speak of because they would rather be doing their work than anything else' (p. 51). Roe (1951b) also noted that 'this one thing alone [persistent dedication to work] is probably not of itself sufficient to account for the success enjoyed by these men but it appears to be a *sine qua non*' (pp. 233–234).

Rossman (1931), who conducted research on 710 inventors, showed that their most salient trait was perseverance, and concluded that working eight hours a day, five days a week would never make a man an inventor. MacKinnon described his creative architects as typically zestfully committed to their profession. R. B. Cattell (1963, 1971) agreed with Havelock Ellis (1904), Kretschmer (1931), and Galton (1869) that, over and above intelligence, the highly creative person possesses some very characteristic personal qualities, such as energy and zeal, almost amounting to fanaticism. Calvin Taylor (1988) told of a scientist who suggested the only way to stop his creative colleague from working on a problem was to shoot him!

Moreover, it is clear that the intense effort expended by creative achievers is not merely undirected hyperactivity or discharge of emotional energy. It is aimed: it is aimed at excellence. Creative achievers are not only conscientious, but also typically ambitious. They have high levels of aspiration (Barron, 1968; Gough, 1964; Helson & Crutchfield, 1970; MacKinnon, 1978; Stein, 1974). They are constructively critical, and are typically less contented or satisfied than others are (Barron, 1968; J. Rossman, 1931; Van Zelst & Kerr, 1951).

Findings relating to achievers in youth correspond well with those relating to adult creators. Cox (1926) pointed out that her ten most eminent subjects were conspicuous for their persistence, but extremely high scores were obtained by her sample as a whole on all items pertaining to will, tenacity and perseverance.

It was also apparent to Cox and her co-workers that the persistence of their subjects was aimed at excellence. The highest average score for their whole sample was obtained on the item

Desire to excel at performances (whether of work, play or otherwise) in which the person has his chief interest. Desire to do well, whether to excel others or for the work's sake. (p. 173)

In the light of the foregoing discussion, it would be reasonable to suggest that one of the major determinants, if not *the* major determinant, of creative achievement is motivation, and Cox is among those who would agree. Her overall conclusions to her study of geniuses (creators and leaders) in youth were

the following traits and trait elements appearing in childhood and youth are diagnostic of future achievement: an unusual degree of persistence, tendency not to be changeable, tenacity of purpose, and perseverance in the face of obstacles – combined with intellective energy – mental work bestowed on special interests, profoundness of apprehension, and originality of ideas – and the vigorous ambition expressed by the possession to the highest degree of desire to excel. (p. 180; italics in the original, numerals omitted)

These findings are not surprising. They are consistent with the facts relating to the *enormous productivity* of creative achievers – which indicate that creators spend a major part of their waking hours at work. The suggestion that creativity depends on persistent effort and practice is reminiscent of Edison's oft-quoted remark to the effect that genius is 99 per cent perspiration – and this in turn echoes the words of an ancient (unnamed) poet who lived several hundred years before Plato:

Before the Gates of Excellence the high Gods have placed sweat. (Hamilton, 1960, p. 76)

# 7

## *The creator's motivation*

As a young child Goethe already had the idea that hard work can accomplish anything. He seemed astonished by the fact that no-one else seemed to realize this simple fact (Gedo, 1972). Paul Valéry asserted that stubborn labour was an important component of creativity, and took great exception to the suggestion that poets receive the best part of their work from muses (or other such imaginary creatures). He called that a concept of savages. His own labour was stubborn, we know – Valéry made 250 typed drafts of the poem *La jeune Parque*, which is generally considered to be his masterpiece (Grubbs, 1968, p. 91).

The stubborn labour of creative achievers is attributed to what one calls 'motivation'. But to understand the development of creativity one needs to do more than give the tendency to engage in stubborn labour a name. One needs also to address what Chambers (1964) called the central problem in this area: what are the well-springs of the creator's strong motivation?

How and when does the motivation of the genius arise? What is it that sustains it? And how does it relate to their creative ability? Obviously, any attempt to explain the important influences acting upon the development of genius should give attention to such questions. However, even though it is continually recognized that the creator's most salient characteristic is persistent motivation, workers in the field have given relatively little attention to investigating its origin and nature. One of the explanations for this neglect is no doubt to be found in the current tendency to view creativity as a matter of spontaneous unstereotyped reactions to the demands of daily life – with the need for self-actualization playing some vaguely defined role.

Another explanation is to be found in the current tendency to conduct investigations relating to creativity in a laboratory or classroom. Some researchers think it unnecessary to consider baseline individual differences when exploring the determinants of creativity. As Amabile (1983) explained, social psychologists do not look at consistencies in behaviour (or motivation) for 'it is the purpose of social psychology to investigate the impact of social and environmental factors on most people or on the "average" person' (p. 63). Accordingly, contemporary researchers have based their pronouncements about the motivation to create on their observations of the effects of situational variables on children and unexceptional adults performing trivial tasks (e.g. Amabile, 1983, 1985; Hennessey & Amabile, 1988; Torrance, 1988).

It is unfortunate that facts emerging from empirical research should have offered such a blinkered view of the determinants of creativity, for social influences may, and apparently do, have a lasting effect on relatively enduring traits as well as on temporary states. As we have seen in previous chapters, there is a great deal of evidence to show that creativity is an enduring trait. Even though there may be some ups and downs in creators' output over their lifespan, it would be foolish to ignore the fact that highly creative people produce not only works of quality, but also quantity – and you would be wise to put your money on those who have been very creative in the past when you bet who will be creative in the future. There is ample evidence to show that creative achievers tend to persist in creating, and to ignore obstacles or to push them out of their way. They manipulate their own situational variables to make their lifestyle favourable to their own brand of creative productivity. The 99 per cent perspiration referred to by Edison – the sweat before the Gates of Excellence – does not have its counterpart in structured situations, where subjects are invited to solve 'creative' problems under the watchful eye of an investigator with a stopwatch. That sweat is a style of life.

Discovering the motivation underlying the sustained effort that is so typical of creative achievers therefore requires more than an examination of situational variables affecting average people in a classroom. It requires, to begin with, a examination of common factors in the backgrounds, early experiences and characteristics of people who have been productive. After that one needs to consider those factors in the light of general principles governing motivation – to see how common factors in the lives of creators may determine a tendency to persevere and excel.

This chapter therefore discusses various theories of motivation, and applies them to some of the noticeable common themes in the lives of creative achievers.

## Theory relating to the role of 'intrinsic satisfaction' in the motivation to create

Broadly speaking the terms 'intrinsic motivation' and 'intrinsic satisfaction' refer to the need for and pleasure gained from actually engaging in a behaviour, whereas 'extrinsic motivation' and 'extrinsic satisfaction' refer to the need for and pleasure gained from *the results* of the behaviour.

Modern theories relating to the motivation underlying creative behaviour propose that intrinsic motivation is more powerful than extrinsic motivation, and relevant research (much of which is reviewed by Amabile, 1983) seems to support the suggestion that intrinsic rewards are more effective for promoting creativity than extrinsic rewards are. People will feel and be most creative when they are motivated primarily by interest, enjoyment, satisfaction, and the challenge of the work itself, and not by external pressures or evaluation, says Amabile. External rewards (or expectations of external rewards) in fact dampen creativity.

Research in this area (e.g. Amabile, 1983, 1985; Hennessey & Amabile, 1988) has shown that subjects (children, students and adults) are indeed more likely to be creative in the classroom when there are no expectations of extrinsic rewards contingent on their performance, and the explanation given is that expectations of extrinsic rewards tend to compete with intrinsic motivation: subjects who expect extrinsic rewards try to gain them with as little effort as possible. Even thinking about extrinsic reasons for being creative lowers their actual creativity (Amabile, 1985).

Although these principles may apply in the laboratory (to people who are sufficiently interested in extrinsic rewards to have their intrinsic motivation and performance disturbed by the thought of them) it is important to remember that this research is typically conducted in artificially controlled situations where the extrinsic rewards offered are merely short-term satisfactions such as special privileges (e.g. being allowed to play with a polaroid camera or favoured toys), tangible gifts (e.g. candy) and praise from the researchers. Moreover, the subjects are usually unexceptional people who engage in the exercise either because they are conscripted, or because they respond to open invitations to participate in the research. (Their motivation for participating is extrinsic.) One should therefore be wary of generalizing the rather simplistic conclusions of this type of research to explain the creative achiever's tendency to stubborn labour. And one should perhaps also give a little deeper consideration to the concept of intrinsic motivation if one wishes to explain how it contributes to an enduring tendency to create.

On reviewing psychological literature relating to intrinsic motivation, one finds the concept to be rather amorphous. At least three broad interpretations have been placed on the term. For one, intrinsically motivated behaviour has been described as *an end in itself* as compared to extrinsically motivated behaviour that leads to another end, reward, or goal. Second, intrinsic motivation is described as underlying actions which are *directed toward* (*self-chosen*) *goals*. Third, intrinsically motivated behaviours may be regarded as those that satisfy an *instinctual intellectual need to master the environment*. Although these three views of intrinsic motivation are not mutually exclusive, they have somewhat different implications, and therefore require separate attention.

## *Suggestions relating to the concept of 'behaviour as an end in itself'*

When 'intrinsically motivated behaviour' is interpreted as behaviour which is simply 'an end in itself', a very wide range of enjoyable activities may be regarded as intrinsically satisfying. Psychological origins of this concept of intrinsic motivation may be found in the work of Woodworth (1918), who drew attention to the fact that behaviour which had been extrinsically rewarded may continue to run by its own drive in the absence of any extrinsic rewards; for example a man who used to walk to his place of work because it saved the cost of a bus ride may continue to walk even when he is wealthy and owns a car – simply because he enjoys walking. This notion of doing something 'for its own sake' was later given the name of 'functional autonomy' by Allport, who proposed that the motives of the mature person are intrinsic in the sense that they have become divorced from their original biological needs, and the relevant behaviour is then 'functionally autonomous'.

It is easy to understand the concept of functional autonomy as it applies to everyday life. For example, most of us are able to appreciate that we enjoy eating and sexual activity as ends in themselves – not because they preserve us as individuals or as a species. The suggestion that creative activity is necessarily functionally autonomous is however questionable. Allport was happy to accept it, however. To Allport (1961) it was out of the question that creative behaviour could be extrinsically motivated. By way of simple explanation, he wrote:

How hollow to think of Pasteur's concern for reward, or for health, food, sleep, or family, as the root of his devotion to his work. For long periods he was oblivious of them all, losing himself in the white heat of research. And the same passion is seen in the histories of geniuses who in their lifetime received little or no reward for their work. (p. 236)

As Allport suggested, it seems Pasteur's activities were not directly related to biological needs. (Few would claim that Pasteur's creative efforts were aimed at biological goals, such as food or sleep etc.) But it is doubtful whether his behaviour was simply an end in itself. Anyone reading a biography of Pasteur will find that he was continually under external pressure to solve certain problems and reach certain goals. If a motive may be inferred from the result of the behaviour, then it may be inferred that Pasteur was motivated to achieve those goals. 'Nothing', he said, 'is more agreeable to a man who has made science his career than to increase the number of discoveries, but his cup of joy is full when the result of his observation is put to immediate practical use' (Vallery-Radot, 1937, p. 150).

Is creative behaviour then never an end in itself?

In childhood, independent intellectual activity that builds skills in a relevant domain may originally be an end in itself. Children who are exposed to relevant values and examples may engage in self-rewarding independent intellectual behaviour such as painting or experimenting, with no goal in mind and gain a simple delight in it. As Amabile and others have suggested, children do take a delight in constructive activity when they are not pressed to engage in it. But theorists who suggest that the production of creative works results simply and directly from a similar type of motivation are leaving large gaps in their reasoning.

The creative life-work of the adult must be much more than an end in itself. If anything is to be achieved by it, it must be goal-directed. And once it becomes goal-directed, creative work may at times be frustrating and tiring. Serious creative work usually involves some tedious ritual activities and repetition of work that has so far failed to achieve the required goal. To support his contention that creativity often involves pain, Steinkraus (1985) offered many quotations from the writings of creators who have testified to the suffering they have endured to achieve their goals. Among these quotations is Coleridge's confession that every line of his poem 'Christabel' had been produced by him with labour pangs: 'I turn sick and faint when I reflect on the labour I have expended on the mere endeavour to avoid and remedy imperfections', wrote Coleridge. In similar vein, Stephen Spender explained 'I dread writing poetry, for, I suppose the following reasons: a poem is a terrible journey of painful effort of concentrating the imagination' (1954, p. 125), and Flaubert confessed 'you have no notion what it is to sit out an entire day with your head between your hands beating your unfortunate brains for a word' (quoted by Steinkraus, 1985, p. 45).

Flaubert was often able to write only very little, and that with great difficulty. When writing *Madame Bovary* (which is often held to be the most creative novel yet written because it was so far ahead of its time), he confessed at one stage in a letter to Louise Colet:

I have written no more than 25 pages in all in six weeks . . . I have gone over them so much, recopied them, changed them, handled them, that for the time being I can't make head or tail of them . . . Sometimes I don't understand why my arms don't drop from my body with fatigue, why my brains don't melt away. I am leading a stern existence, stripped of all external pleasure, and am sustained only by a kind of permanent rage, which sometimes makes me weep tears of impotence but which never abates. (1851/1974, p. 326)

As with Pasteur, Flaubert's motivation to work exceeded his motivation to engage in other activities that were satisfying in themselves. He loved his work 'with a love that is frenzied and perverted, as an ascetic loves the hair shirt that scratches his belly' (p. 326), probably because his work was indeed more than an end in itself. It allowed him to test himself and produce something to show that he could pass the test: 'All my life I have lived with a maniacal stubbornness, keeping all my other passions locked up in cages and visiting them only now and then, for diversion. Oh, if I ever produce a good book I'll have worked for it! Would to God that Buffon's blasphemous words [le génie est une longue patience] were true' (p. 325).

On considering the facts relating to creative achievers one is indeed confronted with the suggestion that 'functionally autonomous' behaviour may lead to goal-directed behaviour, as well as the other way around. It seems a type of behaviour that is an end in itself in childhood may later become extrinsically motivated. By actively engaging in functionally autonomous activities, children may develop their knowledge and skill, and may then become eager to use that knowledge and skill to gain rewards such as recognition, a place among the 'elite' of the discipline – and self-esteem. And so the functionally autonomous constructive activities that were an end in themselves in childhood may pave the way to goal-directed creative life-work of the adult. But, *if play is to become productive, the underlying motives must change, so that the activity is directed to a goal.*

Unlike Allport, Apter (1982) clearly distinguished behaviour that is an end in itself from goal-directed activity – suggesting that on some occasions a particular type of activity may be an end in itself and at other times a means to an end. When behaviour is directed towards a goal the state is 'telic' explained Apter. But when the person is primarily concerned with continuing the sensations associated with the activity, the state is 'paratelic'. Similar behaviour may be related to telic and paratelic states on different occasions. During paratelic states, feelings of meaningfulness, significance and goal achievement are avoided as far as possible, as reaching a goal may terminate the satisfaction gained from the activity. Apter explains that 'a good test of whether a given person's activity is telic or not is whether the person concerned would willingly give it up in exchange for any goal which that activity may have' (p. 51).

Apter's thesis is that each state is relatively stable, but it is always possible to switch to the opposite state when satiation with the current state occurs (which implies that goal-directed activities may at times become satisfying in themselves, and vice versa). Although everyone is likely to experience both states from time to time, it would also appear that some people spend more time in one than the other.

We have Einstein's testimony to the fact that, even after creative skills have developed, a creator may indulge in intellectual activity in a paratelic state. He confessed:

When I have no special problem to occupy my mind, I love to reconstruct proofs of mathematical and physical theorems that have long been known to me. There is no goal in this, merely an opportunity to indulge in the pleasant occupation of thinking. (Ducas & Hoffman, 1979, p. 17)

Note that Einstein referred here to unconstructive leisure activity – not to his creative enterprise.

Although there are likely to be shifts between telic and paratelic states during creative activity, creative production is obviously not primarily conducted in a paratelic state. I have suggested that it is unlikely, for example, that Pasteur or Flaubert would have sacrificed their goals to the immediate satisfactions of the ongoing sensations afforded by their creative activity. Lack of concern for goals would prevent the completion of creative works – and creators typically complete a great number of products.

On the basis on the foregoing discussion, it may be argued that the persistent motivation underlying productive creativity cannot simply be ascribed to satisfaction gained from activity which is purely 'an end in itself'. However, there is a possibility that the tendency to engage in creative production *may have its roots in independent activity in childhood that builds knowledge and skills* – when goals were not yet well-defined and the activity was to a large extent paratelic. If one is to be persistently motivated to create, the tendency to engage in the relevant intellectual activity must, however, be sustained – and it may be reinforced by growing expectations of goal attainment.

*Suggestions relating to the concept of 'self-defined goals'*

A second commonly held concept of intrinsic motivation does allow that intrinsically motivated behaviours are aimed at goals, suggesting that the goals must relate directly to the behaviour. Among such goals are 'beating one's own record' or improving on one's previous perform- ance. The motivation underlying such goals is described as 'intrinsic' because it offers a sense of subjective freedom rather than imposing an obligation. It allows one to adjust the demands of the activity to one's capacity for dealing with them. An exhilarating activity like skiing lends itself well to this type of intrinsic motivation.

Csikszentmihalyi (1982) explained that when capability exceeds opportunity, boredom results – but when opportunity or goals exceed capability, anxiety results. Self-directed activity offers not only the satisfaction of a sense of personal control, but the optimum experience afforded by a balance between capability and opportunity.

Although it is frequently implied that the optimum experience described by Csikszentmihalyi is invariably experienced in creative activity, it seems that productive creativity does not always allow such experience. Creative production is likely to include some rather boring as well as some excessively demanding experience – some relatively easily attainable subgoals and some which are at least temporarily beyond the creator's grasp. Nevertheless Csikszentmihalyi's concept of optimal experience applies well to motives underlying independent intellectual activity in childhood, for independent activity allows children to match their goals and their pace to their own capabilities.

*Suggestions relating to the concept of 'mastery motivation'*

Intrinsically motivated behaviour has further been described in terms of an *instinctual intellectual need which finds satisfaction in mastery of the environment.*

At the beginning of the present century motivation was largely associated with instinctual drives that served the survival of the species and, at that stage, instinctual behaviour was seen mainly as consumma- tory and protective. But, a long time ago, Aristotle suggested that men have a natural 'desire to know' (Deci, 1975); Francis Bacon wrote that 'all knowledge and wonder (which is the seed of knowledge) is an impression of pleasure in itself' (Bacon, quoted in the *Oxford dictionary of quotations*, 1974, p. 24) and it had been noted by teachers such as Maria Montessori (1912) that children gained pleasure from exercising their cognitive capacities. In 1918 Karl Bühler wrote of the 'functional pleasure' inherent in actions that did not lead to the satisfaction of any known biological need. In 1938 Murray proposed that people had a 'creative need', which he described as an instinctual need to adapt to new situations and produce new ideas and objects. Subsequently researchers on animal behaviour concluded that not all instinctual drives were directly related to preservation. Living organisms also had an instinct to develop their ability to master the environment (e.g. Dashiell, 1925; Harlow, 1953; Hendrick, 1943; Nissen, 1930).

In 1950 Berlyne published a paper on curiosity, and many turned their attention to the tendency to explore novel stimuli. Harlow (1953) and Woodworth (1958) noted that the tendency to explore in general does not become satiated, but the exploration of a specific place or stimulus does. This implies that *exploring objects or facts from various points of view will be more satisfying than repeatedly focussing on the same aspect.*

R. W. White (1959) brought together the various notions relating to instinctual intrinsic needs in terms of 'competence' or 'effectance' motivation to deal effectively with the environment. He pointed out that in young children the effectance motive may be undifferentiated, but *with experience it becomes differentiated into more specific motives.* These suggestions were further elaborated with regard to intrinsic motivation in general and in particular with regard to the motive to create. The motivation to create was explained in terms of above-average levels of needs relating to mastery motivation, such as curiosity, inquiry, exploration, novelty, complexity and order (Barron, 1968; Helson & Crutchfield, 1970; MacKinnon, 1978; Maddi, 1965; Maddi & Berne, 1964; Schachtel, 1959). For example, Barron (1963) suggested that creative people are challenged to make new order out of their own experience and abilities. Accordingly, they are attracted to complex or disordered sets of stimuli, and gain pleasure from reducing them to order.

It is clear that creators do tend to exercise their cognitive skills in childhood. Although not all are favourably disposed towards school, there is much to suggest that they typically enjoy and engage in independent intellectual or constructive activities – which might be interpreted in terms of a mastery motive. But there is also little question that all normal children attempt to manipulate and master the environment. The fact remains, however, that individuals differ with respect to *how well* they master various aspects of the environment. As White (1959) pointed out, effectance motivation differentiates. It is not sustained when actions produce little effect, or when a situation has been exploited to the point that it no longer presents new possibilities. One factor that enhances the probability that particular actions will be effective, and that new possibilities will be discovered is competence.

This means that competence is likely to enhance the intrinsic satisfaction and reinforce the motivation to master.

It seems, therefore, that a well-founded sense of competence is likely to be one of the major factors that lead children to engage in relatively complex tasks and set themselves increasingly higher goals. As we have seen, a *well-founded sense of competence* is characteristic of productive creators, and this is likely to be an important factor in maintaining their motivation to excel. Moreover, as creators are usually competent in a specific domain in childhood, they are likely to sustain intrinsic motivation and develop a motive to excel *in that domain*.

## Theories relating to the role of psychodynamic tendencies in the motivation to create

Somewhat in contrast to theories relating to the intrinsic satisfactions are psychodynamic theories, which focus on general motives underlying the development of the personality, rather than motives pertaining to particular types of activity.

As mentioned in chapter 1, it was Freud's contention that the general motive underlying the development of the personality is to maximize gratification of instinctual needs (especially sexual and aggressive needs) while minimizing the possibility of punishment and guilt. To Freud, the motivation to create is supplied by energy that has been derived from instinctual sexual needs and sublimated into culturally valued work, so as to minimize punishment and guilt. George Bernard Shaw apparently agreed that creators are able to divert their sexual energies into creative enterprise, maintaining that

The world's greatest books get written, its pictures painted, its statues modelled, its symphonies composed, by people who are free from the otherwise universal domination of the tyranny of sex. (Quoted by Kenmare 1960, p. 158)

And research findings offer some support for the idea that creative activity is a substitute for sexual activity. A relatively large proportion of creators apparently engage in little connubial sexual activity, which is the only sexual outlet generally approved by society – and is therefore the best way of satisfying sexual instincts while minimizing guilt.

Francis Bacon put a rather more practical complexion upon the matter, however, implying that connubial activities and their products simply get in the way of creative (and other) enterprise:

He that hath wife and children hath given hostages to fortune for they are impediments to great enterprises, either of virtue or mischief, certainly the best works, and of greatest merit for the public have proceeded from unmarried or childless men. (Bacon, 1685/1980 p. 149)

In contrast to Freud, theorists of a more existentialistic or Humanistic persuasion regarded the motivation to create as a manifestation of a monolithic drive to free and actualize the self (with the implication that actualization involves optimal development and balance between various aspects of the personality). This applies to Rank's suggestion that creative behaviour represents a healthy resolution of a conflict between fear of life and of death, and also to Fromm's (1955) suggestion that productive creative behaviour is the outcome of a balance between closeness and independence. MacKinnon's (1965) brave attempts to show support for Rank's theory, were unfortunately not very convincing, and his findings that extremely creative architects are less 'neurotic' than others are in conflict with a large body of findings suggesting that neurosis is more prevalent among highly creative individuals than in the general population.

Research findings also offer little in support for the views of Fromm, Maslow and Rogers, who suggested that the development of a productive or self-actualizing creative personality depends on understanding, a loving interaction between child and parent and/or satisfaction of lower needs. As we have seen, some extremely creative people enjoyed little affection, acceptance or emotional satisfaction in their childhood homes.

It seems, therefore, that the suggestion that creativity represents the achievement of personal balance, and 'becoming everything one is able to become' is indeed wide of the mark for explaining creative achievement. Findings show clearly that, if not mentally unbalanced, creative achievers are definitely 'one-sided' or 'single-minded'. They do not generally become 'everything they are able to become'. They tend to devote their energies to a particular type of creative activity to the exclusion of other involvements, they often have unsatisfactory interpersonal relationships, and a relatively large number have committed suicide (see Prentky, 1980).

Adler's suggestion that creativity is related to co-operation, mutual trust, respect and understanding in the childhood home does not typically apply to creative achievers. Neither (as we shall see in the following section) does his suggestion that creative activity is the outcome of a healthy tendency to perfect the personality through serving mankind. But his suggestion that the motivation to create might be initiated by feelings of imperfection does have empirical support. This suggestion has been echoed by Barron's (1968) proposal that creative people are concerned about their personal adequacy and are motivated to prove themselves, and is upheld by observations such as Lombroso's (1895) long sad list of physical and mental problems in men of genius and by findings of modern research. Goertzel and Goertzel (1962) reported that one quarter of their subjects had one or more physical disabilities. It was shown, moreover, that geniuses often have other handicaps such as orphanhood, emotional insecurity or rejection to contend with in childhood. To the list of their problems one might also add socially censured sexual orientations and impotence.

## Suggestions relating to the role of 'extrinsic satisfactions' in the motivation to create

As I mentioned earlier in this chapter, 'extrinsic satisfactions' are those derived from the results of a behaviour, rather than from the behaviour *per se*. Despite what psychologists have said to the contrary, productive creative behaviour apparently offers various types of extrinsic satisfaction. Financial reward is seldom one of them, but even financial reward provides some motivation for creators. Speaking of working for money, Anthony Trollope (1974) noted that those who preach the doctrine that an author or artist should not work for money are like clergymen who preach sermons against the love of money but know that love of money is a distinctive characteristic of humanity. 'Such sermons', he says, 'are mere platitudes called for by customary but unintelligent piety. All material progress has come from man's desire to do the best he can for himself and those about him' (p. 246).

But money is of course not the only or major extrinsic motivator. As we have seen from the results of studies relating to the societal and socio-cultural backgrounds, creative achievers seem to be motivated to become like models who are admired by themselves and esteemed by society at large. 'I have certainly also had always before my eyes the charms of reputation', wrote Trollope (1974).

> Over and above the money view of the question, I wished to be more than a clerk in the Post Office. To be known as somebody, to be Anthony Trollope, if it is no more, is to me much. The feeling is a very general one, and I think beneficient. It is that which has been called 'last infirmity of noble mind'. The infirmity is so human that the man who lacks it is either above or below humanity. I own to the infirmity. But I confess that my first object in taking to literature as a profession was that which is common to the barrister when he goes to the bar, and the baker when he sets up his oven. I wished to make an income on which I and those belonging to me might live in comfort. (p. 246)

As Trollope implied, creators aspire to win fame and self-esteem by seeking recognition and admiration from discerning people whose opinion really matters. These are particularly valuable incentives for people who have suffered (real or imagined) rejection, neglect, aversion or other intimations of imperfection. People who have been made to feel somewhat inferior to others in some respects may be motivated to seek public confirmation that they are superior to them in other respects.

According to George Orwell, the first reason for writing is

Sheer egoism. Desire to seem clever, to be talked about, to be remembered after death, to get your own back on grownups who snubbed you in childhood, etc., etc. It is humbug to pretend that this is not a motive, and a strong one. Writers share this characteristic with scientists, artists, politicians, lawyers, soldiers, successful businessmen – in short, with the whole top crust of humanity. (1957, pp. 315–316)

It was Auden's (1956) opinion that

Every writer would rather be rich than poor, but no genuine writer cares about popularity as such. He needs approval of his work by others in order to be reassured that the vision of life he believes he has had is a true vision and not a self-delusion, but he can only be reassured by those whose judgment he respects. It would only be necessary for a writer to secure universal popularity if imagination and intelligence were equally distributed among all men. (1956, p. 22)

Perhaps Auden's best-known comment on the subject is that 'no poet or novelist wishes he were the only one who ever lived, but most of them wish they were the only one alive, and quite a number fondly believe their wish has been granted' (1956, pp. 21–22).

The suggestion that creators are motivated to gain recognition has been supported by various empirical findings, for example, Cox (1926) found that, from a young age, artists and musicians enjoyed admiration from the crowd. We have also seen that some creators are exhibitionistic, even though socially withdrawn. Findings relating to contemporary scientific creators suggest that, even if they are relatively unconcerned about the opinion of the 'crowd', they persistently seek professional recognition (Merton, 1973; Roe, 1965; J. Rossman, 1931).

The strength of a need (such as hunger) is often identified and assessed by withholding a relevant commodity (food) and watching how this affects the person concerned. Judging by what happens when recognition is withheld from productive creators, one gains the impression they generally have a strong need for it. Examples of jealousy, frustration and anger when recognition of their work is at stake are legion. Merton and Barber (Merton, 1973), found that priority was hotly contested in 92 per cent of the simultaneous scientific discoveries before 1700. Although the proportion of legal contests has somewhat decreased since then, a notable degree of interpersonal rivalry and animosity has very frequently been displayed when recognition was at issue in science. For example, Halley described the astronomer Flamsteed as a lazy malicious thief (Merton, 1973). Flamsteed described Newton as always insidious, ambitious and excessively covetous of praise. Newton bitterly accused Hooke of demanding more credit than was his due (Westfall, 1980). Einstein lamented: 'That alas is vanity. You find it in so many scientists. You know, it has always hurt me to think Galileo did not acknowledge the work of Kepler' (Cohen, 1979, p. 41).

Although few scientists are likely to admit their hunger for recognition, many have difficulty in hiding it. Merton (1973) explained that, whenever an autobiography or biography made the point that the creator was little concerned with priority, there was a reasonably good chance that one would find him, a few pages later, embroiled in some contentious episode involving priority.

Contentious protection of priority is, of course, not peculiar to scientists. Acts of jealous aggression against one another by writers, artists or composers are also legend, and sometimes animosity is aroused by the achievements of others, even when their own priority is not at stake. Poe, for example, not only charged Longfellow for copying his own *Haunted place* in the *Beleaguered city*, but also for plagiarizing Tennyson's *Death of the old year* in his *Midnight mass for the dying year* (Hayward, 1974).

Jealousy is not necessarily confined to creative achievers in the same field. Throughout life, Goethe brandished his hatred for Newton, constantly denigrating him both as a man and as a scientist, with comments such as 'Newton's method of investigation must astonish, indeed horrify, everyone who is not demoralized'. Although no-one apparently tried to prevent Goethe from publishing his writings (including comments on Newton) he beseeched

What is this freedom of the press, for which everyone cries and sighs so insistently, if I am not to be allowed to say that Newton deceived himself as a young man and then spent his whole life perpetuating this self-deception. (Quoted by Friedenthal, 1965, p. 395)

Creators may even display their animosity to the world at large, as did Schopenhauer, who declaimed: 'If I could only satisfy my desire to look upon this race of toads and vipers as my equals it would be a consolation to me' (quoted by Hayward, 1974, p. 216).

Beneath the animosity of creators and behind the protestations that they have no desire to be accepted by others, one sometimes, however, catches a glimpse of the frustrated need that arouses these negative feelings. One moment we find Poe declaring

I write from mental necessity to satisfy my taste and my love of art. Fame forms no motive power with me. What can I care for the judgement of a multitude every individual of which I despise?

but later we find him lowering his mask, to reveal

It was false what I said. I love fame I dote on it. (Quoted by Hayward, 1974, p. 196)

Some creators admit indirectly that they want the public to love and respect them. Stephen Spender (1954), for example, maintained that every serious creative writer is in his heart concerned with reputation. And in his elegiac poem, 'Lycidas', John Milton declared

> Fame is the spur that clear spirit doth raise
> (That last infirmity of noble mind)
> To scorn delights, and live laborious days
>
> ('Lycidas', 1637, li. 70)

A few are rather more direct: Tolstoy, for example, confessed 'I felt the need to be known and loved of all the world . . . so that they would troop around me and thank me for something' (quoted by H. Gardner, 1973, p. 334).

Merton (1973) summed up the scientific creator's hunger for recognition as being generated from within but craving satisfaction from without, explaining that vanity is the outer face of the inner need for assurance that one's work really matters, that one has met the hard standards maintained by at least some scientists. Joy gained through scientific discovery and through recognition by others are stamped out of the same psychological coin.

Although Adler (1927) suggested that creative ambitions are dedicated in a philanthropic spirit to the welfare of mankind, and popular writings on men of genius promote this image, it seems that this sentimental notion has little foundation with regard to highly creative individuals. Some creators (including Einstein, Hardy and many of the 700 inventors studied by J. Rossman, 1931) confessed that the welfare of mankind had little to do with their creative efforts. The creative mathematician G. H. Hardy (1969) faced the matter squarely, declaring

Ambition has been the driving force behind nearly all the best work of the world. In particular, practically all substantial contributions to human happiness have been made by ambitious men . . . If a mathematician, or a chemist, or even a physiologist, were to tell me that the driving force in his work had been the desire to benefit humanity, then I should not believe him (nor should I think the better of him if I did). (p. 79)

## Some additional suggestions relating to the motivation to create

The foregoing discussions lead to the conclusion that the motivation to create may be initiated by satisfactions inherent in independent intellectual activity, but it is maintained by expectations of the extrinsic rewards that are gained by using the knowledge and skill that are thereby developed. Although this may explain why creators are motivated to produce something of value, it does not clearly show why they endure all the hard work that creativity demands, rather than gaining more immediate satisfactions with less effort. Many of us would be extremely happy to produce something of enduring value and become famous – but few of us dedicate ourselves single-mindedly to achieving that goal. For one, this is because we are too busy with activities that promise other satisfactions through relatively little effort. Traditional theories do not explain why some people would be more inclined than others to sacrifice relatively easily attained satisfactions, such as those gained through social involvements. They fail to show why some people 'scorn delights to live laborious days', as Milton put it. Something other than the promise of intrinsic satisfactions and fame is needed to explain the powerful, unrelenting, unidirectional impetus so clearly seen in the lifestyles of creative achievers. Something must detract from competing delights. And it is my contention that this role is played by threat.

### The role of threat

'As a boy', wrote George Orwell,

I had no money, I was weak, I was ugly, I was unpopular, I had a chronic cough, I was cowardly, I smelt . . . The conviction that it was *not possible* for me to be a success went deep enough to influence my actions until far into adult life . . . But this sense of guilt and inevitable failure was balanced by something else: that is, the instinct to survive. Even a creature that is weak, ugly, cowardly, smelly and in no way justifiable still wants to stay alive and to be happy after its own fashion. (Orwell, 1957, pp. 45–46; Orwell's emphasis)

Although adaptation to the environment involves mastery as well as adjustment, it primarily involves avoidance of extinction. Survival needs take precedence over needs for growth (as even the existentialists and

Humanists admit). For the very young, being alone relates closely to extinction, and is threatening. In the course of development, various experiences may become associated with being alone, including indications that one is out of favour with, or unattractive to, others. In general any signs that one is unable to achieve what is desired by others may relate to being abandoned – which is extremely alarming to the young.

Sustained threat implies stress, which has been described as a state where the well-being of the individual is endangered and all one's energies must be devoted to protecting that well-being (Cofer & Appley, 1964, p. 463). As often noted, the most distressing element in the experience of stress is the perception of an imbalance between demands upon one and one's ability to meet those demands – one is in fact *unable to control the situation* (McGrath, 1970; Rutter, 1983).

Much has been written about the reduction of the harmful effects of threatening or potentially stressful situations through somehow being able to control the situation. Experiments on animals and humans show that subjects who are allowed to control the level of threatening stimuli show less subjective discomfort and secrete lower levels of cortisol than those who are exposed to similar stimuli without being able to control them (e.g. Lundberg & Frankenhauser, 1978). The collection of papers dealing with stress, coping and development in children published by Garmezy and Rutter (1983) is replete with examples illustrating that the development of coping mechanisms in response to threat depends on the child's ability to control the situation – particularly to somehow control the actions of others (see, e.g., Levine, 1983).

There are, however, some circumstances over which a child (or an adult) is unable to gain control, and perception of one's inability to control a situation involves the release of adreno-corticotropic hormone (Henry & Meehan, 1981). Raised levels of this hormone are associated with what has been called a sense of 'learned helplessness', which is characterized by depression and submission (Seligman, 1975). But another effect of the experience of lack of control, which has special importance for adaptation, is an increased ability to learn. Behavioural experiments have shown that conditioning or learning may sometimes be more rapid as a result of the adreno-corticotropic hormone effect (e.g. Henry & Meehan, 1981). Henry and Meehan explain adaptive value of depression in the following terms:

Depression occurs when an animal perceives a mismatch and is out of place in either the environment (lost) or the social hierarchy (when abandoned by an attachment figure, such as a mother). Within limits depression is a response of great survival value. In a social animal with a high learning capacity, depression enables it to learn fresh patterns of behaviour and so avoid repeating an undesired experience. (p. 316)

When people experience threat, pain or insecurity in certain situations over which they have no control, but find they are able to exercise control in another situation, they might cope by *avoiding* the whole range of potentially uncomfortable situations, and seek control in the area where they have better control. An avoidance response does not, however, remove the source of threat. It does not even alter the perception of threat. Nor is an avoidance response extinguished, as it continues to be reinforced by a sense of successful prevention of distress. So, as Lazarus (1974) explains, the tendency to appraise certain situations as threatening becomes very deep-rooted, because the source of threat is not clearly perceived when it is avoided. Beliefs and attitudes are based on previous experience. The experience may eventually be forgotten, but the attitudes are retained through constant reinforcement of avoidance behaviours.

Emery and Csikszentmihalyi (1982) have suggested that a life theme may originally develop as an attempt to cope with the experience of stress, and tend over the years to become part of the personality. It is possible that, in some people, such a life theme may involve *avoidance of social situations which have been perceived as threatening and engagement in 'safe' intellectual pursuits*. And it is likely that this applied to Einstein.

It is clear from Einstein's scant autobiographical notes that his independent intellectual activities in childhood had a palliative function by providing a sense of security that he failed to find in his social and personal world. He later revealed:

I believe with Schopenhauer that one of the strongest motives that lead persons to art and science is flight from everyday life, with its painful harshness and wretched dreariness . . . With this negative motive there goes a positive one. Man seeks for himself, in whatever manner is suitable for him, a simplified and lucid image of the world, and so to overcome the work of experience by striving to replace it to some extent by this image . . . This is what the painter does, and the poet, the speculative philosopher, the natural scientist, each in his own way. Into this image and its formation, he places the centre of gravity of his emotional life, in order to attain the peace and security that he cannot find within the narrow confines of his swirling personal experience. (Quoted by Holton, 1971, Appendix, p. 108)

Although few modern psychologists may accept that threat or stress plays an important role in the development of the motivational habits of creative people, it has indeed long been noted that happiness, and escape from unhappiness, may be gained from intellectual activity. Aristotle maintained that rational pursuits provide man with his most noble and perfect pleasures, completely unmixed with pain. In these terms intellectual activity may be described as a palliative avoidance response.

Psychologists of various persuasions, including early and modern psychoanalysts such as Anna Freud (1937) and Storr (1983), have also noted the palliative effects of intellectual behaviour. Csikszentmihalyi (1982) proposed that, when intensely engaged in such behaviour 'there is neither need nor opportunity to reflect on oneself – the self as an object of awareness recedes while the focus of attention is taken up by the demands of the activity and by the response given to them' (p. 22). Whyte (1978) explained that self awareness aims to eliminate the discomforts that cause it, and man will go to any length to escape self-awareness. 'Learn to know yourself by all means, when you feel it necessary, but then turn to something in which you can forget yourself', said Whyte (1978, p. 36).

We have ample reason for believing that, as children, many creators were threatened by rejection or other forms of emotional insecurity, and there are clear examples of their discovery of the palliative effect of intellectual activity in their writings. Gustav Flaubert advised: 'Read, do not dream. Plunge into long studies; there is nothing continually good but the habit of stubborn work. It releases an opium which lulls the soul' (1851/1974, p. 322). Somerset Maugham (bereaved in childhood, and unable to find satisfying love in his numerous homosexual encounters) asserted that 'It is the inestimable privilege of the creative artist to win in creation release from the pains of life' (1958, p. 105). As a child, Charles Babbage (1864/1969) discovered that intellectual activity distracts the mind from pain – a principle he put into practice in later life. In his autobiography he confided:

Although I may not have put into words the principle, that *occupation of the mind is such a source of pleasure* that it can relieve even the pain of a headache; yet I am sure it practically gave an additional stimulus to me in many a difficult enquiry. (1864/1969, p. 14; italics in the original)

Edison (1948/1968) stated bluntly: 'As a cure for worry, work is better than whisky, much better' (p. 58).

It is also clear that Einstein's search for security through contemplating the certainties in physical phenomena became a life theme. In his autobiographical notes (1949/1979b) he explained:

When I was a fairly precocious young man I became thoroughly impressed with the futility of hopes and strivings that chase most men restlessly through life. Moreover, I soon discovered the cruelty of that chase. (1949/1979b, p. 3)

In childhood he first sought refuge in religion, but having failed to gain a sufficient sense of certainty there, he found it at the age of twelve in a little book of Euclidean geometry. The discovery that geometric theorems could be proved with certainty made an 'indescribable impression' on him. Long after he admitted

that the religious paradise of youth, which was thus lost, was a first attempt to free myself from the chains of the 'merely personal', from an existence dominated by wishes, hopes and primitive feelings. Out there was this huge world, which exists independently of us human beings and which stands before us like a great eternal riddle, at least partly accessible to our introspection and thinking. The contemplation of this world beckoned as a liberation, and I soon noticed that many a man whom I had learned to esteem and admire *had found inner freedom and security in its pursuit* . . . The road to this paradise was not as comfortable and alluring as the road to the religious paradise; but it has shown itself reliable, and I have never regretted having chosen it. (1949/1979b, p. 5; italics mine)

In a letter to his sister we gain a glimpse of Einstein as a young adult, still suffering discomfort from his inability to control social and personal problems, and seeking refuge in the intellectual pursuit of the physical world:

What depresses me most of course, is the [financial] misfortune of my poor parents. Also it grieves me deeply that I, as a grown man, have to stand idly by, unable to help. I am nothing but a burden to my family . . . Really, it would have been better if I had never been born. Sometimes the only thought that sustains me and my only refuge from despair is that I have always done everything I could in my small power, and that year in, year out, I have never permitted myself any amusement or diversions except those afforded by my studies. (in Ducas & Hoffman, 1979, p. 14)

In a later letter he remarked:

As in my youth, I sit here endlessly and think and calculate, hoping to unearth deep secrets. The so-called Great World, i.e. men's bustle, has less attraction than ever, so that each day I find myself becoming more of a hermit. (in Ducas & Hoffman, 1979, p. 17)

Underlying this theme one may see a search, not only for security, but also for a sense of his own worth.

Among Roe's (1953) conclusions to her research on eminently creative scientists are that 'certainty of his own worth is any man's greatest need. Though some of them may find it only there, scientists do find this certainty in science' (p. 53).

Some people may cope with stress by gaining control over a part of the environment, thereby affirming a sense of their own worth. Some may need further affirmation, and they set out to show they are able to surpass others and gain public recognition.

## The role of tension reduction

To further our understanding of the creators' motivations, it is as well to take a deeper look at the basic nature of pleasure – and see how this could apply to creative achievement.

It is generally agreed that pleasure and displeasure are related to tension, but there has been little consensus as to the exact nature of the relation. Freud suggested that tension causes discomfort and people are generally motivated to reduce it. The Humanists argued that this is a very primitive view of humanity, and that healthy people in fact gain pleasure from tension and therefore seek to increase it. Psychologists of a Humanistic persuasion describe the intrinsic satisfaction in a task in terms of a rise in tension.

The view adopted and elaborated upon in the following sections of this book was originally put forward by Murray and Kluckhohn (1953). These authors suggested that neither a tensionless state, nor a state of tension is generally most satisfying: *pleasure results from the actual reduction of tension*. The more tension is reduced, the greater the pleasure.

Taking this a little further – one may assume that, if tension reduction is pleasurable, then *anticipation* of tension reduction would also be pleasurable. Therefore tension would be exhilarating when *there is anticipation of tension reduction* – but it would *not* be pleasurable when one feels there is little hope of being able to reduce it.

This principle applies well to the suggestion that competence reinforces mastery motivation. To the competent person, a challenging task promises greater reduction of tension than a simple task does, and a competent person would therefore be likely to have relatively high levels of aspiration. Moreover, the principle of pleasure through tension reduction also applies well to aesthetic satisfaction – which plays an important, but too seldom recognized, role in the motivation to create.

## The role of aesthetic satisfaction

As I mentioned, creators appear to be aesthetically sensitive even in childhood. Numerous adult creators, both artists and scientists, have testified that they gain enormous pleasure from perceiving and producing something of beauty. This raises the question – what does 'beauty' mean? And how does it afford pleasure? The following sections briefly consider some possible intellectual, emotional and socio-cultural sources of aesthetic pleasure.

*Intellectual sources of aesthetic pleasure.* The Pythagorean definition of beauty was 'the reduction of many to one' – a concept that implies integration of elements into a harmonious whole. This corresponds with Poincaré's (1908/1954) suggestion that the experience of beauty is an intellectual experience of harmonious order among parts. A similar notion of beauty is expressed by the Gestalt theorists in terms of 'the law of Pragnanz', which implies a tendency to simplify. To the Gestalt psychologists, the beauty of a set of stimuli inheres in harmonious relations among the parts, and between the parts and the whole. When this is lacking, tensions are set up, which motivate one to restructure the relations among the elements, to create harmony and thereby reduce the tension.

When composing his little pieces as a child, the young Mozart sought harmony by looking for 'notes that like each other'. Notes that 'like' each other do so for very practical reasons: there is a simple mathematical relation between the frequencies of the vibrations they set up. Other simple relations contributing to harmony among the elements of aesthetic products include 'symmetry' and 'closure'. Some of these relations are clearly spelled out by Gestalt psychologists and logicians. But others, such as those underlying cultural traditions, cannot be expressed in mathematical or logical terms. Dutch gables, for example, do not harmonize well with pagoda-type roofs, but the explanation for this is cultural rather than formal: culture rather than nature has determined here what parts 'like each other'.

Unfortunately, much of the psychological research on the elusive subject of aesthetics has been conducted by presenting unexceptional subjects in the laboratory with a selection of artificial stimuli and asking them to state their preferences. This type of research aims mainly to show why certain stimuli are generally more aesthetically pleasing than others are. For more than a century researchers have, for example, tested the effects of repeated exposure to aesthetic objects. Some found that repeated exposure to an object (such as a picture) increased one's appreciation of it. Others found that familiarity bred contempt: repeated exposure resulted in tedium and lack of appreciation. In an effort to reconcile these findings, Berlyne (e.g. 1971) suggested that when one is repeatedly exposed to a relatively complex aesthetic product, pleasure will increase as it becomes more familiar (and easier to 'understand') –

until it becomes too familiar. At this point pleasure decreases with repeated exposure. Aesthetic pleasure involves a balance between opposing sets of variables, he explained. In the one set are variables that introduce order and certainty into the structure and reduce its complexity – such as symmetry. These decrease tension. The opposing set consists of variables that add complexity to the product and reduce its certainty. These increase tension.

Berlyne further suggested that all such variables fall on a single dimension ranging from extreme simplicity and certainty (which is not arousing) to extreme complexity and uncertainty (which is very arousing). There is a curvilinear relation between arousal and pleasure. In other words, pleasure derived from an aesthetic product is greatest when complexity and arousal are at intermediate rather than extreme levels. Extreme complexity and uncertainty are too arousing and extreme simplicity is not sufficiently arousing to cause pleasurable aesthetic reactions. As one gains repeated experience of a very complex product, it may, however, become less arousing – which means that, for a while, one gains more pleasure from each exposure to it, but after a while the optimal point is reached, after which the product becomes less pleasing with each exposure.

When one comes to think of it, Berlyne's model may be interpreted in terms of the principle that pleasure inheres in reduction of tension: *the greater the actual reduction of tension, the greater the pleasure.* In these terms we can see that when one perceives a stimulus as extremely complex it offers little pleasure because one feels incapable of reducing the tension it arouses – and when one perceives the stimulus as extremely simple it arouses little tension to reduce.

The notion that an aesthetic experience involves a discharge of tension is not new. Among those who have suggested that art captures attention, arouses tension and then purges it was Aristotle, who used the word 'katharsis' with respect to aesthetic experience. This apparently applies to science too, for Einstein wrote that 'music does not influence research work, but both are nourished by the same source of longing, and they complement each other in the release they offer' (in Ducas & Hoffman, 1979, p. 78).

The reader may notice that the above discussion says little about creators' enduring aesthetic sensitivity and their persistent urge to produce something of beauty. As we have seen, creators are not only aesthetically sensitive they also tend to be emotionally unstable. Moreover aesthetic sensitivity is particularly noticeable in those groups in which the instability is most marked – artists and writers. Even in the absence of reliable statistical correlations this leads us to wonder how emotional instability might relate to aesthetic sensitivity.

One suggestion is that, as creators are prone to experiencing high levels of emotional tension, and are also well versed in the formal demands and techniques of their discipline, *they are motivated and able to discharge their tensions by reducing intellectual complexities to harmonious wholes.*

*Emotional sources of aesthetic pleasure.* Although intellectual appreciation of harmonious forms is important to aesthetics, one should not, however, ignore the more primitive side of aesthetic reactions. There is obviously more to such reactions than a shift on the perceptually complex–simple dimension and reduction of intellectual tension. Aesthetic appreciation must also be affected by emotion and culturally acquired reactions.

When considering the emotional nature of aesthetic reactions, it is particularly important to realize that aesthetic reactions are not restricted to humans. Humans might develop aesthetic appreciation through understanding, which allows reduction of intellectual tensions, but in addition to intellectual reactions to the formal relations in a beautiful work are *instinctual reactions*, which arouse tensions that give rise to a positive emotion: a feeling of attraction; a feeling of love. All organisms are naturally attracted by certain stimuli that arouse tension and offer promise of tension reduction. Many are able to produce clearly discernible stimuli of that nature. Birds, for example, present beautiful plumage but also sing lovely songs, perform attractive dances and adorn their homes with pretty pieces; even fish exhibit attractive colours – all of which enhance their chances of arousing and discharging sexual tensions.

To the evolutionists, the production of such attractive stimuli is the animal equivalent of the human arts. The original aim of art, said Darwin is to excite a feeling of liking in the opposite sex. It is part of the natural urge to promote the survival of the species and has a sexual character. It operates in the service of 'sexual selection', which, Darwin explained, is one of the natural mechanisms promoting survival of the fittest. Sexually appealing characteristics which usually relate to fitness and reproductive capacity make one individual a more likely candidate than others for selection by members of the opposite sex. As individuals endowed with these natural physical attractions are more likely than those with deformities to be chosen as mates and to produce progeny, this selective tendency naturally preserves the fitness of the species.

Built into the genes of animals are inherited reflexes (what one calls 'instincts') to create certain 'artistic products' that make them appealing to the opposite sex and enhance the probability of their mating. However, all members of a species have rather similar tastes: each species of animal responds in a stereotyped fashion only to a narrow range of stimuli, most of which signify fitness and readiness for mating.

This does not apply to the same extent in humans, however. Although humans are attracted by physical characteristics signifying fitness, fertility and readiness for mating, they have a far more flexible and variable conception of sexual appeal than animals do. A rotund woman displaying explicit signs of physical fitness for childbearing might be regarded as sexually attractive in a society where food supply is uncertain, but she may be regarded as monstrously lacking in agility and grace in a sophisticated society where adaptation and fitness to rear young have become assessed from more than a purely physical point of view. Specific views on sexually appealing characteristics vary moreover not only from one culture to another, but also in the same culture and within subcultures from time to time. Various types of beauty and sexual appeal are appreciated as 'fashions' come and go. But some characteristics are never regarded as attractive – in any culture. Among them are signs of physical or mental disorder, inability to cope with social expectations, and various other weaknesses associated with extinction of individual and species.

As we have seen from research findings cited in the previous chapter – these characteristics are in fact often found in creative achievers. And this makes them poor candidates for sexual selection. Yet they too are endowed with instincts that urge them to be attractive so that they might be loved. If naturally unattractive, they may be urged to produce something of beauty as an extension of themselves – to attract love. In other words, creating beauty not only serves the purpose of reducing intellectual tensions but also arousing feelings of attraction (sexual tensions and promise of tension reduction) in others.

Freud suggested that one may see in some corner of the fantasies of exceptional (and unexceptional people), 'the lady' at whose feet all their triumphs would be laid. It seems, however, that one should not be specific about the gender of 'the lady'. Nor perhaps should one restrict the aim of producing something of beauty to sexual selection – even in the service of survival. Most of us have experienced the enormously strong aesthetic appeal of young children (an appeal that may well preserve them from extinction by parents and neighbours). Most of us have also experienced the appeal of aesthetic stimuli sent out by birds, fish and other beautiful animals. This gives reason to suggest that survival of the species may be served by the 'arts' of animals in more ways than through sexual selection. Animals have avoided extinction by arousing aesthetic appreciation in humans who love, pet and protect them. This may apply to some people too.

*Cultural influences on sources of aesthetic pleasure.* It is now widely agreed that the lability and intensity of one's emotional reactions depend largely on genetic factors. Moreover, it appears from research findings relating to creators that people who are prone to intense emotional reactions are often aesthetically sensitive. This suggests that the basis for the *intensity* of aesthetic reactions may be to some extent organic. Even if this is true, however, it does not mean that all emotionally labile people are aesthetically sensitive or that aesthetic sensitivity depends entirely on emotional sensitivity. People not only vary with respect to their intensity of emotional arousal, but also with regard to what arouses them and what particular forms their emotional reactions take. The latter depends largely on social influence.

As already explained, human emotions are not merely innately programmed stereotyped reactions to specific survival-related stimuli, as is the case with lower animals. In humans, not only intellectual appraisal, but also the *type of emotional reaction* elicited by a particular stimulus depends largely on socialization. Responses to the sensuous and formal qualities of works of art are affected by what one has learned to expect and to value. As Koestler (1964) explained, aesthetic appreciation implies a complex system of values and judgments, which embodies various criteria of excellence including technical, psychological and cultural values. Some of these values distort others. For example, one places less aesthetic value on a faithful copy of a painting than on the original, although the visual stimuli offered by the two are practically identical. One's appreciation is affected by the knowledge that there is only one highly prized (and perhaps highly priced) original. Sometimes, says Koestler, one is mainly appreciative of the fact that one is engaged in appreciating a work that is highly valued by others. A man who reads Kierkegaard may be moved not so much by what he reads as by the fact that he is reading it – if it is the 'in' thing to do. His intrinsic satisfaction in this exercise might be the less if Kierkegaard's works were less highly esteemed by those who appear to be intellectually elite.

As we have seen in preceding chapters, social influences on aesthetic tastes typically begin to operate on creators in their childhood homes, and are further exerted by teachers, mentors, and other models. The global and pervasive effect of cultural influences on aesthetic values is perhaps most clearly shown by the rise and fall of particular artistic styles in the culture. But creators are moved by more than the fact that they know what is currently appreciated and what is the 'in' thing to appreciate. Although they acquire cultural values they also change them. They mould the intellectual perceptions and emotional reactions of those that follow them. Even if they add little knowledge to their culture, they change the way in which people view and evaluate knowledge. As Wordsworth put it, each great mind 'must himself create the taste by which he is to be relished'.

## Conclusions

This chapter has attempted to cast some light on the nature of various motives that seem to play complementary roles in sustaining the unidirectional impetus seen in the lives of creative achievers – pulling and pushing them to engage persistently in their creative work.

Intrinsic motives, which have at their source an instinctual need for mastery, seem to lead creators as children to seek pleasure in independent intellectual activities that are suited to their abilities – and to put the stressful, uncontrollable aspects of their lives out of their minds. These activities lead to a particular type of competence or talent, which interacts with their need for mastery, leading them to set themselves ever higher goals and aspire to excellence.

Extrinsic motives, which have at their source instinctual needs for the survival of individual and species, contribute to the single-minded perseverance of creators by urging them to avoid the stressful aspects of their lives and to seek love and esteem through producing something highly valued by society at large and also elicit love or admiration from individuals.

Although none of these motives might be sufficient in itself to sustain the stubborn labour of creators, the combination is relatively powerful. The pull and push are in the same direction.

Some of the suggestions discussed in this chapter will be further developed in the next, where the development of creative ability is explained in terms of a common pattern of influences in the early lives and characteristics of eminently creative people.

# 8

## The developmental pattern

As Gruber and Davis (1988) suggest, it is important in each creative life to have an appropriate coincidence of knowledge, purpose and affect (emotion). The findings discussed in previous chapters give one a fairly clear indication of the nature and interaction of those influences in the lives of creative geniuses – and we have now reached a point where we can combine the conclusions emerging from the findings into a composite developmental pattern.

Obviously, not all creators have exactly similar backgrounds, early life experiences, or personal characteristics, and it would be senseless to describe their development in terms of a wide assortment of specifics: but, underlying the specifics, are a few clearly discernible common factors. In this chapter, those factors are outlined and explained. Figure 8.1 provides a schematic representation as a frame of reference.

The pattern depicted in figure 8.1 may be briefly described as follows: in childhood, creators are typically influenced by some of the events, mechanisms and agents (listed at the top of the figure) that result in the development of factors (A), (B) and (C). More specifically, one or more of the items in the first set of events, mechanisms and agents (on the left of the figure) may influence (A), which is the acquisition of a *sense of values that places learning and achievement high among desired goals*; the next pair (in the centre) influence (B), which is *precocious development of some sort of intellectual ability or talent*, such as reading, artistic talent, musical talent, constructive ability or scientific ability; and any of the third set of events, mechanisms and agents (on the right) may lead to (C), which is stress.

Although the *specific events*, mechanisms and agents affecting the development of (A), (B) and (C) may vary from person to person, facts presented in previous chapters give reason to believe that *their effects* – that is (A), (B) and (C) – are common to productive creators, and the interaction of these effects leads to (D), which is persistent independent activity and desire to excel (described in chap. 7). From (D) develops

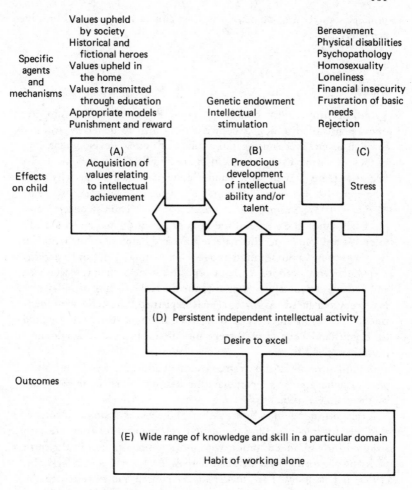

Figure 8.1 *Factors influencing the development of creative genius*

(E) – a wide range of knowledge and automatic skills in the relevant domain, and a habit of working alone. (The question as to why (E) should result in creative inspiration will be dealt with in the final chapter.)

The arrows in figure 8.1 indicate that (A), (B) and (D) interact and are mutually enhancing. Although (B) and (C) have no direct effect on one another, their interaction contributes to (D).

The following sections recapitulate and elaborate upon the determinants and effects of (A), (B), (C) and (D) in the light of general principles governing human behaviour and facts relating to creative achievers.

## Values

Values determine what one considers worthy or unworthy, and give one a sense of direction and incentive. They are generally acquired through several mechanisms in the course of human development. One of these mechanisms is 'identification'. In middle childhood one usually begins to identify with parents and people in authority, especially those who appear to be powerful, admirable and admired by others (see, e.g., A. Freud, 1937; Sarnoff, 1962; Stoke, 1950). A child's concept of an ideal self – the child's idea of the kind of person he or she would like to be – is fashioned after the characteristics and opinions of such models. By identifying with admired models, emulating them and adopting their values and ideals, the child incorporates some of their characteristics and becomes in some way similar to them – and a feeling of self-worth is thereby enhanced. As Slater (1961) explained, 'the child who identifies ... is saying in effect "I want to be like you. If I were, I would have you (and your virtues) with me all the time, and would love myself" ' (p. 113).

A similar tribute is paid to strong animals and wise men by primitive peoples, who aspire to incorporate the desired virtues of these beings by the simple expedient of eating them.

Ideals relating to one's future self are, however, not simply incorporated by direct contact and emulation (or ingestion). They are also acquired through identification with more remote models in the form of living, historical, and fictional heroes. As Murray and Kluckhohn (1953) put it: '[ideals] are imaginatively created and recreated in the course of development in response to patterns offered by the environment – mythological, historical, or living exemplars. Thus the history of the ideal self may be depicted as a series of imaginative identifications, of heroes and their worship' (p. 40).

Albert and Runco (1986) had something particular to say about creative achievers in this regard. These authors suggest that, because of the frequent conflict within their families and the frequent loss of a parent in childhood, creators as children often have a relatively large variety of heroes and models, many of whom they do not even know.

Other mechanisms involved in the acquisition of values are reward and punishment – both direct and vicarious. If, for example, one is rewarded for engaging in intellectual activity, or has seen others being rewarded for so doing, one is likely to place high value on that activity.

There is a good deal of support for the suggestion that creators-to-be are typically influenced by agents who transmitted values (relating to intellectual achievements) through the various mechanisms mentioned above. Sociometric studies indicate that creative achievers are usually born into societies in which relevant role models and incentives are in good supply. Nomothetic studies reveal that they are born into the particular socio-economic strata and families (such as professional-class and Jewish families) in which the value of intellectual achievement is upheld. Case histories show that, as children, they are usually exposed to some influential adult acquaintances, teachers and mentors, who provide appropriate examples and encourage them to take an interest in subjects that allow scope for creative achievement – and that they are typically subjected to parental styles of control likely to instil a sense of the virtue of intellectual endeavour.

It seems therefore that values may play an important role in the development of creative genius, by promoting a desire to excel in some intellectual endeavour, and suggesting that a sense of self-worth will be achieved by engaging in intellectual activities.

## Precocious development of ability

Whereas values point out where one should aim, appropriate ability gives one a good chance of successfully achieving the aim.

There is ample evidence cited in foregoing chapters to support the suggestion that creators typically develop some talent or intellectual skill at an early age, even if not extremely intelligent or able in all respects. As indicated in figure 8.1, mechanisms involved in promoting precocity are *genetic endowment* of biological potentials, and *early intellectual experience*. From what we have learned of their backgrounds, it is apparent that creators' precocity could well be attributed to interaction of genetically endowed potentials and environmental stimulation. Moreover, a circular chicken-and-egg interaction may arise, where precocious intellectual ability not only results from, but also leads to encouragement and tuition by adults (see H. J. Walberg, 1988). As Feldman (e.g. 1986, 1988) explained, prodigies are the product of an interacting set of forces, including natural capacity, parental interest and effort, and appropriate introduction to the relevant domain.

Genetic potentials cannot be empirically demonstrated with any certainty, but there is a great deal of evidence to show that whatever potential creators may have had was fostered and promoted through early intellectual stimulation by various mechanisms and agents. Sociometric and nomothetic studies show that they typically come from societies and families that build a good supply of knowledge and cultural materials, and make a point of teaching and encouraging the young to use them. A disproportionate number of creative achievers are first-born children and/or are placed in a favourable position to receive special attention from adults, at least for a while. Case histories reveal that eminent creators usually interact to a considerable extent with adults in their childhood, and that some are also deprived of the company of peers (which is usually less intellectually stimulating than interaction with adults). There are, moreover, indications that intellectual interests are casually acquired through constant exposure to intellectual conversations and participation in the intellectual activities of adult models, and there are also examples of coercive stimulation and intensive training.

Although there are numerous accounts of the delights of learning experienced in the childhood home, it is also apparent that not all creators initially experienced their early tuition as delightful. Some, as we have seen, had it thrust upon them rather forcibly. Nevertheless, there is a strong possibility that, early in childhood, coercive training may have laid down a firm basis for precocious development of an intellectual skill in some eminent creators. Testimony to this effect is offered by Norbert Wiener, who explained that, by learning mathematics at an early age from his father, his 'energies were released for later serious work at a time when others were learning the very grammar of their professions' (Wiener, 1953, p. 290). Churchill (1930/1983) also expressed the view that thorough grounding may pave the way for exceptional performance, referring thus to his somewhat unsuccessful early experiences at Harrow,

by being so long in the lowest form, I gained an immense advantage over the cleverer boys . . . They all went on to learn Latin and Greek . . . But I was taught English . . . We practised continually English analysis . . . It was a kind of drill . . . Thus I got into my bones the essential structure of the ordinary British sentence – which is a noble thing. (*My early life: a roving commission*, 1930/1983, pp. 24–25)

To whatever mechanisms and agents precocious development of skill may be attributed, it is likely to encourage a child to engage in relevant self-directed pursuits. The writer Norman Podhoretz (1967) testified to the importance of ability in promoting the development of motivation, saying

The desire to write, if real, arises in the first place from the ability to write.

A child, for example, may show himself to be unusually articulate on paper, and will then be encouraged by teachers or parents to exercise this power. I choose the word 'exercise' deliberately, for articulateness on paper is a gift which does not differ greatly in principle from the gift of physical coordination we call athletic skill: like a muscle it needs to be exercised not only for it to develop but because it exerts a pressure of its own on the possessor to use it. (pp. 248–249)

As Podhoretz implied, intellect is not only the processor but also the product of experience. Therefore precocious intellectual development in some area would not only provide a head start, but would also encourage activity which further widens the gap between the child and his or her age-mates. Precocity would be self-generating – as indicated by the arrow from (D) to (B) in Figure 8.1. It would contribute to high evaluation of achievement – (B) to (A). And it would also contribute to the ambition to excel – (B) to (D) – as Bertrand Russell well illustrated by confiding:

As soon as I realized I was intelligent, I determined to achieve something of intellectual importance if it should be at all possible, and throughout my youth I let nothing whatever stand in the way of this ambition. (1967, pp. 36–37)

In sum therefore, values (A), and matching precocious ability (B), are likely to be self-generating and to afford a sense of incentive and confidence that contribute to (D), a tendency to engage in independent intellectual behaviour and ambition to excel.

## Stress

It seems that stress – indeed *distress* – may add unidirectional impetus to a tendency to engage in independent intellectual activities and the desire to excel.

Among the discernible mechanisms and agents responsible for distress in the early lives of creators-to-be are internal diversity or disturbance in the society, financial insecurity (chap. 3); bereavement, rejection, corporal punishment, over-possessive or over-demanding parents, lack of emotional satisfaction or security, isolation, ugliness, physical handicaps or disease (chap. 4); psychopathology, a tendency to homosexuality or other sexual problems and emotional sensitivity (chap. 6). The use of the word 'discernible' is perhaps inappropriate. These factors are very noticeable in most biographical material. And so is the distress experienced by the young creator-to-be.

Some of these distressing circumstances lead children directly to independent intellectual activity, by preventing them from engaging in alternative activities. In the usual course of events children with relevant values and ability enjoy *some* independent intellectual activity – but they do not usually concentrate their energies on such pursuits. There are other things to be done and enjoyed. Their time and energies are spread across various diversions, such as entertainments, sports and social activities, which offer a variety of intrinsic and extrinsic satisfactions. In some children, however, the pull of extraneous attractions is counteracted by some distressing physical impediment that restricts them to a limited range of activities. Edison, who was regarded as stupid by his father and 'addle-brained' by his teacher, attributed the development of his own creative ability to the fact that he was hard of hearing in childhood. Although his (partial) deafness prevented him from performing well at school, it led him to realize that almost any book will offer some entertainment or instruction, and drove him to read all the books in the Detroit library. A number of other creators were driven to intellectual activity in childhood because some or other physical handicap prevented them from engaging in, or at least from enjoying, other childhood activities. Indeed, the frequently noted positive relation between short-sightedness and intelligence, which is commonly attributed to genetic factors (e.g. Karlsson, 1978), might well be an instance of this phenomenon.

Other types of distressing circumstances may lead indirectly to independent intellectual activities, by preventing or discouraging contact with people. Children who have experienced unsatisfying interpersonal relationships, bereavement, rejection, cruelty, and those who feel unattractive or unable to meet social demands, are likely to move away from people, avoiding further interpersonal involvements and thus guarding against repetition of painful experiences. To these children, intellectual activity may offer refuge from an actual threat or from contemplation of it – as was the case with Joseph Conrad, the motherless boy who read his books outside his father's sick room, and Einstein who escaped from 'personal wishes, hopes and feelings' to his pursuit of the laws governing the physical world. Intellectual distraction may offer not only immediate comfort but also more enduring benefits, as Edward Gibbon (1789/1966) implied when describing his gratitude for the care he received from an aunt after his mother's death:

Pain and languor were often soothed by the voice of instruction and amusement: and to her kind lessons I ascribe my early and invincible love of reading, which I would not exchange for the treasures of India. (p. 36)

But where care is not forthcoming from others and trust has failed, creators may call upon their own resources to find some comfort and beauty. Such transference of faith from others to oneself is very poignantly illustrated in Nietzsche's description of his own brave efforts to weather his feelings of emotional isolation.

Ten years have passed – not a drop of water has reached me, no moist wind of love – a *rainless* land . . . Now I ask wisdom not to grow niggardly in this aridity: you yourself must overflow, you yourself must shower down dew, you yourself must be rain for this yellow wilderness. (Translated by Hollingdale, 1965, p. 267; italics in the original)

Intellectual pursuits offer palliation and compensation. They allow one to be guided by satisfactions relating to 'optimal experience' where demands match one's ability to meet them, and one can proceed at one's own pace in a preferred direction. This is important to children who for some reason or other lack a sense of control in certain areas of their life. But it seems that creators in distress not only turn to intellectual activity for palliation and compensation; they also seek to find there a sense of positive control, mastery and self-esteem. As explained in chapter 7, such needs may lead a person to aspire to excellence.

## Independent intellectual activity and the desire to excel

We have briefly considered what leads creators to engage in intellectual activities and to aspire to excellence. This section indicates how these activities and aspirations lead to the acquisition of a wide range of knowledge and skills in the relevant domain, and a habit of working alone – the path from (D) to (E).

Although many creative achievers may have disliked school, it is clear that they generally enjoyed learning, and gained a great deal of satisfaction from proceeding independently with their subject of interest (see chap. 4). In some cases this extracurricular activity would promote academic success, but the benefits of independent intellectual activity are not necessarily reflected in academic achievement. For one, the subject of the child's interest may not form part of the school curriculum. Where the subject is in fact taught at school, extracurricular activities may not build the particular range of responses required by the teacher.

The suggestion that self-directed intellectual activity in childhood makes a major contribution to adult life-performance is supported by the fact that extracurricular activities in childhood are better predictors of life performance than academic achievements are (C. W. Taylor *et al.*, 1985). If bright children are furnished with relevant literature and materials they may be able to gain a *relatively wide view of their particular subject of interest*. It permits them to explore various approaches, ignore rules and try out new ways of dealing with material and facts. Children, as we know, tend to become bored with constantly exploring the same aspect of a matter, although their tendency to explore in general does not become satiated.

Moreover, bright, inquisitive children who spend a major part of their time engaged in a specific type of intellectual activity are not only likely to encounter a wider variety of knowledge of their particular subject, but also to *encounter the same knowledge in a wider range of contexts*. As James Clerk Maxwell, the notable British physicist explained,

> there is no more powerful method for introducing knowledge into the mind than that of presenting it in as many ways as we can. When the ideas, after entering through different gateways, effect a junction in the citadel of the mind, the position they occupy becomes impregnable. (Everitt, 1983, pp. 135–136)

Furthermore, when precocious children who value intellectual achievement work independently, *they acquire knowledge that is not necessarily shared by their peers* who adhere to a school curriculum. If they are able and aspire to excellence, they are moreover likely to explore more advanced material than their peers do – and, as noted in chapter 4, productive creators typically read more *advanced* books than those usually enjoyed by children of their age.

## A wide (but specialized) range of knowledge and skill and a habit of working alone

### A wide range of knowledge and skill

One of the possible outcomes of persistent engagement in independent intellectual activity is the acquisition of wide knowledge and skill, which puts children ahead of their peers in the particular domain of interest. As explained in later chapters, the creative process is usually regarded as a new combination of existing knowledge. This leads one to conclude that people who gain a wide range of knowledge have a relatively good chance of being creative. They will have acquired a large universe of items from which possible new combinations could be drawn.

We return, however, for the moment, to another possible outcome of persistent intellectual activities in childhood. Independent intellectual activities may occupy the time that age-mates spend on more diverse pursuits, and it therefore causes the gap between children involved and their peers to widen in more than one direction. Although children who become absorbed in solitary intellectual activities may become more skilled in certain areas, they are likely to become less socially skilled and less 'well-rounded' than their age-mates. It is clear that creative achievers as children are not 'good all-rounders' (see, e.g., H. J. Walberg, 1988). As we have seen, they typically disliked team games and were incompetent at sport. Their knowledge and skill may also be relatively scant in other respects. This apparently happened to Edward Gibbon (1789/1966) who 'arrived at Oxford with a stock of erudition that might have puzzled a Doctor, and a degree of ignorance of which a schoolboy would have been ashamed' (p. 43).

A further possible outcome of independent intellectual activity is the development of a habit of working alone.

## A habit of working alone

According to the cultural historian, Arthur M. Schlesinger (1960), 'everything that matters in our intellectual and moral life begins with an individual confronting his own mind and conscience in a room by himself' (p. 103). And it is apparent that most eminent creators would agree. Among those who are quoted by Hock (1960) in this regard are Lord Byron, who asserted that 'society is harmful to any achievement of the mind'. Richard Wagner explained that calm and quiet are a master's most imperative needs and confessed that 'isolation and complete loneliness are my only consolation and my salvation' (p. 108). Edward Gibbon wrote that 'conversation enriches the mind, but solitude is the school of genius' (1789/1966, p. 337). The greatest of all inventors, Thomas Edison (1948/1968), agreed that 'the best thinking has been done in solitude' (p. 56); and Voltaire obviously also held this opinion. Before completing his *Candide*, he locked himself up for three days and opened the door only to take in meals and coffee (Hock, 1960).

'Aloneness', as we have seen, is not merely the effect of the circumstances in the life of creators: it is often also part of their personality – for the creator is frequently apart and withdrawn even in the presence of others, and makes a deliberate attempt to seek solitude. One of the most beautiful comments on the aloneness of great geniuses is Wordsworth's reference to the statue of Newton (in Trinity college chapel) as

the marble index of a mind forever Voyaging through strange seas of Thought, alone (*The prelude*, bk iii)

Zilboorg (1959/1972) explained the importance of solitude for creativity by suggesting that isolation allows the development of sustained trends of thought, and that working alone minimizes interruption. Interruption, it seems, is one of the major enemies of creative thinking. Among the conditions listed by Walter Bradford Cannon as unfavourable to the development of his scientific 'hunches' was 'being interrupted or feeling that there may be an interruption at any time' (1976, p. 68). Charles Babbage (1864/1969) devoted an entire furious chapter of his autobiography to the harmful effects of outside disturbances on his concentration during creative work. The tale is often told of Samuel Taylor Coleridge (c. 1797/1954) losing from memory the greater part of his poem *Kubla Khan* through being disturbed by 'a man from Porlock' who came to discuss something with him at a crucial moment. Among others who have complained that the damage wrought by interruption may require a considerable time to undo is Tchaikowsky (1906/1970) who lamented: 'Dreadful indeed are such interruptions. Sometimes they break the thread of inspiration for a considerable time, so that I have to seek it again – often in vain' (p. 58).

Marie Curie (1936) wrote that from youth her husband, Pierre, needed to concentrate with great intensity in order to obtain precise results from his work. It was impossible for him to interrupt or modify the course of his reflection to suit the external circumstances. Edwin Land, research director of the Polaroid corporation, explained his own need for uninterrupted privacy in the following terms:

I find it very important to work intensively for long hours when I am beginning to see solutions to a problem. At such times atavistic competencies seem to come welling up. You are handling so many variables at a barely conscious level that you can't afford to be interrupted. If you are, it may take a year to cover the same ground you could cover otherwise in sixty hours. (C. W. Taylor, Smith & Ghiselin, 1963, p. 69)

Darwin took firm steps to avoid being disturbed: his family were strictly forbidden to enter his study (F. Darwin, 1929). Many other creators, including Goethe, found some way to isolate themselves. Goethe declared:

Nothing will change the fact that I cannot produce the least thing without absolute loneliness. Once again I made the experience that I can work only in absolute solitude, and that, not only conversation, but even the very presence in my house of loved and esteemed persons at once diverts my poetic source. (Hock, 1960, p. 108)

The suggestion that creative activity is facilitated by solitude is not, however, kindly taken by modern workers in the field: the current tendency is to attempt to promote creativity through group interaction. Although the findings relating to creative achievers suggest they are typically unsociable, withdrawn and not inclined to associate with group activities, it is nevertheless assumed that group interaction would facilitate creative thinking.

In contrast to psychologists, however, the cultural historian Arthur Schlesinger (1960) was sceptical of the benefits of group interaction in creative endeavour. '"Togetherness" is the banner under which we march into the brave new world', wrote Schlesinger, but committees or group tactics are 'essentially means by which individuals hedge their bets and distribute their responsibilities resulting in dilution of insight and the triumph of mishmash' (p. 103).

Even findings of research on ordinary people have supported Schlesinger's views. In addition to the personal testimony of creative achievers, controlled research has shown that people are likely to come up with better ideas when they work alone. It has been shown, for example, that nominal groups (i.e. a number of individuals working independently, whose responses are pooled) produce better ideas than do the same number of people interacting as a real group (Chatterjea & Mitra, 1976; Renzulli, Owen & Callahan, 1974; Street, 1974; D. W. Taylor, Berry & Block, 1958). This applies even to groups of subjects who have previous experience of working together in real life (Dunnette, Campbell & Jaastad, 1963). On the basis of studies by herself and her students, Amabile (1983) concluded that the presence of others undermines creativity in the laboratory, if the others are present as an audience (i.e. if the others give attention to the work).

There are obviously variations in the degree of solitude required by various types of creators, and it is clearly easier for artists and writers to work alone than for scientists to do so – particularly where scientific projects require teamwork and the control of complicated systems of equipment. Sometimes it is necessary for creators to work while being observed by others. Collaborators do not, however, necessarily interact or work in one another's presence all the time. Although collaboration may involve discussion of strategies and schemes of work, much of the creative thinking underlying the planning and execution of collaborative projects may be done in privacy. A team of people may develop good products by building upon one another's ideas; but, as Nobel Prize winner Bernado Houssay (1961) pointed out, each idea comes from within the mind of one person:

The most remarkable piece of research apparatus is the human brain. Some people want to buy every piece of equipment known to science. They believe that with a beautiful building filled with modern equipment they have a first rate research institute. That is superstition. The greatest discoveries have been made by men working alone. (p. 36)

## The question of women creators

Before leaving the subject of the essential determinants of creative ability, we turn to an age-old question 'Why are women so under-represented among the geniuses of history?' Almost all the subjects of the studies discussed in this book are male. Where are the Alberta Einsteins, Frederika Nietzsches, Leonora da Vincis and Pablita Picassos in our histories of civilization? Charles Darwin admitted that his sister was brighter than he was (F. Darwin, 1929); Adele Galton (while herself still a child) tutored her famous brother (Pearson, 1914). Why did Mesdames Darwin and Galton not take their place in history?

In the view of the ancient Greeks (especially the males) women are in every respect inferior to men (as are servants and children). Aristophanes illustrated women's lack of inventiveness by putting the following words into the mouth of Praxagora:

They dip their wool in hot water according to the ancient plan, all of them without exception, and never make the slightest innovation. They sit and cook, as of old. They wear out their husbands as of old. They buy sweets as of old. (Dickinson, 1973, p. 46)

Before going any further it should be mentioned that studies of women who have in fact been exceptionally creative reveal that their early circumstances and their personality characteristics are very similar to those of male creators. Creative women usually come from professional-class homes, and have a strong respect for cultural values. They typically suffer financial and other forms of insecurity, and they are usually intellectually stimulated by their fathers, who are seldom emotionally warm (see Helson, 1971). The parents of highly creative women are typically involved in intellectual pursuits, particularly reading (Bachtold & Werner, 1973). Like creative men, creative women are more introverted, aloof and self-sufficient than less creative women and people in general (see, e.g., Bachtold & Werner, 1970; Helson, 1971). They prefer contemplation to social interaction and favour working alone. Biographies of highly creative women suggest that the pattern of influences acting on the development of creators is similar for males and females (for a brief example see the biographical notes on Virginia Woolf by Haviland, 1984).

It seems, in fact, that the pattern of influences acting upon the development of creative ability in women is similar to that which determines the development of creativity in men.

Assuming that creative careers would in fact follow a similar course in both sexes, one is now able to see why so few women have become eminently creative in the past: the first factor contributing to the development of creativity appears to be a sense of *values* relating to creative intellectual achievements. Although women may have learned to value creative achievements, these achievements have traditionally been regarded as a male prerogative. The role models of intellectual excellence were men. Even in those societies where intellectual achievements were valued, the women's own 'real' achievements were defined in terms of motherhood and nurturance. Their cultures and their families have traditionally persuaded women to gauge their worth in terms of their ability to serve and please others.

Much the same applies to the development of *intellectual precocity* (which is the second factor influencing the development of creativity). Traditionally girls have been afforded less intellectual stimulation than boys have. In the past even precocious girls were given less education, less encouragement and fewer rewards for indulging in intellectual pursuits than boys were. Institutional structures denied women access to cultural materials and to eminent masters, and in the home they were given less independence than boys. Their intellectual interests were regarded as mere hobbies or aberrations – more useful perhaps for keeping them out of mischief than for preparing them for a future career.

These factors mitigate against the development of creative ability in girls. But perhaps even more potent restraints on women's creativity are the very practical considerations that hamper their chances of exercising their developing creative ability. At the time when the first notable works of creators are typically produced (in their twenties), most women are burdened by maternity and the care of young children. Even if a woman is able to hand over the care of her children to a surrogate, she is not usually able to completely forget family and domestic matters and 'lose herself in the white heat of research' as was possible for men like Pasteur, or to lock herself in a room only to open the door to those bearing food, as was possible for Voltaire. The fact that Taylor Coleridge lost his magnificent work through the interruption of the man from Porlock has repeatedly been recorded with an appeal to public sympathy. But women are constantly held up by 'men from Porlock' who demand their attention and interrupt their thoughts. They have no wives to insulate them from outside intrusion or to relieve the burden of the trivial domestic demands and social obligations that a family household entails.

Certainly not the least of the women's problems is freeing themselves from interruption by children – a luxury that relatively few women are afforded. The Romans had a saying, 'libri aut liberi' (books or children), recognizing that one could generate knowledge *or* (not *and*) children. George Bernard Shaw obviously agreed, explaining that 'people of high character and intelligence cannot be plagued with children . . . The child at play is noisy and ought to be noisy: Sir Isaac Newton at work is quiet and ought to be quiet' (Kenmare, 1960, p. 71).

In addition to these impediments to the development of a woman's abilities and aspirations, are those imposed by affiliative tendencies. From an early age girls are typically more interested than boys are in personal relationships, and they display a greater need to be with people (see, e.g., Hutt, 1972). The formation of an identity in adolescence depends on different factors in males and females. Typically, when forming an identity, young men test out who they are by assessing their competence and knowledge, forming a belief about the world and planning for their future careers. But girls are more likely to define themselves in terms of the satisfaction they will gain from getting along well with people and being important to favoured people (Gilligan, 1982; Hodgson & Fischer, 1979).

McAdams and Bryant (1987) referred to 'intimacy motivation' in terms of a need to spend time 'thinking about other people and one's relationships with them, engaging in a large number of conversations with others, and experiencing considerable positive affect in the presence of others' (p. 397). Research has consistently shown that women, especially young women, tend to have a high level of this need, they are more inclined than men to seek companionship and emotional intimacy (Hodgson & Fischer, 1979; Kacerguis & Adams, 1980; La Voie, 1976; Marcia & Friedman, 1970; McAdams & Bryant, 1987; Toder & Marcia, 1973; Waterman, 1982). Although creative achievers may find that being alone brings a welcome feeling of *solitude*, young women are therefore often likely to find it engenders a feeling of *loneliness*. And this is an important reason why women are often denied solitude. They deny it to themselves.

Although John Steinbeck was no doubt referring to the human race rather than the male sex, it seems that he made a valid comment about the creative process when he wrote that 'it lies within the lonely mind of man' (Steinbeck, quoted by Arnold, 1959/1972, p. 44).

## Implications and issues

In a book on creativity, one may expect to find some advice on how to promote it; and the reader may be wondering how one could possibly apply anything that has so far been discussed to educational and child-rearing issues. However, unlike most books on the subject, this one is not aimed at providing solutions to the problem of how to enhance creativity – and the pattern of influences discussed in the foregoing sections in fact carries both negative and positive implications for the feasibility of doing so.

Among the negative implications are that stress or discomfort in childhood is a powerful motivator that leads to the persistent single-minded lifestyle of creators. Few would regard the suggestion that discomfort plays a role in the development of creative ability as useful for promoting creativity. Indeed, many psychologists apparently find it too uncomfortable to accept that the development of something as highly valued as creativity has anything at all to do with something as unpleasant as stress. Innumerable examples of reluctance to consider any negative aspects of the determinants of creativity are to be found. Usually the defence takes the form of empirical findings showing that gifted children (or people who perform well on creativity tests) are more secure, happy and healthy than others. Gifted children do not necessarily become creators, however. Something is needed to translate talents into the power to create. That something demands work – work that builds the skills upon which creative production rests. And it is short-sighted to reject out of hand the notion, unpleasant though it may be, that some imbalance or lack of comfort in childhood might bring forth initiative, resourcefulness, and a motive to achieve self-esteem and recognition – which makes people work – to achieve excellence.

Among other defences typically used against the suggestion that discomfort is a factor in the development of creative ability are empirical findings showing that the performance of unexceptional people deteriorates when they are subjected to potentially stressful situational variables. This may also apply to eminent creators. They probably don't work well under stressful conditions (as their remarks about solitude imply). It is perhaps important to reiterate and emphasize that *I do not propose that stress plays a facilitating role in actual creative performance: I suggest that it motivates the creator-to-be to develop skills and excel.*

Few would disagree that it is a social duty to prevent children from suffering distress wherever possible. But it would be foolish to be led by one's finer inclinations (and research findings based on shaky operational definitions) to conclude that a happy, secure childhood and a kind, social environment are necessary to creative achievement. Anything essential to the development of creative ability would not be absent in the lives of highly creative individuals, and it is clear that many people who did in fact produce creative work of the highest order lacked acceptance, love and other such benefits in childhood.

On the other hand, one should obviously not conclude that some discomfort in childhood invariably leads to creative achievement. Extremely few emotionally deprived or distressed children become creative, or even take a step in that direction. There is a great deal of empirical support for the suggestion that emotionally disturbed children are not even able to concentrate. Those who are severely deprived may become psychologically disturbed, or socially and intellectually inadequate. Many who are moderately deprived are merely nonentities. Therefore, even though stress may be a catalyst in the development of creative ability, it would be dangerous to assume that it promotes creative achievement in those who lack the necessary resources.

One must, of course, accept that, regardless of what precautionary measures are taken at a societal level, a number of the children in the society will be subject to stress. One comfort to be taken from the foregoing chapters is that stress has not only negative outcomes and that 'unhealthy' people need not consider themselves incapable of creativity. The following is quoted from a short letter written by William Allen (1987) to the editor of *Psychology Today*:

As a writer and teacher of creative writing, I believe that many if not most of the gifted writers I've known have some degree of manic depression.

In cases of individuals with vision and focus, no matter what the field, channeled manic-depression has doubtless served as an engine to help advance humankind. Articles such as Holden's should help creative people with mood-swings be more accepting of themselves and more productive. (p. 5; his reference is to Holden, 1987)

As stress is unwelcome but often unavoidable, we conclude this second part of the book – which has mainly to do with the development of creative achievers – with some thoughts on issues relating to the other factors that seem to play a role in their development: development of intellectual talent and values.

## Issues relating to development of intellectual talent

Several current issues relating to the early education of talent may be considered in the light of the foregoing chapters: broad education versus special talent development; discipline versus freedom, and acceleration versus non-acceleration of gifted children.

*Broad education versus special talent development.* The major purpose of school education is to give pupils a general background as a basis for later specialization. Apart from the obvious necessity for children to develop a number of basic skills, it is often not possible to know where their special domain-relevant talents lie until they have had a fairly broad range of learning experience. Even the precocious intellectual skill of some geniuses was not noticed by teachers.

Occasionally, however, it becomes apparent that a certain child is especially talented in a certain domain. (This would have applied, for example, to the young Mozart, and also to Einstein whose mathematical ability was apparent in late childhood.) Occasionally, too, one finds a child that is unable to meet standards in certain domains. What should one do then?

A commonly held view is that, regardless of special talents or shortcomings, children should be educated to be 'good all-rounders' or 'whole people' etc. J. W. Gardner (1973) has suggested that children who have a high level of ability in a particular area are sometimes forced by a 'tyranny of talent' to narrow their outlook and 'not discover other talents'. Although this may be true in the abstract, one should, however, bear in mind that no talent is a free gift waiting to be unwrapped. Any talent must be stimulated and exercised to develop and show itself. If energies are diffused across various domains, one may become a Jack-of-all-trades without displaying any noticeable talent at all. There is some doubt, for example, whether Mozart would have benefited from dissipating his energies over a variety of domains. Leonardo da Vinci? Yes! But there are extremely few Leonardos in the history of mankind (and he did not have to gather as much scientific knowledge as the scientists of today). Today, specializing in a single domain is probably *less damaging than developing a narrow rigid perspective within the domain.*

The answer as to whether broad or specialized education is preferable must, of course, depend on the further issue of whether one wishes to achieve balance or excellence. Unfortunately it seems that one needs to make a choice – and that choice must depend on the particular needs and circumstances of the individual. Bloom and Sosniak (1981) have presented a very persuasive case for allowing children who are especially gifted in a certain domain to specialize and concentrate their efforts on that domain. These authors suggested it would be worthwhile for teachers to give well-considered private support for the development of obviously salient talents or interests, and argued that forcing children to devote time and attention to subjects in which they have little talent or ability may be demotivating and have a negative effect on talent development.

Case histories and personal testimony of creative achievers certainly support Bloom and Sosniak's suggestions, which seem to apply not only to what they have observed about the development of talent, but also to what I have observed about the development of creativity. Especially intellectually able children who for some reason are unable to achieve balance or uninterested in doing so, might benefit by gaining a sense of control and esteem through achieving excellence in a certain quarter. Moreover, as H. J. Walberg (1988) reminds us, heterogeneous human resources and division of labour enhance both individual and national welfare.

*Discipline versus freedom.* At one extreme of educational policies is an authoritarian ideology that favours 'drilling in' traditional knowledge and skills according to a set curriculum. At the other is a child-centred ideology that favours leaving children free to decide what they wish to learn, and allows them complete freedom of expression. The 'freedom of expression' approach is usually associated with the development of creativity, and a popular view is that forcing children to learn certain skills, techniques, knowledge and standards may restrict them from being creative.

Examination of the lives and opinions of creators makes it clear, however, that the basic rules and techniques of a discipline are the necessary bases from which creative leaps are made. Exciting though it may be to believe that creativity wells up naturally from primaeval feelings, there is very little indication in the facts relating to the lives of creators that significant ideas emerge from untutored minds. Primitive feelings may well up, to be sure – but they are not necessarily creative. Usually they are merely primitive. Culturally valuable creative ideas are, indeed, more likely to emerge from sophisticated scepticism.

Facts relating to eminent creators have shown, however, that independent learning is one of their most favoured and effective pursuits. I have argued, moreover, that independent activity may offer scope for a width of experience in the area of interest – a width that curricula and classroom experience may not afford. One should, however, perhaps beware of over-generalizing in this respect, and draw a distinction between potential creative achievers and others. Independent learning is not necessarily favoured by all children, and many who are given freedom to do as they please are not in fact pleased to embrace intellectual activity with the same fervour as future creators do. The nature of, and interest taken in, extracurricular activities will depend to a great extent on the individual's needs, values, and competence – which, as we have seen, are to a large extent influenced by early experience in the home.

Amabile and co-workers (e.g. Amabile 1983, 1985; Hennessey & Amabile, 1988) have spoken at some length of the social facilitation of creative performance in a classroom. In this situation, social facilitation of creative performance takes the form of deferring judgment, with-holding extrinsic rewards and avoiding social pressure – all of which may have a beneficial effect in structured situations. But if one wished to promote culturally valued creativity in the long term, and under natural conditions, it would be as well to use more naturally enduring forms of social facilitation – among which are domain-relevant modelling, pace setting, standard setting, tuition, and also constructive feedback as to where children are not meeting required standards. Withholding judgment may make children feel at ease to express themselves freely in the classroom – in the short run. But in the long run it may result in lowering of standards.

Facts relating to creative achievers suggest that creativity will be facilitated by first endowing children with basic knowledge and disci-pline, and then giving freedom to those who wish to work independently, allowing them to call upon expert advice, feedback, literature and materials (*quality* of advice, feedback, literature and materials is important). The development of transcendent creativity is not obstructed by discipline, or even drilling: it is impeded by confinement to a narrow perspective – to a limited range of information and poor standards.

Creators are not merely different. Indeed, being different has become a new convention. Creators are not relieved of the responsibility of being knowledgeable, skilled and adaptive to prevailing needs. Great minds are indeed disciplined – but they are not confined.

*Acceleration versus non-acceleration.* Another issue relating to development of intellectual talent is that of acceleration versus non-acceleration of the gifted child's intellectual development.

The facts suggest that deliberate intellectual stimulation favours the development of giftedness (e.g. Stanley & Benbow, 1986). Stanley and Benbow assert that they do not know of any single careful study of actual acceleration that has shown it not to be beneficial, although armchair articles about the dangers of acceleration abound.

Among the 'armchair' views is that deliberate acceleration of intellectual development may result in emotional or intellectual disturbance (the child will become a 'mad genius'). This view may be based on observations of famous people who were in fact mad geniuses – people who were not only intellectually stimulated but also emotionally traumatized in some way (that led them to seek further intellectual stimulation and motivated them to excel).

In combination, intellectual stimulation and emotional deprivation may well produce genius – but it is not an infallible method, and one would be well advised not to try it. Feldman (e.g. 1988) noted that families of child-prodigies tended to show stress. Moreover, parents who 'push' their children to acquire intellectual skills *as well as subjecting the child to emotional stress* might well succeed in producing people who are neither able to find satisfaction through social interactions nor to attain success through intellectual endeavour. Although some may succeed in deliberately creating a genius, as, for example, the fathers of Wiener, Mill, Pascal, Witte and others did, Wiener (1953) warned he would not ask all children to pay the price, for

this price cannot be paid by a weakling, and it can kill . . . Before I should even think of subjecting any child, boy or girl, to such a training I should have to be convinced not only of the intelligence of the child, but of its physical, mental, and moral stamina. (p. 292)

## Issues relating to values

Although Rogers would have it that there should be no conditions of worth placed upon a person by others or himself, the fact remains that in human (and animal) societies there are. Few of the people one deals with in the normal course of daily life separate one's worth and value from one's behaviour. And it would be dangerous to society (if not to individuals themselves) if there were no values or conditions placed on behaviour. Moreover, unconditional bestowal of worth places the virtue in the beholder rather than in the beholden. I have little doubt that to be unconditionally valued is less rewarding than being aware that one has met conditions of worth and has earned self-esteem. When worth is freely given there is no challenge met, no tension reduced, but merely a lack of tension. If one aims at promoting creativity in a society, it is not sufficient to provide the comfort that one may rely on others for unconditional positive evaluation. It is necessary to indicate clearly how positive evaluation may be earned and to place particularly high value on those who have produced something of value for the culture.

The standards by which self-worth may be earned in a culture are revealed by what is valued – and by *who* is valued and honoured. In 1960 Schlesinger lamented that 'ours is an age without heroes' (p. 95) and 'the century of the common man has come into its own' (p. 97). But, says Schlesinger, 'let us not be complacent about our supposed capacity to get along without great men' (p. 105).

Although this may be the age of the common man, I am not entirely in agreement with Schlesinger's suggestion that ours is an age without heroes – or that there ever will be one. There seems to be in man an abiding need for human, superhuman and divine models who represent universal ideals and point out the direction for attaining self-worth. Although the modern human heroes may not be men of creative genius, they do exist. Most of the heroes in history books are leaders, soldiers and statesmen whose fame rests on their victories over people rather than over nature. Many of the contemporary heroes accorded recognition on television and other news media are sports stars, political leaders or cult leaders. Children are currently exposed to the blatant evidence that physical prowess or merely causing a public sensation may make one a cultural idol, and/or bring one large financial rewards.

Although the work of creative achievers may be recognized by those within the particular discipline and a few other cognoscenti, there is relatively little public celebration of their contributions. A notable exception was America's beautiful public tribute to Edison. Over the United States on the evening of Edison's funeral there was a symbolic darkening of all but the essential lights for a minute. The elevated trains and the tramcars stood still. The torch on the Statue of Liberty was extinguished. Then, across the whole land, the light that America owed to Edison blazed out again (R. W. Clark, 1977).

Despite occasional reference to their work, however, creators seldom receive media coverage, as do politicians and sports stars or entertainers. Creators, especially scientists, are often very private and very busy people, whose works are understood only by few. Einstein is among the few scientists who attained a public image. He resented it. 'The cult of individuals is always, in my view, unjustified' he wrote (1921/1979a, p. 302).

There is, nevertheless, at least one way of justifying the cult of individuals who represent intellectual achievements. They might provide explicit examples of values and ideals which inspire the young to follow their direction. 'We feed on genius' wrote Emerson. 'Great men exist that there might be greater men' (Schlesinger, 1960, p. 104). This would, however, apply not only to genius but to whatever the young define as 'great'. Therefore, as Selye (1960) suggested, those who make valuable contributions to the culture should be accorded public recognition and privileged positions, to demonstrate cultural values to the next generation.

And, as we have seen, it appears that the transmission of cultural values to children occurs largely in the home.

# Part III

# Creative thinking and inspiration

Parts I and II addressed two versions of the question of what makes a person creative: 'On what basis are people designated as creative?' and 'What determines the development of creative ability?' The focus now moves from the creative person to the creative process, and here we consider two other versions: 'What processes are involved in creative thinking?' and 'What causes creative inspiration?'

The following chapters discuss traditional theory and present some new ideas about the creative process. These new ideas go further than the old ones in explaining why some people tend to be creatively inspired.

# 9

# Stages in creative problem-solving

Many of the psychologists and scientists who have investigated the nature of the creative process have looked upon it as a special case of 'problem solving', and a number of researchers have analysed the creative process by identifying a typical sequence of stages that people go through while solving problems.

Early investigators in this field based their conclusions on the introspective accounts offered by famous scientists who recorded facts about their own creative thought processes. Among these scientists was Hermann von Helmholz (1896), who is known for his creative contributions to both physics and physiology. Towards the end of the last century Helmholz described his experiences of problem solving in terms of an initial *investigatory stage*, during which he became saturated with the relevant facts; a *stage of rest and recovery*, during which he gave no conscious attention to the problem, and finally a *stage of illumination*, when he had sudden unexpected insight into the end goal of the problem. Subsequently two creative French mathematicians, Henri Poincaré (1913) and Jacques Hadamard (1945) described their own experiences of creative problem-solving in much the same way. Among those who have drawn up descriptive lists of stages in the creative process, are Dewey (1910); J. Rossman (1931); Osborn (1953); Johnson (1955); Merrifield (Guilford, 1967); R. B. Cattell (1971); and Mansfield and Busse (1981). Some of these sets of stages are briefly indicated in table 9.1.

The most frequently cited model of stages in the process of problem solving was formulated by Wallas (1926), who, following the introspective speculations of Poincaré and Helmholz, described problem solving in terms of four stages: (1) *preparation*; (2) *incubation*; (3) *illumination*; and (4) *verification*. This scheme is still frequently used as a conceptual model of problem solving and forms the basis of the following discussion. First, however, we consider a primary stage not mentioned by Wallas – the stage of *problem finding*, which has recently become the

Table 9.1. Stages in the problem-solving process

| Author | Stages described | | | | | |
|---|---|---|---|---|---|---|
| Helmholtz (1896) | | initial investigation | rest and recovery | sudden illumination | consequences considered | solution accepted |
| Dewey (1910) | feeling a difficulty | defining difficulty | | suggested solution | consequences considered | |
| Poincaré (1913) | sensing difficulty | long period of diligent work | unconscious work | emergence of hypothesis; receptivity to subconscious ideas | application of techniques | |
| Wallas (1926) | | preparation | incubation | illumination | verification | |
| J. Rossman (1931) | observation of difficulty | survey of information | | solutions formulated | solutions critically examined | new ideas formulated, tested and accepted |
| Osborn (1953) | orientation to problem | preparation; analysis; formation of hypotheses | incubation | synthesis; combining ideas | verification | |
| Johnson (1955) | | preparation | analysis | production | judgment | |
| Merrifield et al. (1962) | | preparation; analysis | | production | verification | |
| Cattell (1971) | clarifying and deciding on problem; mounting effort (tension) | | incubation (depression) | solution (often poorly communicable) | working out detail; tidying communication | re-application |

subject of special psychological interest in problem solving. Particular attention is then given to the most 'creative' stage described by Wallas – the stage of inspiration – which has intrigued students of human thought throughout the ages.

## Problem finding

It is often held that the most crucial aspect of creative problem-solving is *finding* the problem, and that sensitivity to problems is a notable characteristic of creative people. Indeed, problem finding has been described as a creative process in itself (e.g. Arlin, 1975; Bunge, 1967; Dillon, 1982; Getzels and Csikszentmihalyi, 1975; Mackworth, 1965), and notable scientists have subscribed to the view that finding problems is more creative and more important than solving them. For example, Albert Einstein and Infeld (1938) expressed the opinion that

the formulation of a problem is often more important than its solution, which may be merely a matter of mathematical or experimental skill. To raise new questions, new possibilities, or regard old problems from a new angle, requires imagination and makes real advance in science. (p. 83)

### Conceptions of problem finding in empirical investigations

As one can see in the first column of table 9.1, the first stage in dealing with a problem is sometimes described in terms of 'sensing some difficulty'. This is one way of describing the finding of a problem. In the same vein, but more explicitly, problem finding has been defined in terms of *discovering some gap or inconsistency in existing knowledge* (e.g. Henle, 1974; James, 1890; Torrance, 1979).

This conception makes it difficult to investigate problem finding at first hand, as researchers are unlikely to be on the spot when creators find gaps in the existing universe of knowledge. For contemporary research, 'problem finding' is therefore often simply construed as 'question-asking', so that it might be investigated in structured situations. Researchers using the question-asking approach require their subjects to ask a variety of questions about given items, such as simple geometrical figures or household objects (within a stipulated time limit). Valued problem-finding responses on such as task include 'How would one determine the distance around a rectangle?'; 'What is the area of a rectangle?'; and 'Are there dimensions of a rectangle that make it more pleasing to the eye than other dimensions?'

This type of 'question asking' differs considerably from what Einstein and Infeld (1938) were referring to when discussing the importance of finding new problems, and I have very strong reservations as to whether the ability to ask a variety of questions about simple figures or household objects would transfer to discovering important inconsistencies or gaps in existing scientific knowledge. It seems doubtful whether findings relating to the differences between people who are good and people who are not so good about asking questions in structured classroom situations would add much to our knowledge of problem finding in the sciences.

Another interpretation of 'problem finding', has come from the desire to investigate artistic problem-finding in a classroom situation. In such cases art students have been designated as good problem finders if they handle relatively many given objects before composing a still-life painting; examine the objects intensively rather than superficially, and select objects that other people tend to leave alone. Such investigations also appear to have little to do with finding inconsistencies or gaps in existing knowledge.

How then could one explain the ability to *find important gaps and inconsistencies in the current knowledge relating to science and the arts?*

Consider the suggestion that problem finding arises out of a systematic set of *expectancies*. Everyone at times experiences a sudden gap or disparity between a present event and what past experience has led one to expect. This type of experience leads one to feel that something is at fault with one's knowledge and assumptions – for the current event cannot be interpreted in terms of what one knows. Apparently this is what happens when eminent scientists begin to discover a problem. Einstein (1949/ 1979b) put it thus:

wondering appears to occur when experience comes into conflict with a world of concepts already sufficiently fixed within us, whenever such a conflict is experienced sharply and intensively it reacts back on the world of thought in a decisive way. (p. 9)

What this implies is that one cannot distinguish a significant problem from trivial variations in the situation unless there is some well-established knowledge and a well-structured set of expectations. In other words, problems and important questions arise out of knowledge, not ignorance. As William James (1890, vol. II) put it:

We feel neither curiosity nor wonder concerning things so far beyond us that we have no concepts to refer them to or standards by which to measure them. (p. 110)

In modern psychological terminology this phenomenon may be described in terms of mental models. The modern psychological theory of 'mental models' has its origins in the work of Craik (1943), who described such models as mental phenomena with a relational structure similar to the real phenomena they represent. Mental models are *analogues* of physical phenomena – they allow one to generate images of real events, and to mentally represent the systematic variations occurring in real events.

To build mental models that represent one's environment in everyday life the mind is ever dedicated to forming associations, and gathering and ordering perceptions into meaningful patterns. This applies no less to artistic and scientific endeavour. Gerald Holton (1962) explained that

in science, as in art and philosophy, our most persistent intellectual efforts are directed toward the discovery of pattern, order, system, structure, whether it be as primitive as the discernment of recurrent seasons or as sweeping as a cosmological synthesis. The search for constancies in the flux of experience is so fundamental and so universal a preoccupation of intelligent life itself, that in common with many of the Greek philosophers, we may regard the mind as the principle that produces order. (p. 217)

As mental models are analogues of external realities, and embody natural laws, they enable one to imagine what would happen under various circumstances. Consequently they allow one to avoid danger. Experience leads one to picture, for example, what would happen if one touched a hot stove, put one's foot on the accelerator while taking a sharp corner, or switched off the electricity while one's brother was busy on the computer. Johnson-Laird (1983) pointed out that 'the richer and more veridical the mental model, the greater will be the organism's chances of survival' (p. 402). It implies that the higher on the evolutionary scale and the more experienced the individual, the more likely it is to anticipate danger and avoid it successfully.

An important function of mental models is to provide 'templates' against which incoming information can be matched. When there is a mismatch between incoming information and a mental model, one is aroused. In other words, one is alerted by a difference between what one expects and what actually happens – not only by an uncommon or unexpected stimulus, but also by the absence of an expected one (the reader may have had the experience of being alerted by the cessation of a continuous sound). The absence of expected events can be extremely arousing. Consider what would happen if the sun failed to rise one day! The mismatch between that event and very firmly established models of expected systematic realities would probably arouse every adult in equatorial regions to panic. Babies and Eskimos in winter would, however, be unconcerned: the former because no model has developed, and the latter because their mental models allow for the sun to take leave of absence in winter.

It has, in fact, been demonstrated at a physiological level that incoming information that corresponds with existing expectations is not mentally arousing (for details, see the review by John & Schwartz, 1978). The expected is not arousing, as it carries little new information. Mismatches between current events and expectancies are, however, arousing. When expected events fail to occur, electric potentials are emitted in certain brain regions (see the review by John & Schwartz 1978). This suggests that a model of past events has been constructed and acts as a monitor in the system that generates electric potentials when there is a mismatch between expected events and actuality.

When referring to the importance of problem finding in creativity, Mackworth (1965) pointed out that intensive study of problem solving without regard to problem finding will add little to our understanding of originality, as the supreme problem solvers of today are machines. Since Mackworth made this statement, however, machines have been programmed not only to solve problems, but also to *search for and find them* (see, e.g., Langley *et al.*, 1987). As Langley *et al.* point out, problem finding by computer is simply a particular instance or variant of problem solving.

Computers can find problems because they can be programmed to discover regularities and laws in sets of given data, and also to find discrepancies. It seems reasonable to suggest, however, that discovery of laws, relations, and discrepancies must depend in the first place on *what data have been fed in to the programs*. And the same must apply to problem finding in humans.

Much of the foregoing discussion applies to problem finding in general, and especially to science. There is, however, another aspect of problem finding that may be applied especially to art. Problem finding relates not only to discrepancies between current events and a mental model of reality, but also to *discrepancies between current events and the mental model of a goal*. Models of goals serve as sources of feedback. When events are not proceeding according to a planned goal, or when one's actions do not result in a desired effect, one is alerted to adjust them accordingly.

The American artist Yasuo Kuniyoshi (1954) thus described the artist's encounter with (and search for) problems:

There are numerous problems that beset the artist in his work. Consciously or unconsciously each artist tries to solve them. Lately I have come to the stage where I actually take a problem and try to solve it. For instance I was interested in painting a dark object within the dark. In order to carry this out successfully it may take me several years. (p. 55)

Before leaving the subject of 'problem finding' we should note that problem finding is not always a precursor to problem solving. In art, and in science too, problems may occur during the course of a work, when gaps or inconsistencies develop between current realities and the model of one's goals. As Flanagan (1972) pointed out: 'The scientist asks a question and then looks for the facts to answer it. The facts may answer the question. More likely they suggest an entirely new question' (p. 106).

Obviously one cannot be too definite about the position or about the determinants of the 'problem-finding stage' in the creative process. But, one thing may indeed be stated with a considerable degree of certainty. It is not likely that creators will find significant problems at any stage before they have had a fair degree of experience of the relevant subject, so that the questions they ask reflect the recognition of gaps, inconsistencies or lack of harmony – questions that reflect recognition of new challenges rather than ignorance.

Moreover, ability to find problems significant to creative production would not only be determined by experience and knowledge, but also by the tendency to *seek problems*. As Schank (1988) put it: 'creativity and learning derive from the need to correct failures, and understand anomalies in the world. We can create solutions, correct failures and understand anomalies only by identifying where we have been wrong' (p. 229).

The tendency to seek problems is, moreover, likely to be fuelled by desire to excel. Those who wish to transcend or improve upon existing knowledge would be likely to go out in search of problems. Less motivated people would tend to avoid, gloss over or explain away anomalies.

*Conclusions relating to problem finding*

The foregoing leads to the conclusions that

1. discovering pattern, order and structure, endows one with a sense of certainty and control, and it also enables one to *build veridical mental models*;

2. finding problems occurs when one has constructed a mental model of reality and *some current perception does not match this model*;
3. the richer and more veridical a mental model, the better basis it provides for problem finding;
4. discovering important problems in fields of creative endeavour must depend on a minimum degree of cognitive development that allows one to make observations and learn basic skills, and above all on *relevant experience* that helps to build elaborate veridical models;
5. the ability to find significant problems would therefore be *likely to vary*, not only over individuals, but also to some extent within the individual – over various areas of knowledge;
6. the ability to find problems would develop through the *desire to excel* and improve upon existing knowledge.

## Problem solving

We now turn briefly to the four stages in problem solving described by Wallas (1926), and then give some special attention to the stage of inspiration.

The first of Wallas's stages, the stage of *preparation*, is described as a fact-finding stage, where all the facts necessary for achieving a solution to the problem are marshalled. 'Preparation' may include searching for relevant facts, exploring, experimentation and reformulation of the problem. This may take minutes or years.

The stage of *incubation* is most economically described as a stage during which the problem is set aside and no longer given conscious attention. Then comes the stage of *inspiration* (or illumination) – the sudden experience of insight; the invasion by external forces described by the ancients; the 'satori' or sudden flash of enlightenment celebrated by the Japanese; the 'aha' experience observed in the laboratory.

Less dramatic is the stage of *verification*, which involves checking the solution of problems, editing and generally tidying up the product, making it fit for public presentation.

Although the stage of verification is often the most lengthy and important, the 'illumination' or 'aha' stage is generally regarded as the critical incident of 'creative' thinking. Most attention has therefore been focussed on this stage of the creative process – not only by psychologists, but also by creators and those who have chronicled notable events in the history of the sciences and arts. Popular tales abound, including the tale of Archimedes gaining sudden insight while bathing, leaping from the water, and rushing naked through the streets crying 'Eureka'. There is also the tale about Newton's sudden insight into the laws of universal gravitation on seeing an apple fall from a tree in his mother's orchard.

Although these tales may be apocryphal, what they imply with regard to the subjective experience of the event is backed up by first-hand reports from creative achievers – *the person concerned was not working on the problem when the solution sprang to mind.*

Numerous dramatic and interesting tales are told about famous creators having sudden flashes of enlightenment concerning the solution to a problem while they were otherwise engaged. In what follows I let some eminent creators describe their own experiences.

The illustrious creative mathematician, Henri Poincaré (1908/1954) wrote several personal accounts of moments of inspiration, including the following description of his insight into the nature of Fuchsian functions:

> The changes of travel made me forget my mathematical work. Having reached Coutances, we entered an omnibus to go to some place or other. At the moment when I put my foot on the step the idea came to me, without anything in my former thoughts seeming to have paved the way for it. (p. 26)

Among other mathematicians who described personal experiences of sudden insight, was Gauss, who explained in a letter to a scientific journal how a mathematical proof that had been evading him for years suddenly became apparent:

> Finally, two days ago, I succeeded, not on account of my painful efforts, but by the grace of God. Like a sudden flash of lightning, the riddle happened to be solved. I myself cannot say what was the conducting thread which connected what I previously knew with what made my success possible. (Quoted by Hadamard, 1945, p. 15)

Heading his paper on the 'Law of induction' Gauss wrote 'Found 23rd January 1835 – 7:00 am before rising' – which implies he might have been sleepy at the time.

Jacques Hadamard thus described his own inspiration occurring while half-awake, concluding that

> One phenomenon is certain and I can vouch for its absolute certainty: the sudden and immediate appearance of a solution at the very moment of sudden awakening. On being very abruptly awakened by an external noise, a solution long searched for appeared to me at once without the slightest instant of election

on my part – the fact was remarkable enough to have struck me unforgettably – and in a quite different direction from any of those which I had previously tried to follow. (Hadamard, 1945, p. 119)

Poincaré described incidents of inspiration before falling asleep, and also while walking. So did Sir William Hamilton, who thought of a new mathematical method while strolling in the streets of Dublin with his wife.

Musicians have also reported being assailed by ideas when riding, resting or walking. A letter allegedly written by Mozart (reprinted in Ghiselin, 1954, pp. 34–35) tells that his ideas flowed most abundantly when he was alone, 'say, traveling in a carriage, or walking after a good meal, or during the night when I cannot sleep'. In a letter to Tobias von Haslinger, Beethoven told that a canon had come into his head while he was dozing during a journey by carriage. As soon as he awoke he could not recall it. But on returning the next day in the same carriage, the same canon flashed into his mind – this time while he was wide awake (Shapero, 1954).

For years Wagner had been contemplating the idea of *The ring*, and had been attempting to make a start for many months when, sick with dysentery, he found his way into a hotel. The next day, having had little sleep the preceding night, he flung himself onto a couch, falling into a trance-like state. It felt, he said, like sinking into a great flood of water.

The rush and roar soon took musical shape within my brain as the chord of E flat major, surging incessantly in broken chords . . . I awoke from my half-sleep in terror, feeling as though the waves were rushing high above my head. I at once recognized that the orchestral prelude to be the 'Rhinegold', which for a long time I must have carried about within me, yet had never been able to fix definitely, had at last come to being within me. (Quoted by Whyte, 1973, p. 35)

When it comes to poets, we recall the famous case of Samuel Taylor Coleridge who on wakening from a profound sleep induced by an anodyne seemed to have in his mind a poem he had composed. As he eagerly began to write it out he was interrupted by a man who came on business from Porlock.

Of his *Iphigenia*, Goethe wrote:

This morning when I was riding over from Zento, I had the great good luck to invent (between sleeping and waking) a limpid plan for 'Iphigenia auf

Delphos'. There will be a fifth act, the likes of which cannot often be seen. I was happy like a child. (Quoted by Hock, 1960, p. 65)

One might expect dramatic tales of inspiration from musicians and artists, who have courted their muses over the ages: but perhaps the most dramatic and oft-repeated stories of inspiration have come from scientists.

The German chemist Kekulé thus described his revelation concerning the structure of the benzene molecule.

I was submerged in reveries. Before my eyes the atoms began to dance. I had always seen them in motion, those little beings, yet I had never succeeded in describing the manner of their motion. Today I saw how two smaller ones frequently joined as couples, how larger ones embraced two smaller ones, and how all of them turned about in a whirling dance . . . This is how the structure theory came about.

He realized the structure resembled a ring.

I turned my chair toward the fireplace, and dozed off. Again the atoms danced before my eyes; now my mind's eye distinguished larger formations, of manifold shapes; long rows often more tightly joined. Everything was in motion, writhing and coiling in serpentine fashion, and lo and behold . . . what was this? One serpent grasped its own tail, and mockingly that thing whirled before my eyes . . . the benzol ring! (Quoted by Hock, 1960, p. 66)

Among the tales of 'multiple inspiration' is that of Otto Loewi, who awoke one night to find himself possessed with a brilliant solution to a problem that had been bothering him. He jotted down a few notes on a notebook beside his bed, but on waking the next morning he found that the notes were totally illegible. Loewi went to his laboratory to see if some sense might be found of the scrawl while working on his project – in vain. However, the next night he woke with the same flash of insight – and this time carefully recorded the ideas that led him to win the Nobel Prize.

Descartes had his major revelations come to him one night through no less than three consecutive dreams that appeared to him to have come from above (Whyte, 1978).

In his brief autobiography Darwin reported 'I can remember the very spot in the road, whilst in my carriage, when to my joy, the solution [of his problem] occurred to me'. Russell Wallace, who published the theory of natural selection with Darwin, was also affected by sudden inspirations and concluded that 'Ideas and beliefs are not voluntary acts' (quoted by Whyte, 1973, p. 38). Wallace reported as follows on how his own solution to the problem of selection came to him after pondering upon it for some time

No light came to me till February 1853 . . . During one of my fits [of fever] while again considering the problem of the origin of species, something led me to think of Malthus's *Essay on Population,* which I had read about ten years before, and the positive checks – war, disease, famine, accidents, etc. It then occurred to me that these checks might also act on animals . . . while vaguely thinking how this would affect any species there suddenly flashed upon me the idea of the survival of the fittest. (Quoted by Hayward, 1974, p. 133)

Dreams and hypnagogic states are apparently fertile fields of inspiration for scientists. Cannon and Helmholz reported having repeated experience of answers to their problems on waking. On one such occasion Cannon had an idea as to how he might construct a device for automatically recording clotting of blood. Herschel 'discovered' the planet Uranus through a dream; Leibnitz dreamt of the basic idea underlining his conception of a world system; and Niels Bohr dreamt of his atom model.

As one can see from the foregoing examples, the circumstances surrounding the experience of inspiration are rather consistent, and there was good reason for MacKinnon (1978) to refer to the phenomenon of sudden inspiration as the 'bath-bed-bus syndrome'. It typically occurs when the subject is in the bathroom, in bed or in a vehicle (and perhaps we should add walking). We will return later to consider why these particular circumstances should favour sudden creative insight.

## Empirical research on the stages of problem solving

Psychologists generally feel their conclusions to be more 'scientific' and on relatively sound logical footing when based on measures of quantitative data – such as numerical indices of the frequencies with which various phenomena occur. As the creative solving of important problems is not amenable to such quantification, research in this area has been conducted on subjects who were invited or conscripted to solve 'creative' problems in a classroom setting under controlled conditions.

A much quoted early empirical investigation of this nature was conducted by Patrick (1935, 1937), who confirmed that when given tasks in the laboratory, minor poets, scientists and control subjects all seem to go through overlapping stages resembling those described by Wallas. Patrick's findings have not, however, gone unchallenged. It has been suggested, for example, that her observations were fitted into her prior conception of Wallas's four stages (Eindhoven & Vinacke, 1952). On the basis of their own observations Eindhoven and Vinacke suggested that the 'stages' in problem solving are merely components of a single process rather than a sequence of steps or processes, a suggestion supported by Ghiselin (1963) after studying the introspective reports of geniuses. Self-reports, in fact, often suggest that creative processes are unified and overlapping rather than following a stage-like progression. To give Wallas his due, he too pointed out that 'even in exploring the same problem, the mind may be unconsciously incubating one aspect of it while it is consciously employed in preparing for or verifying another aspect' (Wallas, 1926, pp. 70–71).

Any argument as to the sequence and duration of stages in problem solving is, however, likely to be sterile, as problems vary across many dimensions. Nevertheless, allowing for the fact that not all problem solving follows the same course, and also allowing that some creative acts may not at all fit the problem-solving models mentioned in the foregoing discussion, one cannot help but recognize that the personal accounts by eminent creators relating to 'inspiration' following a period of 'incubation' have too much in common, and are too numerous to be ignored, or glossed over. Although R. W. Weisberg (1986) is of the opinion that stories or 'myths' about incubation should be set aside, we must beware of throwing the baby of consistent subjective experience out with the bath water of invalid explanation. One of the most intriguing questions that has arisen from the problem-solving approach to creativity is 'Why should a period of incubation promote inspiration? – *if indeed it does so.*' It obviously seems so. Why does it seem so?

As laboratory studies on the stages of preparation, incubation and inspiration are rather artificial, it is unlikely that the answer will be found there. The situation and the problems presented in classroom studies are quite different from those involved in highly creative work. After conducting research in this area and analysing the research of others, Olton (1979) concluded that experimental evidence of incubation under controlled conditions is unreliable, and it is not possible to obtain evidence of incubation in the classroom. As it is also impossible for researchers to make direct observations of the incubation and inspiration of eminent creators, the only relevant data to work on when studying the phenomenon of creative inspiration are retrospective personal reports of eminent creators. And eminent creators have almost invariably attributed their own inspiration to the invasion of external metaphysical forces, or to internal forces emanating from the unconscious mind.

Even if one is obliged to accept subjective *descriptions* of inspiration, one is, of course, not bound to accept subjective *explanations*, and from time to time psychologists have attempted to explain incubation and inspiration in terms of cognitive or psychoanalytic theory. What follows are some loosely grouped cognitive explanations of the effects of incubation on inspiration. Psychoanalytic explanations are discussed in chapter 11.

### How does incubation bring about inspiration?

Perhaps the simplest explanation of the role of incubation is that it dispels fatigue. This suggestion was originally put forward by Poincaré (1908/1954) who proposed that 'the rest has given back to the mind its force and freshness' (p. 27). It was, however, met with little enthusiasm, even by Poincaré himself, who continued the above by suggesting 'it is more probable that this rest has been filled out with unconscious work and that the result of this work has afterward revealed itself' (p. 27). Another argument against the 'fatigue' suggestion is that the incubation period is often far longer than necessary for dispelling fatigue (Guilford, 1967; Poincaré, 1908/1954).

A second explanation of the role of incubation is that it helps to disperse the effects of what is known in psychology as 'Einstellung' or 'set'. These terms refer to a temporary rigidity: a tendency to perceive problems in a particular way and to persist in using a particular strategy for solving them, even if the strategy is not quite appropriate for the problem at hand.

Some while ago Luchins (1942) demonstrated in a systematic series of experiments that problem-solving 'sets' become established through recent success with the use of a particular strategy. School children do much the same by asking their victims to pronounce M-A-C-D-O-N-A-L-D, then to pronounce M-A-C-I-N-T-O-S-H, and finally to pronounce M-A-C-H-I-N-E-R-Y.

Although it has been widely agreed that set-effects may be dispelled during incubation, there has been some difference of opinion as to how this occurs. Woodworth (1938) proposed that a period of incubation may dispel the set by *reducing the 'recency' value of inappropriate strategies*. It seems, however, that sets often tend to persist, even in the absence of recent success, possibly as the effect of previous learning and habit-formation.

Among other suggestions offered to explain the establishment of sets is that certain current trends of thought *persistently activate certain habits and long-term memories* leaving other more useful memories unactivated and temporarily inaccessible to consciousness (see, e.g., J. R. Anderson, 1985). In accordance with this view, research has shown that people engaged in solving problems tend to recall very little information beyond that which is directly related to the problem, even though they are able to remember more useful information (see research cited by R. W. Weisberg, 1988).

To explain the dissipation of sets, it has been suggested that unimportant information is selectively lost from active memory when the problem is put aside (e.g. B. F. Anderson, 1975; Simon, 1966; Woodworth & Scholsberg, 1954). It was Simon's opinion that selective forgetting aborts unproductive lines of thought, and allows whole 'chunks' of relevant information to be recalled from long-term memory. As Simon explained, the span of active memory is limited, but through experience (during the stage of preparation) there is 'familiarization' with the information in the particular domain. This familiarization allows associated items of information to become integrated into larger units or chunks. Consequently larger units of relevant information can be drawn into active memory and worked on.

Related to the above view is the fact that memory becomes transformed as time goes by. Sensory details are usually remembered in the short term. After a while the detail is forgotten and only the meaning is remembered. Moreover, memories become integrated with other information (J. R. Anderson, e.g. 1985). It is therefore feasible to suggest that, in time, one begins to perceive a problem in terms of the meaning rather than the detail, and this may facilitate the solution. It has further been suggested that, in time, the problem itself may become restructured in the mind (e.g. Ohlsson, 1984). In other words, one may suddenly look at the problem in a different way and be able to see it in terms of a different question, the answer to which is relatively simple.

Among currently favoured suggestions is that external or internal stimuli (even emotions) to which the problem solver is exposed during the period of incubation may cause a change in set or provide a hint which activates mental tendencies that were inactive when the problem was first worked upon (e.g. Bastik, 1982; Maier & Burke, 1967; Nicholls, 1972a). This suggestion enjoys considerable support from personal testimony and anecdotal literature, in which the solutions to famous problems are described as being triggered by current events, contextual stimuli, or endogenous phenomena. As we have seen, several eminent creators testified to the value of hints provided by dreams, and Newton's insight into the universal laws of gravitation is said to have been triggered by a falling apple.

In accordance with the notion that inspiration is elicited by a 'hint', it has been argued that in fact *nothing occurs during the stage of incubation.* The memory system is merely lying in wait for some cue that would initiate the recall of some useful item of knowledge (see, e.g., Langley and Jones, 1988; Olton, 1979). This implies that the critical influence, the event or hint that triggers the inspiration occurs only at the moment of inspiration. If a cue is sufficiently important, said Olton (1979), it might initiate processing of associated information in long-term memory and bring it into active memory – *even if the subject's attention was not focussed on the cue.* Langley and Jones suggest that an important cue may allow the problem solver to notice a similarity between the current problem and something already known – and this may help the problem solver to find the solution by using an analogy (see, e.g., Dreistadt, 1968, 1969; Langley & Jones, 1988). (We will return to the subject of analogy in problem solving in the following chapter.)

Although each of the above explanations may explain some aspect of inspiration, none explicitly accounts for one of the most noticeable regularities in autobiographical descriptions of inspirations – the situation in which creative insights so often occur: the bath-bed-bus-type of situation. When suddenly inspired, eminent creators were usually sleepy, asleep, drugged or lulled by monotonous stimuli – in other words, *in a low state of arousal.* If we are interested in discovering the mechanisms involved in the classical type of 'Eureka' experience, we should consider the implications of this consistent finding.

A relevant suggestion may be derived from the work of Easterbrook (1959) (who was not in fact particularly interested in problem-solving behaviour). Easterbrook suggested that the *level of cortical arousal is inversely related to span of attention*, and this theoretical assumption has since continued to receive empirical support (e.g. M. W. Eysenck, 1984). It has been consistently shown that as arousal increases, there is a progressive reduction in the range of cues observed and used.

It has also been shown (e.g. Luria, 1973/1984) that when a subject is *actively engaged in solving a problem*, the level of cortical arousal is relatively high. This means that while actively engaged in solving a problem one's attention is narrowly focussed: one's range of awareness is likely to be relatively constricted. Even if one shifts the focus of one's attention, only a narrow range of cues will be utilized at any one moment. Remote cues will not be perceived simultaneously, and synthesis of remote concepts is relatively unlikely.

When one is in a low state of arousal (during a period of incubation), however, one's attention is likely to be wide and diffused, and a relatively wide variety of 'irrelevant' cues is likely to be simultaneously accessible to awareness. This would apply to endogenous cues (in current imagery) as well as to those in the environment. And bringing supposedly 'irrelevant' cues together in the current stream of thought may provide a vital link to a new perception of a problem. In other words, *lowering of cortical arousal makes one open to simultaneous perception and association of hitherto unrelated items.*

In a similar vein, Martindale (1981) suggested that when arousal is high few 'cognitive units' are highly activated. But during low stages of arousal many and various cognitive units are activated to a lesser degree. In other words, when cortical arousal is relatively low, one's span of awareness is relatively wide.

The above suggestions might explain why new and varied insights occur while one is ruminating on a problem in a desultory fashion, or when one is engaged in what Olton (1979) called 'creative worrying' – keeping the problem more or less at the back of one's mind but musing about it from time to time. But the personal reports of many creators indicate they were not thinking about the problem at all when the insight occurred. We are therefore still left with the question of *why it seems that a solution to a problem springs to mind when one is not thinking about it.* None of the above explanations account for that important fact. Indeed none are explicit about the 'unconscious' nature of inspiration.

Before considering some old and new explanations of unconscious aspects of inspiration, we make a short detour in the next chapter – to take a look at some traditional theories relating to specific processes involved in the critical stage of creative problem-solving. It is necessary to know something of these theories and related facts when considering the part played by low arousal and 'unconscious' processes.

# 10

## Specific abilities and processes involved in creative problem-solving

Traditional theories relating to specific creative processes fall into roughly three major categories: in one category are theories that represent creative thinking in terms of distinguishable intellectual factors; second are those that describe creative thinking as an associative process; and third are those that depict it as an emergence of primitive insights from the unconscious mind. Although the correspondence between these views may not be immediately apparent, there is indeed considerable overlap to be seen on closer inspection.

The first two categories are discussed in this chapter and traditional views of unconscious processes are discussed in the next.

### The factor-analytical approach

The name of Joy Guilford is bound to turn up in any protracted discussion of creative thinking, for it was Guilford who aroused so much interest in research on creativity in the middle of this century. His theory of intelligence and creativity dominated the factor-analytical approach in the sixties and seventies, and is the best-known example of the first category mentioned above. Guilford systematically elaborated the ideas that

1. intelligence is not a unitary variable but a cluster of very specific intellectual abilities; and
2. creative abilities are part of intelligence, but they are distinct from the mental abilities that are usually measured by intelligence tests.

To understand Guilford's (e.g. 1950, 1963, 1964, 1967, 1970, 1971, 1975, 1976, 1982, 1986) concept of creative thinking, it is necessary to have some idea of his general concept of intelligence.

### Guilford's view of intelligence

When Guilford began his work on the structure of intellect it had already been noticed (by, for example, Binet and Henri, 1896, and

202

Thurstone, 1950) that intelligence, or at least what various intelligence tests measure, is not a unitary variable. Guilford had found that the correlations between various intelligence scores were often zero, and concluded they were not measuring the same thing. In an attempt to be scientifically objective, Guilford (e.g. 1967) subjected the scores of numerous people on numerous items to a factor analysis. Zero correlations between most of the factors obtained re-affirmed his belief that intelligence is a composite of many distinct factors rather than a hierarchy of abilities depending on a dominant 'g' factor.

Although distinguishable, many of the factors identified by Guilford appeared, however, to have certain common properties, and he decided that each had three qualities or dimensions. The first of these three dimensions is the dimension of operation, which has to do with the way in which information is processed. It has five categories:

1. *cognition*;
2. *memory*;
3. *divergent production* – which relates to originality, and involves a broad search for information and generation of numerous novel answers;
4. *convergent production* – which relates to focussed search, and produces known, certain, correct or expected responses like those usually demanded in conventional intelligence tests;
5. *evaluation* – which has to do with decisions relating to suitability, goodness, accuracy, etc.

The second dimension is that of content, which relates to the kind of information that becomes processed. There are four categories on this dimension:

1. *figural*;
2. *symbolic*;
3. *semantic*; and
4. *behavioural*.

The third dimension is the dimension of product, which relates to the form of the information after processing. On this dimension are six categories:

1. *units*;
2. *classes*;
3. *relations*;
4. *systems*;
5. *transformations*; and
6. *implications*.

The intersection of the operation, content and product categories provides for $5 \times 4 \times 6$ ($=120$) hypothetical three-dimensional intellectual abilities or factors.

## Guilford's concept of creativity

Guilford construed creativity as problem solving, but after unsuccessful attempts to demonstrate reliable differences between people as regards their problem solving ability, he concluded that problem-solving involved a number of separate abilities:

| | |
|---|---|
| *Sensitivity to problems* | – the ability to recognize problems |
| *Fluency,* which involves: | |
| ideational fluency | – the ability to rapidly produce various ideas to meet requirements |
| associational fluency | – the ability to list words associated with a given word |
| expressional fluency | – the ability to organize words into phrases and sentences |
| *Flexibility,* which involves: | |
| spontaneous flexibility | – the ability to be flexible even when there is no necessity |
| adaptive flexibility | – the ability to be flexible in solving a problem |
| *Originality* | – the ability to produce novel, uncommon, or clever answers |

Guilford (1975) explained that, although any content or product category of his factor model might be involved in creative thinking, the operation category of divergent production is the most important to the abilities listed above. In his Structure of Intellect model, divergent production may be combined with a product and a content category in twenty-four ways, and these twenty-four combinations or factors are collectively known as *divergent thinking.*

## Guilford's creativity tests

Guilford was not the first to conceptualize and measure creativity in terms of intellectual abilities differing from those measured by traditional intelligence tests. Even before the turn of the century Dearborn (1898) had noticed that scores on tests of 'productive imagination' were relatively independent of scores on intelligence tests. At the beginning of the century Terman (1906) concluded that inventive qualities were distinct from intelligence, and Chassel (1916) derived tests for originality. A few decades later Guilford developed a battery of tests for measuring divergent thinking, using some of the tasks originally designed by Thurstone. Each of the tests in Guilford's battery was designed to measure a particular factor. For example, a test for measuring *divergent production of semantic units* requires testees to name all the things they can think of that are white and edible.

The literature on creative problem-solving reveals that Guilford's test items, or modified versions of them, are still in very wide use. His concepts of fluency, flexibility and originality also form the basis of the well-known creativity test battery designed by Torrance (1974). Nevertheless, although Guilford must be applauded for his thorough and systematic investigations, the value of his contributions to the understanding of creative thinking is questionable.

First the *criterion-related validity of his tests* may be questioned in terms of empirical findings. Factor analyses of scores on the Guilford tests have shown that they do indeed represent separate factors (see the review by Barron & Harrington, 1981). Moreover, correlations between scores on the creativity tests and intelligence tests are generally low (Flescher, 1963; Getzels & Jackson, 1962; Guilford, 1967; Herr, Moore & Hasen, 1965; Torrance, 1962; Yamamoto, 1964). This is, of course, to be expected, as the tests were developed on this basis. The trouble is that when scores on creativity tests are compared with *other ratings of creativity* the correlations are also generally low (e.g. Beittel, 1964; Merrifield, Gardner & Cox, 1964; Piers, Daniels & Quackenbush, 1960; Skager, Schultz & Klein, 1967; Torrance, 1962; Wallach & Kogan, 1965; Yamamoto, 1964). On reviewing many of the studies relating to the distinction between creativity and intelligence, Wallach and Kogan (1965) concluded that few studies offered evidence of divergent or convergent validity of the creativity tests. Most important, however, is the fact that there is usually an almost zero correlation between scores on these tests and various criteria of creativity in adult creators (Gough, 1964; MacKinnon, 1961; C. W. Taylor *et al.*, 1961). The test is predictive of the criterion *only where the criterion of creativity somewhat resembles the tasks in the test* (e.g. J. M. Elliot, 1964).

Psychologists nevertheless favour the use of routine procedures that allow quantification, and as criteria for creativity are notoriously difficult to establish (R. B. Cattell, 1971; Hocevar, 1981; Mansfield & Busse, 1981; Shapiro, 1968), Guilford-type tests are still used extensively for measuring and predicting creativity. This means that creativity is often defined, assessed and predicted in terms of test performance.

Guilford was not particularly disturbed by using such artificial criteria of creativity. 'So long as we maintain the role of scientist we are not concerned with whether the products [of creative thinking] are socially valuable', he said (1975, p. 37). It is, however, strange that he neglected to consider the role of motivation, which he recognized as being of major importance to creative achievement. Although he stressed that goals, motivation, interest and incubation contributed to discovery, invention and problem solving, Guilford nevertheless measured creativity in terms of timed-test scores.

. Myron Allen demonstrated that the validity of Guilford's tests may be questioned not only in terms of their predictive power but also in terms of their conceptual representation (construct validity). For Allen's study Guilford prepared simple descriptions of twenty-eight of his most important factors (see Guilford, 1963, pp. 115–117). A group of productive scientists were then asked to rank the factors according to their relevance for scientific creativity. Although it was expected that they would consider divergent production as most relevant to scientific creativity, they in fact favoured *convergent* production in the operation category.

Others (e.g. Austin, 1978; R. B. Cattell, e.g. 1971; Mansfield & Busse, 1981) have also argued that creative thinking is not essentially divergent thinking, as it involves selecting among alternatives rather than generating many alternatives. James Austin (1978), the neurologist, pointed out that 'sensing which ideas to ignore is probably more important than generating many of them' (p. 104); 'it is not sufficient for a scientist to come up with an original idea. The idea must be evaluated against fact' (p. 75).

Contending that measures of creativity derived in artificial test-situations offer no way of predicting the *quality* of a person's future creative work R. B. Cattell (1971) lamented that 'in the intellectual tests designed by Guilford's students, and many others who have worked on creativity in this decade, creativity has finished up by being evaluated simply as oddity or bizarreness of response relative to the population mean or as output of words per minute' (pp. 408–409). In real life, said Cattell, creativity is not merely a matter of producing unusual responses: particularly in the sciences, creation has to be judged by hard standards.

It may, of course, be argued that even if productive creativity does not demand a great many unusual responses within a limited time, it does require at least some new ideas. Productive creativity must involve at least some 'divergent thinking'. I believe it important to recognize, however, that the divergent thinking essential to productive creativity need not be expressed by emitting many unusual responses during problem solving. *Essential to creative thought is the divergent experience and thinking that helps to build a wide range of relevant knowledge (elaborate veridical mental models) and skill (automatic responses) – well before the creative insight occurs.*

## Associationistic approaches

The suggestion that learning depends on forming associations and that thinking follows paths of associations, stems back at least as far as Aristotle, who suggested that thinking involves chains of images that are linked because they represent things that are somehow associated. It was Aristotle's opinion that things become associated on the basis of their *similarity* (which means they have some elements in common), *contrast* (which also means they have some elements in common) or *contiguity* (which means they had previously occurred in temporal or spatial proximity).

There is now little argument that associative processes play an important role in creative thinking: much of the theory relating to the creative process suggests that creative thinking is a matter of forming new associations, *new syntheses or new combinations of elements of existing knowledge* rather than producing something that is new in every respect.

The notion that creative thinkers combine items of existing knowledge because they become aware of some similarity or overlap between them has been favoured for some time. William James (1890, vol. 2) was very decisive on this point. He explained that it takes a Newton to notice the law of squares, a Darwin to notice the survival of the fittest, because such discoveries require a remarkable eye for resemblances, and that men of genius are particularly able in this regard. Some of the insights into superior mental functioning that support this view come, paradoxically, from studies of mentally retarded people. It seems that the skill in which mental retardates are critically deficient is classification and generalization. This means they are unable to recognize similarities and make appropriate transfer from one situation to another (Gallagher & Courtright, 1986). Very simply, the Japanese physicist, Hideki Yukawa (1973), elucidated the role of these processes in creative thinking:

Suppose there is something which a person cannot understand. He happens to notice the similarity of this something to some other thing which he understands quite well. By comparing them he may come to understand the thing which he could not understand up to that moment. If his understanding turns out to be appropriate and nobody else has come to such an understanding he can claim that his thinking was creative. (p. 114)

The observation of similarities is obviously also important to artists and poets. Coleridge reported that

though [my brain] perceives the difference in things, yet it is eternally pursuing the likenesses, or, rather, that which is common [between them]. (Quoted by Gerard, 1954, p. 240)

In the following sections we first consider various traditional theories relating to the role of association in creative thinking, giving special attention to the classical or 'learning-theory' approach; the remote-association approach; and the analogical-thinking approach. (The 'creative' reader may note some similarity and overlap between these.) We then glimpse some exciting new developments in the sphere of 'artificial creativity' – the work done by people who have taught machines to make non-trivial scientific discoveries.

*The classical associationistic approach*

The classical associationistic interpretation of creative thinking suggests that a problem solver engages in mental and/or physical trial-and-error behaviour, generating sequences of responses associated with a problem until, by chance, an appropriate response is made (or an appropriate idea is found). In line with this approach is Skinner's (e.g. 1976) interpretation of the creative process and Campbell's (1960) theory of 'blind variation and selection retention'. Their views can be most simply explained in terms of evolution. They suggest that a variety of responses is produced through a process analogous to mutation, and selection occurs through retention of those responses which survive the test of fitness. Campbell allowed that the selection of the fittest responses may occur unconsciously.

These suggestions are not far removed from Guilford's concept of divergent thinking, and are clearly reflected in the second of the two main principles adopted in many creativity training-programmes. This principle states that quantity breeds quality, therefore one should generate as many ideas as possible to maximize the probability that some will be useful (e.g. C. H. Clark, 1958; Osborn, 1953; Parnes, 1967a, b; Torrance, 1979).

Deliberate 'trial, error and selection-of-the-best' sequences have undoubtedly occurred in the course of creative production. For example,

Edison spent months trying out hundreds of substances to find the one best suited to his requirements when constructing an element for his electric light bulb (e.g. J. Rossman, 1931). As we have seen, persistence is characteristic of creative achievers. They are likely to try and try again when not successful. Consciously guided trial, error and selection is however a very cumbersome way of finding something new and appropriate, and cannot be the major process underlying creative thinking.

The classical notion of blind variation and selective retention has been elaborated upon in various ways. Briskman (1980) warned that one should not interpret *blind* variation as mere *random* variation. Creators must first put themselves well in touch with the problem and with the requirements of acceptable solutions – and then generate various ideas blindly (in other words heuristically, rather than merely randomly). Perkins (1988) further suggested that selection is *not blind, but, in fact, mindful*. Even though creators may not select ideas or products according to some preconstructed 'checklist', their selection is tacitly guided by principles of elegance, parsimony, power and originality when judging new variations. Simonton (1988) put forward a 'chance-configuration' theory, which is based on the suggestion that the mind is programmed to organize itself, so that mental elements – cognitions and emotions – tend to become integrated and form hierarchical structures. Chance permutations of mental elements vary in stability. The most stable are those in which the items have mutually compatible properties and tend to make up a single element (i.e. become chunked) so that they may act as a single unit in thought. Simonton called such stable permutations 'configurations'. During the course of the creative process, when various ideas or products are generated, the selection of those that will be retained occurs first on the basis of their stability, then on their communicability, and finally on their social acceptance, he said.

## The 'remote-association' approach

The term 'remote associations' refers to the time-honoured notion that creative thinking involves useful combinations of elements from distant domains.

William James (1890, vol. 2) wrote of creativity in terms of the perception of similarities between *remotely related* phenomena. And from his own experience Poincaré (1908/1954), concluded that to create consists of making new combinations of associative elements which are useful . . . Among chosen combinations the most fertile will often be those formed of elements drawn from domains which are far apart. (p. 25)

These conceptions of creative thinking as a *synthesis or combination* of existing knowledge may seem to be somewhat removed from Guilford's notion of divergent thinking. But the two are complementary rather than incompatible. Divergent thinking (before the creative act) may build up a wide range of memories, concepts or elaborate mental models, from which remote elements may be drawn.

The term 'remote-association approach' is usually associated with the work of Mednick (e.g. 1962), who confided that his views on creative problem-solving were influenced by the self-reports of eminent creators. Basing his conceptions of creativity on those of James and Poincaré, Mednick defined creativity as

the forming of associative elements into new combinations which either meet specified requirements or are in some way useful. (1962, p. 221)

The requirement of usefulness was intended to distinguish creativity from mere originality, as an original idea may be merely bizarre rather than creative if it is not useful. For example, explained Mednick, if someone gives 7 363 474 as an answer to the problem 'How much is $12 + 12$?', this is certainly original, but hardly creative. 'It is only when this answer is useful that we can also call it creative', he said (p. 222). This was an unfortunately bad example. As P. W. Jackson and Messick (1973) pointed out, Mednick may have succeeded in showing that originality may be merely bizarre, but he failed to recognize that *there is indeed no creative answer* to the problem of how much is $12 + 12$. Any given answer is simply correct or incorrect.

Mednick (1962) discriminated between creative and less creative individuals in terms of their 'response hierarchies'. Relatively uncreative people are likely to have what is known as a 'steep hierarchy of responses'. In practical terms this means that, when asked to supply associative responses to given words, uncreative people are likely to initially respond at a relatively high rate with stereotyped responses – but soon run out of associations, and give fewer responses in all. Highly creative individuals, on the other hand, are likely to have a 'flat hierarchy' of responses. This means they have fewer well-learned stereotyped responses in their repertoire, but a greater number of remote ones. These people would be likely to respond relatively slowly and steadily to given words, emitting many responses in all.

One might conclude that people who constantly rehearse a limited range of responses are likely to develop a steep hierarchy, whereas those with more varied experience of the subject are likely to acquire a flatter hierarchy of responses in that domain. Therefore Mednick's suggestion that creative people have a flat hierarchy of responses corresponds with the fact that creators tend to work independently and build up elaborate mental models.

In answer to the question of what guides the *combination* of remote elements, Mednick suggested that remote ideas may be brought together through *serendipity, similarity or mediation. Serendipity* is merely a matter of accidental contiguity. To illustrate this principle, Mednick and Mednick (1964) told of a physicist who makes systematic use of the idea that new associations may be formed by accidental contiguity by cutting up indexes of physics textbooks, throwing the fragments into a fishbowl and drawing out several at a time to see whether any new useful combinations emerge. (It was suggested by a member of the audience at the fifth Utah creativity conference that one might also profit from cutting up some existing psychology texts.) The notion of serendipity in forming 'remote associations' is applied in creativity-training programmes in the form of games which require trainees to make 'forced relationships' between a given problem and anything at hand, such as a book or piece of furniture (Parnes, e.g. 1967b).

Mednick agreed with Aristotle and the British philosophers, who suggested that *similarity* among elements of experience, or stimuli that evoke them, might lead to remote associations. But to Mednick the most important of the three ways of bringing remote ideas together is *mediation*. For example, A and B may become associated because each is in some way associated with C. He acknowledged the role of divergent thinking by suggesting that the greater the number of associations the individual is able to generate the more likely it is that some element among them will serve as a mediating bridge.

With the above in mind, Mednick (1962) found that his creativity test 'almost constructed itself' in accordance with his definition of creativity (p. 227). This test, known as the *Remote Associates Test* (RAT) has been very widely used for measuring creativity. It consists of items comprising sets of three words drawn from remote clusters: for example,

| | | | |
|---|---|---|---|
| *Item A* | rat | blue | cottage |
| *Item B* | surprise | line | birthday |

Subjects are required to find a fourth word which could serve as an associative link between the three given words in each item (the answer to the above examples are A 'cheese', B 'party').

On comparing Mednick's test with his theoretical descriptions of creativity, researchers should surely feel some doubt as to whether the RAT really measures Mednick's concept of creative thinking – at least for the following reasons.

1.    Mednick's definition implies that creativity involves originality, but the test items offer no scope for originality. The answers are either correct or incorrect.

2.    Mednick distinguished less creative from more creative individuals on the basis of their respective steep and flat response hierarchies. But the test reflects neither steep nor flat response hierarchies. Only one correct (stereotyped) response is required for each item.

3.    Although Mednick defined creative thinking as forming associative elements into new combinations, responses on the test do not represent any new associations. In the first example above, 'cheese' does not generate a new viable association between 'rat' and 'blue' and 'cottage'. In response to this item one does not, for example, come to the creative conclusion that rats are blue, or that a cottage is related to rats. Nor does a correct response on the second example lead to a creative conclusion that there is a new useful connection between a line and a surprise. Testees are in fact required only to think of traditional combinations. The word 'cheese' is traditionally associated with 'cottage', 'rat', and 'blue'; and the words 'surprise', 'line', and 'birthday' have traditionally been associated with the word 'party'.

Common sense leads one to conclude that the RAT measures the testees' ability to apply general knowledge – especially verbal knowledge. The exercise that best represents Mednick's theoretical views of creativity is the construction of test items. The 'creative' thinking was done by Mednick, not the testees.

It seems that although Mednick's *theoretical* description of creative thinking may correspond well with time-honoured conceptions of creativity, his test does not measure the processes he describes. Correct responses to his test items are merely correct applications of general knowledge. One should, however, bear in mind that *a wide variety of relevant knowledge may, in itself, be an important basis of creative thinking.* And people who devote the major part of their waking lives to their work are likely to acquire a wide range of knowledge in that area.

## The 'analogical-thinking' approach

In psychological literature the terms 'analogical thinking' and 'metaphorical thinking' are used interchangeably, and both are frequently applied to creativity. The description of creative thinking supplied by Hideki Yukawa (near the beginning of this chapter) describes analogical thinking. As the Japanese physicist explained, when one is unable to solve a problem in terms of the circumstances in which it is embedded, one may succeed in solving it in terms of a similar but more familiar set of circumstances.

Somewhat similarly Belth (1977) described analogy as 'the deliberate use of what we know, or know well, to probe into something about which we know little or do not know at all. We examine something unfamiliar or unknown to us within a context of, or superimposing upon it a "map" of what we already know' (p. 77).

The story of Newton and the apple provides a simple example of analogical thinking. It suggests that Newton applied what he knew of the attraction between the earth and the apple to arrive at insights about the attraction between heavenly bodies.

The modern origins of the concept of creativity as analogical thinking are to be found in the writings of Spearman (1931), who described creative ability as 'the power of the human mind to create new content – by transferring relations and thereby generating new "correlates" ' (p. 48), and referred to it in terms of the third principle of cognition, the principle of correlates. This principle states that when an idea and a relation to it are presented, then the mind can generate other ideas with similar relations.

Spearman's model of analogical thinking is formally exemplified by thinking which follows the form A is to B as C is to D – the relation between A and B being the same as the relation between C and D. This type of thinking is tested by 'closed' test items such as Car is to road as boat is to ————? (the relation abstracted in this case being 'proceeds along').

Guilford (1967) constructed tests of this type for measuring 'associational fluency' or 'divergent production of semantic relations'. Factor analysis revealed, however, that such items were closely related to the factor '*convergent* production of semantic units'. This is not surprising, as such closed items require a certain correct answer, allow little scope for originality, and are therefore obviously appropriate for testing convergent thinking or deductive reasoning rather than divergent production. Open items of the form A is to B as ————? is to ————? do, however, allow scope for divergent thinking and originality.

Analogy is obviously used at various levels in productive creativity in real life. For example, constructing formal models in science depends on transferring a set of relations that have been observed in physical phenomena to symbolic content, such as geometrical diagrams or algebraic formulae. Analogical thinking in science does not, however, involve only esoteric symbolic relations such as those represented in algebraic equations. Sometimes it may simply be a matter of transferring relations inhering in familiar phenomena such as sensory-motor experiences onto scientific data. The works of eminently creative scientists including Einstein, Faraday, Maxwell and Fermi, are typically sprinkled with such analogy. Einstein, for example, derived and explained many of his principles in terms of everyday occurrences such as rowing a boat or standing on the platform of a station while a train passed by. He would also conjure up mental images, imagining, for example, what one would see when travelling on a light wave holding a mirror in front of one's face (e.g. Goldberg, 1983). Simple analogy between common experience and scientific observation was especially important to Einstein, for it was his contention that concepts and propositions 'get "meaning" or "content" only through their connection with sense experiences' (1949/1979b, p. 11), and that sensory experience is our only source of knowledge about the world.

Oppenheimer (1956) testified to the importance of analogy in creative scientific thinking in a somewhat similar vein, explaining

Whether or not we talk of discovery or invention, analogy is inevitable in human thought . . . we come to new things in science with what equipment we have, which is how we have learned to think, and above all how we have learned to think about the relatedness of things. We cannot, coming to something new, deal with it except on the basis of the familiar and the old-fashioned. (pp. 129–130)

Analogy is no less essential to artistic and literary creativity. The artist and the writer represent what they have observed about the relatedness of things in real life, by depicting similar sets of relations in their work. The aesthetic quality of such analogies or metaphors may (at least partly) be explained in terms of the suggestion that they *reduce complexity and reduce tension* by transferring the unknown to the known. As creative artists or writers present new ideas in terms of the familiar, they conjure up feelings or experiences well known to their audiences, thus offering them a way to understand the new ideas in terms of what they already know and feel.

We have seen ample reason to believe that analogy is essential to creative thinking – but it would be mistaken to regard them as equivalent. To be creative, analogy must be original and valid – controlled by the particular requirements of the problem at hand. When

Aristotle wrote that whoever is the master of metaphor is the master of thought, he was referring to the generation of original metaphor. When good metaphors are reiterated they may become clichés, reflecting stereotyped rather than creative thinking. And when metaphors are over-used their purpose is lost. Their aesthetic quality is lacking. They reiterate the familiar rather than reducing complexity by transferring the unknown to the known.

Analogy can, moreover, be invalid. In *The Fontana dictionary of modern thought* (Bullock & Stallybrass, 1977) analogy is described as 'a form of reasoning that is particularly liable to yield false conclusions from true premises' (p. 20), and Holton (1986) has described a rich assortment of examples of valuable and faulty use of metaphor in scientific theorizing and teaching. False conclusions are likely to be reached when the analogy is not really or entirely appropriate to the particular problem at hand. As Perkins (1983) pointed out, the deliberate use of analogies may in fact often distract the thinker from the actual constraints. The skill in analogical thinking lies not only in selecting the right model for making a new comparison, but also in *circumscribing* the comparison. Often a seemingly appropriate analogy fits only a part of the relevant circumstances, and it should not merely be taken for granted that it can be extended to the whole.

*Other specific associationistic approaches*

Creative thinking has further been described in terms of various associative, and particularly analogical, processes other than those discussed above. Notable suggestions concerning the associative bases of creativity have been offered, for example, by Koestler, Gordon and Rothenberg. In his massive work, *The act of creation*, Koestler (1964) explained creative thinking as a process of 'bisociation' – which, simply speaking, involves the perception of something in two different (tangential) frames of reference (which have something, but not all, in common). A simple example is a pun.

From a practical point of view Gordon (e.g. 1961) construed creative thinking as a special analogical process which involves 'making the familiar strange' and 'making the strange familiar'. In creativity training-programmes based on Gordon's model, trainees are encouraged to look at familiar events from strange perspectives, and to interpret unfamiliar events in terms of familiar experience.

Rothenberg (1976, 1986, 1987) construed creative thinking as a process of 'Janusian thinking' which is a process of using two directly *opposing* ideas in combination (by means of which paradoxes are created). He suggested that creative people have special capacities for combining two or more different images, ideas or physical entities, and showed that artistic performance in structured situations can be stimulated by exposing subjects to superimposed images (1986).

Schank (1988) in fact presented a paradox, proposing that creativity depends on the use of well-entrenched knowledge structures or 'explanation patterns' that are derived from cumulative past experience and adapted to present situations. Although using an explanation pattern that has been previously useful may be regarded as 'fossilized reasoning' said Schank, it is, in fact, creative to 'misapply' them, that is to use them in a strange situation where they obviously do not belong.

Following Piaget and Gruber, Feldman (e.g. 1988) construed cognitive development as more than a linear accumulation or combination of knowledge. The processes that enable both development and creativity are spontaneous and directed transformations, said Feldman. Of primary importance are the *transformational tendencies of the human mind* that reorganizes itself and also enters into a process of reciprocal transformation with the environment. This means that creativity is neither simply internally nor externally generated. The individual transforms the physical and social environment and is in turn transformed by them.

## Artificial simulation of creative processes

Some exciting new developments in research on creative problem-solving have stemmed from work on 'artificial intelligence' (AI). Researchers in this area have shown that computers are not only able to apply algorithms (reliable formulae), for solving well-defined problems in a routine fashion, but can also use heuristics (short-cut methods that do not guarantee success), for solving ill-defined problems.

Computer simulation of human problem-solving is based on information-processing theory, which describes problem solving in terms of crossing a 'problem space'. *Problem space* refers to the whole range of operations that could possibly help one to progress from an *initial state* (i.e. where one is, or what one knows before solving the problem) to a *goal state* (where one aims to be, or what one wishes to achieve). Theoretically, the most dependable way of reaching a goal is to search systematically through the whole of the problem space (i.e. to try all possible alternatives) to find the desired goal. In practice, such an exhaustive search is, however, often unmanageable, especially if the goal is indefinite (as it is when one aims to discover a universal physical law or compose a symphony). Humans, therefore, generally tend to search *selectively* through a problem space, being guided by theory and experience as to which operations are most likely to be successful, ignoring those possibilities that are unlikely to help them reach their desired goal.

It seems, moreover, that computers are able to simulate certain kinds of selective (heuristic) searches, instead of searching exhaustively through an entire universe of available data for a desired goal. They are able, for example, to use an important heuristic, called 'means–end analysis', for solving ill-defined problems. *Means-end analysis* involves identifying differences between the current state of affairs and the desired goal, breaking up the problem into a number of subproblems with subgoals, and then evoking strategies that are suitable for removing the particular differences between the current position and next subgoal.

Other heuristic strategies simulated by computer are based on the premise that problem solving is largely *analogical*. As we have seen, analogy is a matter of comparing a given set of data with something already known. Analogical problem-solving strategies involve, for example, mapping the relations inhering in a known set of components onto a comparable set of given components. Specific examples are described in Langley *et al.* (1987) and in Langley and Jones (1988).

As William James remarked, men of genius have a remarkable eye for resemblances. Computers have too. They can be programmed to search through data not only for simple resemblances, but also for *similarities and differences in structures, and for regularities and systematic relations*. This enables them to 'think inductively' and derive the general principles governing the data fed into them. It is this capacity that allows computer simulation of creative scientific problem-solving.

*Simulation of creative scientific problem solving.* The idea that creative scientific discovery is a form of (creative) problem solving that can be simulated by computer stems back to the late fifties, to a paper by Newell, Shaw and Simon (1962). It has since been further developed by, for example, Simon (e.g. 1966), Lenat (e.g. 1983), Huesmann & Cheng (1973) and Gerwin (1974). For descriptions of the developments in this field, see Langley and Jones (1988), and especially Langley *et al.* (1987).

Artificial simulation of creative scientific problem-solving requires a rather specific definition of the human thinking processes involved, and the construction of computer programs to simulate those processes. Langley *et al.* (1987) demonstrate their achievements in this area by:

1. describing how certain famous scientific discoveries were originally made;
2. defining the thinking processes that must have been employed by the scientists who made those discoveries;
3. embedding those processes into computer programs;
4. feeding into the program the relevant data and/or scientific laws known to scientists at the time of the discovery;
5. showing that the program can *re-discover* what was originally discovered by the famous scientists.

To exorcise the mystique that is seen to surround artificial intelligence, it is often mentioned that computers are, after all, only able to 'think' because they have been programmed by humans. Humans are of course also programmed to some extent. They are (hard-wire) programmed by their instincts, but they are further programmed by an accumulation of experiences, which transforms the genetically endowed structures and instincts, imposing mental models and pervasive tendencies upon them.

The next chapter considers some traditional views of the unconscious aspects of human creative thinking. These theories relate mainly to what one might construe as the effects of instinctual programming.

# 11

## Traditional views of the role of unconscious processes

When Haydn first listened to his *Creation* he cried 'I have not written this' (Popper, 1972, p. 180).

What accounts for such gaps in the experience of creative production? As mentioned, it has been widely suggested by psychologists and by creators themselves that a major part of creative thinking is unconscious. This notion has not, however, been unquestionably accepted. Guilford (1975) expressed the opinion that attributing certain processes to the 'unconscious' has no explanatory value whatsoever, 'and is rather like sweeping things under the rug . . . If the expression has any meaning at all, I think it should mean facility in retrieving information from memory storage' (p. 47). R. W. Weisberg (1986) was obviously in agreement, suggesting that unconscious incubation is simply a story that should be 'put aside'.

To explain the typical gaps in conscious experience of inspiration (while acquitting ourselves of the charge of 'sweeping things under the rug'), we should at least consider why creators are left with the *feeling* that their ideas have developed unconsciously.

Some traditional views of the unconscious aspects of creative thinking are discussed in this chapter. In the next a new explanation is offered, which considers how one may explain 'unconscious' aspects of creative thinking from an entirely different perspective.

### The concept of an 'unconscious mind'

Although the original conception of the unconscious is often attributed to Freud, the notion of unconscious thinking is in fact thousands of years old. Ancient Greeks and Egyptians expressed the belief that one's actions and feelings are affected by mental activities of which one is unaware. Even the idea that shameful memories are censored and banished to an unconscious part of the psyche (also usually attributed to Freud) was clearly expressed by Dante (Whyte, 1978). The term 'unconscious mind' is however relatively new. It stems from the work of Descartes, who conceptually split mind from matter, and equated mind with awareness. As this dual conceptualization made no provision for unconscious mentation, the concept of an 'unconscious mind' or equivalent was brought into use to form a link between conscious 'mind' and the unconscious organic 'matter' from which the mind emerges. Consequently perhaps, a tendency developed to conceptualize 'the conscious' and 'the unconscious' as nouns, to visualize them as separate structures, regions, or states, and to suggest that a different type of thinking emanates from each.

## Primary- and secondary-process thinking

It has long been agreed that there are two types of thought; one of which is under active control and the other involuntary. Hobbes (1651/1969) referred to the latter as a 'wild ranging of the mind' that is 'Unguided, without Designe, and inconstant' (p. 69). Freud called it 'primary-process' thinking, and suggested it to be the source of creative inspiration.

### The experience of primary-process thinking

The reader has no doubt experienced primary-process thinking when on the verges of sleep or in a febrile state. The experience takes the form of a drifting disorganized succession of fragmented images and ideas in which several images may be fused or concepts may be displaced from their usual contexts and fused with others, so that strange links are formed between ideas that are usually unrelated. The idea or image of one object may become transformed into that of another; emotional attitudes and desires may become displaced from one object to another; an object may become symbolized by another; a whole concept may become symbolized by only one of its parts or by something resembling it. On consideration, it is apparent that this type of thinking involves the specific mental processes (e.g. divergent thinking, analogical thinking and remote associations) that were discussed in chapter 10. It is, moreover, notable that what one calls primary-process thinking and the experience of unconsciously generated creative inspirations occur under the same conditions. Indeed, there is little question that such inspirations arise during primary-process thinking.

## Psychoanalytic conceptions of primary-process thinking

Although apparently unguided, primary-process thinking is not merely random. As Hobbes pointed out, 'in this wild ranging of the mind, a man may oft-times perceive the way of it, and the dependence of one thought upon another' (1651/1969, p. 69). The main credit for formally conceptualizing the organization of primary-process thinking goes, however, to Freud. Following Jones (1953), it is widely conceded that one of Freud's greatest achievements was to show there is structure, meaning and purpose in primary-process thinking – where others had seen only random error or fluid chaos.

Freud attributed primary-process thinking to the expression of emotional urges generated by the id – the primitive, instinctual part of the personality residing in the unconscious. The purpose of the id, said Freud, is to discharge tensions engendered by instinctual libidinal and aggressive drives. When seeking outlets for instinctual urges, the id fails to take the constraints of reality into consideration, however, so these urges have to be controlled by the rational ego, which mediates between instinctual, societal and environmental demands.

The ego attempts to satisfy all these demands through conscious logical, realistic, *secondary-process thinking* which directs one's purposeful encounters and mastery of the external world in accordance with reason, environmental constraints and cultural mores. And to satisfy the demands of both instincts and social prescriptions, the ego has to act as a censor, preventing the socially unacceptable or dangerous aspects of primitive primary-process thinking generated by the id from reaching consciousness while one is interacting with the real world. During daydreaming or reverie, however, ego control and secondary processes relax, allowing the tensions engendered by primitive drives to be partly discharged through primary-process thinking – in imagination. When ego control becomes even further diminished, during hypnagogic states on the verge of wakefulness, in dreaming and under abnormal conditions such as those induced by sensory deprivation, pathology, or drugs, then primary processes intrude freely into consciousness – and thought is experienced as happening to the thinker rather than being actively controlled.

According to Freud and others who held to classical psychoanalytic theory, the effect of secondary-process thinking increases not only along a continuum from sleep to wakefulness, but also with age. As a child develops and gains experience of the environment, secondary-process thinking becomes more powerful, and the thoughts of adults therefore contain less primary-process content than the thoughts of children do. However, when the adult's instinctual energies cannot find approved outlets, they build up, and conscious thought regresses from secondary-process thinking to a more childlike level, allowing the conscious expression of imaginative symbolic fantasies engendered by the id. (The notion that creative thinking is promoted by such 'childlike' primary-process thinking is clearly discernible in Maslow's concept of 'primary' creativity and the other Humanistic theories discussed in chapter 1.)

As mentioned, Freud believed creative adults may be distinguished from others by the fact that they have the ability to keep fantasies generated by primary processes under ego control. This explains why creators might be imaginative without being childish or bizarre. Moreover, Freud's suggestion that energy from frustrated needs builds up and becomes expressed in imaginative fantasy fits well with the fact that creative achievers are often deprived (or deprive themselves) of lower need satisfactions. As Freud, Storr (1983) and many others have shown, literary and artistic works often clearly reflect the particular nature of the creator's frustrated needs. Nevertheless, not *all* creative work is emotionally toned and relevant to sexual or aggressive needs, and classical psychoanalytic theory fails to explain scientific and philosophical creativity.

Among later psychoanalytic interpretations of the role of unconscious processing in creativity are those of Kris (e.g. 1952) and Kubie (e.g. 1958) – both of whom placed less stress than Freud did on primitive drives. Kris was the author of the popular idea that creative thinking is a deliberate 'regression in the service of the ego'. He described this regression in terms of two stages. In the first, the ego withdraws its control, and an attempt is made to gain inspiration from more childish, less socialized, levels of thinking. There is a breaking down of the barriers between the conscious and unconscious, allowing primary processes to emerge into consciousness – and the entry into awareness tends to be experienced as an invasion. In the second stage the barrier between id and ego is re-instated, and the primary-process content is consciously subjected to critical evaluation by the ego, which makes the work communicable and acceptable to others.

The reader will no doubt recognize that the first stage described by Kris corresponds with the experience of inspiration described by the ancients, as well as with the stage of illumination described by Wallas

(1926). The second stage clearly corresponds with numerous reports of creators who have described a 'tidying-up' phase in the creative process, during which the creative product is tested, evaluated and edited. It is Wallas's stage of 'verification'.

Although Kris's theory allowed for more than sexual or aggressive content in creative imagination, the notion of regressing to more childish and less socialized levels for creative inspiration still offered little explanation for high levels of intellectual creativity such as philosophical or scientific creativity – which is still a general shortcoming of theories relating to the role of primary-process thinking in creativity.

Kubie, like Kris, subscribed to the notion that creative processes occur in a 'preconscious zone', but did not favour the idea that creativity is fostered by defensive reactions such as regression or sublimation. To Kubie creativity was a part of healthy adaptive functioning, whereas the unconscious was fixed in unreality, neurotic and distorted. He pointed out an important aspect of preconscious thinking – that in the preconscious, old combinations of facts may be split and reorganized into new facts and principles; and many experiences may become condensed into symbols that can be manipulated far more swiftly than fully conscious thought.

Although this description of 'primary-process' thinking corresponds well with the idea that primary-process thinking is important because it causes new combinations of thought elements, Kubie's suggestion that creativity is a manifestation of psychological health unfortunately does not match the facts revealed by studies of the relation between creativity and psychopathology.

Although various currently popular notions relating to the role of primary-process thinking have something in common with those described above, some questions have been raised, and yet others may be asked about the validity of psychoanalytic explanations of primary-process thinking. For one, *the content* of primary-process thinking is frequently described as consisting of preverbal images laden with aggressive and libidinal emotion, and the degree of primary-process thinking is measured in terms of responses containing libidinal or aggressive elements (e.g. Holt, 1966; Rosegrant, 1982). In fact, however, dreams and fantasies are, of course, sometimes aggressive and sometimes libidinal; but even allowing that instinctual urges may be disguised, it seems that primary processes are not as dedicated to the imaginal expression of primitive drives as psychoanalytic theory suggests. Empirical studies have shown, for example, that the content of daydreams consists largely of fanciful explorations of the future which allow preparation for purposeful action (e.g. Singer, 1978). Only about 10 per cent of dreams are related to sex, and the content of dreams is largely verbal (e.g. Wallace & Fisher, 1983).

Second, as Hilgard (1962) and others have mentioned, primary processes are commonly described as 'drive organized' (implying they are organized by primitive urges which distort the memories of past perceptions), whereas secondary processes are 'conceptually organized' (implying their organization is influenced by logic and reason, which run counter to primitive drives). This suggestion of a dichotomy of dynamic influences acting on primary and secondary processes has also been questioned. 'The usual view of unconscious processes', wrote Gruber (1974), 'is that they express the way in which a person is divided against himself. But a person is not always so divided. When he bends all his efforts toward some great goal, the same problems which occupy his rational, waking thoughts will shape his imagery and pervade his dreams' (p. 246). As explained in the following chapter, findings relating to normal thinking in everyday life support Gruber's suggestion, and indicate that both primary- and secondary-process thinking may be organized by what has been described as 'current concerns'.

Third, primary processes are often regarded as infantile or childlike. Following Holt (1967), it has, however, now been accepted by some that they do not remain infantile but develop with experience, and there have been several attempts to integrate psychoanalytic and cognitive-developmental theories to explain stages in their development (see, for example, Fischer & Pipp, 1984). The development of primary processes is still, however, described as self-centred, organized around drive, need, and emotion, and independent of feedback (e.g. Fischer & Pipp, 1984; Noy, 1969; Suler, 1980). Little has been done to explain the role of learning, environmental feedback and information-processing mechanisms on the development of primary-process thinking. (A remedy for this neglect is offered in the following chapter.)

Fourth, primary-process thinking is generally held to be the supplier of ideas, and secondary processes the censor, controlling the ideas within the constraints of reality and acceptability (e.g. Arieti, 1976; Martindale, 1981; Suler, 1980). However, although it is generally agreed that the output of the primary-process system is inhibited by an opposing system, there is some question as to whether the primary system is selectively blocked by the secondary system simply to avoid the expression of unacceptable thoughts. It seems the secondary system is rather like a controller that depends on sensory input, and stops the flow of irrelevant primary-process traffic while allowing the passage of sensory input into the focus of attention. Primary-process thinking can, in fact, be inhibited by attention to sensory input. And, as we all know, it can be induced by reducing sensory input or by blocking attention to whatever sensory input there may be (Boismont, 1853; Hartman, 1975; West, 1975, among others). This is what happens when we fall asleep or when people are subjected to sensory deprivation and begin to hallucinate.

As West (1975) put it, lack of attention to sensory input results in 'a release into awareness of previously recorded perceptions through the disinhibition of brain circuits that represent them' (p. 310). This implies that the content of primary-process thinking consists of fragments of memory – an implication that has been recognized for a considerable time. Indeed Freud (1900/1973a) suggested that dreams follow paths established by past experience, quoting Hildebrand as saying 'whatever dreams may offer they derive their material from reality and the intellectual life that revolves around that reality . . . in other words from what we have already experienced either internally or externally' (p. 10). All this implies that the content of primary processes is not simply determined by universal instinctive desires but by past experience, both emotional and intellectual.

*The supposed role of the hemispheres in primary-process thinking and creativity*

As mentioned earlier, there has been some argument as to whether creative thinking should be conceptualized in terms of regression to more primitive modes of thought, or rather of free access to unconscious material, and whether creative thinking is a matter of *unconscious or preconscious processing* (e.g. Arieti, 1976; Bellak, 1958; Bush, 1969; Ehrenzweig, 1962; Kubie, 1958; Schachtel, 1973). Such arguments are of course simply academic. They rest on highly abstract concepts that are amenable to various, disparate interpretations – as most highly abstract concepts tend to be. Not all interpretations of the determinants of primary- and secondary-process thinking have been limited to abstract ideas, however. It has also been suggested – at a very concrete level – that *primary-process thinking occurs in the right hemisphere of the brain* and secondary-process thinking occurs in the left. This may be partly the outcome of the tendency to construe 'unconscious' as a noun rather than an adjective, and to imply that 'the unconscious' occupies a specific physical zone. In accordance with this 'regional' view of unconscious and conscious minds is the belief that the *intuitive, imaginative aspects* of creative thinking take place in the right hemisphere, and the completion (verification) of an effective creative product is done either by the left, or by a balanced interaction between the left and right hemispheres (see, e.g., Ehrenwald, 1984; Martindale, 1981; Ornstein, 1972).

Great enthusiasm about the supposed roles of right and left hemispheres has built up since Sperry's (e.g. 1969) findings on subjects with severed inter-hemispherical connections. Sperry showed that people in whom the link between left and right hemispheres had been severed had, so to speak, two minds. Their disconnected hemispheres were independently and often simultaneously conscious, each quite oblivious of the mental experiences of the other. Subsequently Bogen (e.g. 1969), who was one of the surgeons involved in the operations on these patients, applied the idea of hemispheric independence to explain the dual nature of human thought which, for centuries, has been described in terms of various dichotomies such as logical/intuitive; analytic/synthetic; positive/mythic (see Corballis, 1980). These dichotomies have much in common with popular conceptions of the nature of primary- and secondary-process thinking.

Research on brain-damaged people has lent some indirect support to the hypothesis that creativity is lodged in the right brain. It has been shown, for example, that the functioning of the two hemispheres is indeed somewhat specialized. For example, the left hemisphere usually plays the major role in comprehension and generation of *language* (which involves linear ordering of information); the right hemisphere contributes largely to recognition of *spatial patterns* (e.g. Luria, 1973/1984). Such findings have apparently been interpreted to mean that the left hemisphere is specialized for analytical-sequential functions, while the right is specialized for synthetic-holistic functions (e.g. Bogen, 1969; Levy, Trevarthen & Sperry, 1972; Ornstein, 1972). As this suggestion corresponds with the idea that secondary-process thinking is analytic and primary-process thinking is synthetic, it accords with the view that secondary processes occur in the left brain and primary processes in the right. Further, it has been shown that patients with lesions of the right hemisphere have difficulty in understanding the *emotional* components of words or gestures (e.g. Ross & Mesulam, 1979). Such findings have supported the suggestion that emotions are registered in the right hemisphere, and that primary processing must therefore take place in that hemisphere.

Yet further support for this notion comes from the argument that creative thinking is intuitive, emotional and imaginative rather than logical, and intuition is sometimes equated with instinct or emotional feelings (e.g. Bastik, 1982; Hill, 1976; B. B. Rossman & Horn, 1972;

Tauber & Green, 1959). Moreover, intuitive thinking has in common with primary-process thinking that it is condensed, synthetic and cannot be verbally explained. It has therefore been suggested that the right hemisphere plays the crucial role in intuition and is the primary seat of creative thinking.

In accordance with the above, it is now widely accepted that the right hemisphere generates primary-process (and creative) thinking and the left hemisphere is antithetical to it (e.g. Bogen & Bogen, 1976; Ehrenwald, 1984; Hogan, 1975; Ornstein, 1972; Torrance, 1979). The possibility of promoting creativity by stimulating right-hemisphere functions has occasioned a tremendous amount of excitement in psychological, educational and lay circles. In addition, a large number of books, articles and workshops have been dedicated to consideration and enhancement of the specialized functions of the hemispheres (especially the right hemisphere) in the service of promoting creativity. One of the yearbooks of the National Society for the Study of Education (Chall & Mirsky, 1978) was devoted to this topic. We are told, for example, by Haensley, Reynolds and Nash (1986) that 'productively gifted individuals are those, tutored or untutored, who use both processes, but who focus the appropriate process on the stimuli in such a way and at such a point in the sequence that optimal use of both the left and right hemispheres occurs' (p. 136).

It has further been suggested that in the genius the hemispheres work in harmony, rather than 'coming into conflict', where the dominant left hemisphere would have the best opportunity for asserting its superiority (e.g. Ehrenwald, 1984). And various attempts are made in creativity training-programmes to promote the tendency to use the right hemisphere. Ehrenwald recommends, *inter alia*, practising ambidextrous skills, reading both forward and backward, meditation and auto-suggestion.

More dangerously, perhaps, 'left-brain functioning' has been discouraged. It is held that the dominant left hemisphere (which represents reason) may inhibit the functioning of the right, and thereby prevent creative thought. On this account attempts are made to prevent over-development of left-hemisphere functioning. We are warned that early emphasis on left-brain functions, such as reading or mathematical reasoning, tends to inhibit the development of the right-brain functions, or prevents their accessibility to consciousness (Hogan, 1975). In accordance with this view, children who read a great deal and study mathematics from an early age will not be creative. However, as we have seen, that suggestion finds no empirical support – indeed it is *strongly contradicted* by findings relating to eminent creators.

While there is no doubt that each hemisphere has somewhat different roles in higher mental processing, considerable doubt remains as to whether the right hemisphere is more dedicated to primary processing than the left. Arguments (at more and less scientific levels) in favour of the idea that primary-process thinking may be attributed to the right hemisphere are to be found, for example, in Ehrenwald (1984). And arguments against this suggestion are put forward, for example, by Corballis (e.g. 1980), who explains that modern ideas as to the differential contribution of each hemisphere to logic, intuition and creativity do not entirely correspond with neurological findings.

Further, it should be noted that many of the findings relating to the hemispheres come from experiments on subjects with temporary or permanent lesions, and any interference with a system may reduce the possibility of integrated functioning. Even if certain functions are disturbed by lesions in a particular region, this does not show that the region in question is solely involved in those functions. Although only the upper leaves of a plant may wither if its stem is broken, this does not mean that the plant gathers moisture through its stem, or that the stem above the break has a different function from the part below. Moreover, if primary processing did take place in the right hemisphere and secondary processing in the left, then the right hemisphere would be especially active during dreaming. And it has been shown that the left hemisphere is no less active than the right hemisphere during dreaming (e.g. Lavie & Tzischinsky, 1985).

The foregoing discussion leads to the conclusion that the current ratio of primary- and secondary-process thinking should not be viewed in terms of the current balance between the functioning of the two hemispheres. This ratio should rather be interpreted in terms of *level of arousal* (on a continuum from sleep to wakefulness), as Freud's theory suggested. There is little question that there is a relatively high degree of primary-process content in thought when cortical arousal is low. And, as we have seen, inspiration typically occurs when the person concerned is in a state of low arousal.

This brings us to yet another popular psychological interpretation of the role of unconscious processes in creativity – the 'psychedelic' approach – which relates to what is known as 'altered states of consciousness'.

### Psychedelic concepts of the role of primary processing in creativity

Psychedelic (opening the mind) explanations of creative thinking are based on the idea that people seldom or never exploit all the dimensions of their minds. It is held by theorists of this persuasion, for example, that most people tend to restrict their awareness, instead of remaining open to experience offered not only by the environment, but also by their 'own inner beings' (e.g. Maharshi, 1966; Ornstein, 1972; Samuels & Samuels, 1975; Treffinger, Isaksen & Firestien, 1982; Washburn, 1978; Weil, 1972). Maharshi Mahesh Yogi, who developed the 'Science of creative intelligence', the practical aspect of which is the transcendental meditation programme, has explained that the thoughts and experiences that enter our awareness are only surface phenomena – end products of unconscious processes. One can, however, learn to be more fully aware of the events in deeper levels of consciousness, claims Maharshi, and this awareness would allow one to gain 'full enlightenment'. The key to gaining access to deeper levels of consciousness and enlightenment is found by settling the mind down and opening it up – through transcendental meditation.

Descriptions of the experience resulting from such an exercise are much like those of the self-searching experiences reported by some eminent creators. Shear (1982) quoted the following description of a self-searching experience described by Jung:

> The meeting with oneself is at first, the meeting with one's shadow . . . a tight passage, a narrow door . . . But one must learn to know oneself in order to know who one is. For what comes after the door is, surprisingly enough, a boundless expanse full of unprecedented uncertainty, with apparently no inside and no outside, no here and no there, no mine and no thine, no good and no bad. It is the world of water, where all life floats in suspension; where . . . the soul of everything living begins. (p. 158)

Maharshi explained that the mind is a wave on the ocean of being, and described the feeling brought about by allowing the mind to experience its own inner nature in the following terms:

> Experience shows that Being is bliss-conscious, the source of all thinking . . . It lies beyond all relative existence, where the experience or mind is left awake in full awareness of itself without the experience of any object. The conscious mind reaches the state of pure consciousness, which is the source of all thinking. (Quoted by Shear, 1982, p. 156)

In general, experiences resulting from transcendental meditation are described in terms of going to the source of thought and producing a sense of universal unboundedness – reaching beyond time and space. Those who embrace psychedelic disciplines believe this type of experience to be essential, not only to self-knowledge but to the development of one's creative potential.

In addition to transcendental meditation, various other methods have been used for 'opening the mind to fuller awareness of self-knowledge', or something of that nature. One technique involves focussing on a constant stimulus or on a monotonously regular stimulus. Another involves searching for the answer to questions that cannot be answered by using logical thought – such as 'what is the sound of one hand clapping?' Yet another method, used in Zen training, is to 'focus on everything', but not on anything in particular.

Several tales told about the extraordinary habits of famous creators reveal that some of them did regularly use techniques somewhat like those mentioned above. For example, Kant would stare fixedly through his window at a tower in the distance. Schiller liked to have the smell of rotting apples in his desk while he was writing poetry. Other creators, including Poe, de Quincey and Coleridge (and of course Freud), took drugs to enhance their creativity.

All such 'mind opening' techniques have something in common. They induce primary-process thinking – by lowering arousal and/or defocussing attention. The reader may recall that *widening of attention and lowering of arousal go hand in hand*. Focussing on a constant or regular stimulus widens the attention because neural responses to the constant stimulus in time become inhibited (dulled): the sensation and awareness of the stimulus fade through 'habituation'. If, for example, one fixes one's eye on some small object or a distant tower, or even on a smell, one's awareness of it fades; and by destroying the *focus* of attention one *dissipates* attention. This also happens when one focusses on a monotonous regular (thoroughly predictable, unsurprising) stimulus. Moreover, when one 'focusses on everything but not on anything in particular', one diffuses one's attention deliberately. And by addressing questions that cannot be answered through secondary-process thinking, one may induce primary-process thinking by 'blotting out' secondary processes. Of course, drugs induce primary-process thinking with somewhat less effort.

Whenever there is a relatively high degree of primary-process thinking, the qualities of one sensory domain may be transferred to another. This is known as 'synaesthesia', and is basic to artistic creation. For example, in ballet there is an explicit transference of the qualities of auditory stimuli to kinetic and visual patterns. In most art forms there is indeed some symbolic representation of experience in modalities other than the explicit modality. Even in everyday life, synaesthetic effects are basic to metaphoric expressions such as 'cool music', 'blue moods' and 'loud colours'.

The notion that there is a reliable relation between notes and colours goes back at least two and a half centuries. Guided by Newton's analogy between the seven notes of the diatonic scale and the seven primary colours of the spectrum, Castel built a colour organ, believing it is possible to produce 'colour music' that is perceptually equivalent in the two sense-modalities (Marks, 1984). In altered states of consciousness such as mystical trances, psychopathological or drug-induced states, it seems, moreover, that expanded attention leads to a vague awareness of a very wide range of stimuli – and synaesthesia is experienced to an extreme degree. Subjective feelings and sensations from various modalities become interlocked in what one might call 'multiple remote associations'. Various modes of sensation such as sight, sound and feelings of movement tend to merge and become fused. Sensations are not only transferred to other sensory domains but to feelings about the self. One not only perceives a sound as red, but may also perceive one's feelings as red or one's position in space as loud or yellow. Subjective feelings may become so merged with sensations emanating from the environment that a feeling of depersonalization is experienced. It may seem as though one is watching oneself from outside: one may feel that one is one of the objects in the environment – or even that one is part of, and at one with, the universe.

Such experiences occurring during altered states of consciousness are described by those who espouse psychedelic explanations as 'opening one's mind' to deep insights, wider understanding of oneself and the world and, of course, to creativity (e.g. Maharshi, 1966; Ornstein, 1972). As mentioned, such all-embracing universal understanding types of revelations have indeed been experienced by eminent creators – but they are also common to not-so-creative people prior to epileptic seizures, or when affected by pathology or drugs. And we must remember that eminent creators are particularly prone to pathology. Although mind-expanding experiences may bring forth the blissful feeling of being at one with oneself, one's muse and sources of universal enlightenment, they may also produce rather silly delusions.

Martindale (1981) offered an amusing example of how delusive such important-seeming experiences may be. After taking a drug, one of the subjects of 'mind-expanding' research went to the men's washroom – where he experienced a magnificent revelation. On the wall above the urinal was a sign that revealed to him the Ultimate Secret of the Universe. To anyone else it read:

PLEASE FLUSH AFTER USING

*Evaluation of theories relating to the role of primary-process thinking in creativity*

The notion that unconscious processing plays an important role in creativity cannot be ignored. For hundreds of years autobiographical accounts of highly creative scientists, mathematicians, artists and writers have indicated they feel as though their ideas are passively received rather than actively produced by them. Lamartine put it concisely, saying 'It is not I who think; my ideas think for me.' Thackeray, confessed: 'I don't control my characters. I am in their hands and they take me where they please . . . How the dickens did [one of his characters] come to think of that?' (both quoted by Hayward, 1974, p. 123).

Amy Lowell (1954) testified to the pervasiveness of this experience by explaining

A common phrase among poets is 'It came to me.' So hackneyed has this become that one learns to suppress the expression with care, but really it is the best description I know of the conscious arrival of a poem . . . When I am alone, an idea contingent upon something I have seen or done when I am out will announce itself, quite as though it had been biding its time until it had me quiescent and receptive. (pp. 111–112)

Jean Cocteau (1954) used a beautiful metaphor to describe the nocturnal occurrence of this phenomenon

The poet is at the disposal of his night. His role is humble, he must clean his house and await its due arrival. (p. 80)

Common to various traditional theoretical interpretations of the role of unconscious processes in creativity are (explicit or implicit) suggestions that inspiration may be derived from a type of thinking in which the content of thought becomes fragmented and re-integrated or merged, and that this occurs mainly when one is in a low state of arousal. Such explanations lead one to suggest that 'sets' or lowered thresholds, induced by secondary processes in the initial stages of working on a problem, may become dissipated by dislocated, freely wandering, primary-process thinking during a resting period of 'incubation'. We have also seen how the generation of 'remote associations' and meta-phorical thinking occur during primary-process thinking.

A considerable amount of empirical research has been conducted to pin down the effects of primary-process thinking, and to discover the difference between creative people and others as regards their tendency to engage in primary-process thinking (e.g. Bowers, 1979; Hudson, 1975; I. Lewin & Glaubman, 1975; Myden, 1959; Pine, 1959; Singer

& McCraven, 1961; Wild, 1965 – see also studies reported by Martindale, 1981). Much of this research may be and has indeed been questioned on methodological issues, particularly with respect to the criteria of creativity and measurement of primary-process thinking. But methodological errors, although pertinent, do not constitute the main problem.

It is hardly necessary to conduct research to discover whether highly creative people tend to engage in primary-process thinking and gain creative insights from so doing. Everybody regularly engages in primary-process thinking. Personal reports of eminently creative individuals have repeatedly borne testimony to the fact that they engage in primary-process thinking and, moreover, that they are indeed thereby inspired. But in all the excitement about the importance for creativity of primary processing (or whatever unconsciously generated thinking is called), an important consideration seems to have become set aside. The main problem with these studies is that, even if they show conclusively that the tendency to engage in primary-process thinking is greater in creative achievers than in the general population, and even if they show that the creative ideas of eminent creators were enhanced through engaging in primary-process thinking, this would not satisfactorily explain the creator's ability to produce something of cultural value. It could also, no doubt, be shown that ineffectual individuals, drug abusers and those afflicted by psychopathology are more inclined than others to engage in primary-process thinking – without being at all creative. Gilbert Ryle (1982) supplies a very good metaphor to illustrate the point I am trying to make:

Dreamers of dreams may be pathfinders; but they may be mere vagrants; and of those who depart from the pavements, only a few are explorers; the rest are mere jaywalkers. (p. 64)

It is strange that so many theorists and researchers (although recognizing that primary-process thinking is not restricted to creative thinking) assumed that creative people must have particularly *easy access* to primary-process thinking, and/or be able to *shift easily* between primary-process thinking and secondary-process thinking. They also assumed that creative inspiration would be stimulated by inducing primary-process thinking. In this spirit and faith, creativity training-programmes included exercises for promoting primary-process thinking, for inducing harmonious interaction between right and left hemispheres, and for encouraging openness to inner and outer experience – so that the imagination might be enlivened (see Torrance, 1979; Treffinger, Isaksen & Firestien, 1982).

As Ryle (1982) pointed out,

there is a current sentiment which is tending to glorify the notion of imagination with a halo. People are beginning to boast of their imagination as if there were no chance of a lively imagination being a silly one. Scope for originality is also scope for silliness. The genius is an imaginative thinker – but so is the crank. (p. 64)

It is particularly unfortunate that workers in the field of creativity, while focussing on the role of instincts and primitive aspects of unconscious forces, ignored a very important aspect of creative ability. Although instincts may play a major role in the *development of the motivation* to create, they do not *enable* creative thinking.

It is, moreover, unfortunate that researchers have focussed on the strength of creators' inclination to engage in primary-process thinking, when the important question is not whether creative people are more inclined than others are to engage in primary-process thinking – but *why they should do so to greater effect.* Traditional theories have fallen short of explaining why eminently creative people arrive at excellent solutions to intellectual problems through primary-process thinking. It is still far from clear, for example, how scientific inspirations emerge from wild-ranging, primitive, instinctual, emotional, illogical or self-referent thought.

To clarify such matters, one should perhaps consider 'unconscious' aspects of thinking in an entirely different light, and the following chapter attempts to do so, showing how 'conscious', 'unconscious' and 'primary-process' thinking may be explained in terms of automaticity.

# 12

## *Unconscious processing and inspiration: a new interpretation*

As explained in the previous chapter, 'the unconscious' has traditionally been viewed as a primitive, uncivilized or unsocialized part of the personality – a raw source of natural tendencies such as instincts and emotions. This chapter offers a completely different interpretation, which shows that many unconsciously initiated tendencies are well-polished products of learning. But first we consider the meaning of the term 'conscious', which is often used loosely, not only in common parlance but also in psychology.

The word 'conscious' has several somewhat different meanings. It sometimes refers to the *current level of cortical arousal* – as in the phrase 'Peter is now conscious.' Generally, however, it refers to a person's *current awareness of something in particular* – as in 'Peter is now conscious of X'. When used thus, 'conscious' relates to phenomenal experience: and this is the meaning of the word in the following pages. 'Conscious' will refer to *awareness* (of something) and 'unconscious' will refer to absence of awareness of whatever. Note that, in this sense, 'consciousness' refers neither to a general state nor to a region of the brain or mind – 'the unconscious' (used as a noun) has no meaning. At any time a person may be conscious of some things but unconscious of others.

Although countless stimuli in the environment, body and brain are potentially able to produce some experiential effects at any moment, the 'stream of consciousness' has a limited capacity: one is conscious of only a small proportion of what one is potentially able to become aware of. In the words of Nietzsche: 'It is narrow, this room of human consciousness' (quoted by L. L. Whyte, 1978, p. 176). 'Stream' remains a better metaphor than 'room', however, for experience has a sequential quality: one may be aware of something at one moment and unaware of it the next.

Awareness or consciousness of stimuli arising from without and within is *the experiential outcome of ongoing neurological processes*. As such processes cannot be intentionally arrested, their experiential effects cannot be held static. When stimuli from the environment are lacking, or when one's reaction to them is diminished, then one is relatively unconscious of the current environment, but more particularly conscious of the experiential effects of stimuli arising within the brain. When one is awake such endogenous experiences constitute thinking. During sleep they constitute dreams.

The above leads to the conclusion that 'conscious' should not be regarded as equivalent to 'under intentional control'. Dreams, for example, are not under intentional control. They are under automatic control. But one is conscious of them.

## The development and functioning of automatic routines

### Sensory-motor routines

Although this chapter is mainly concerned with thinking, it first considers the automatic aspects of overt sensory-motor activity – and then uses the characteristics of automatic sensory-motor processes as models for explaining the automatic aspects of thought.

Active sensory-motor skills such as knitting, writing, typing and driving involve the performance of complex patterns of action that become so well learned that they can be carried out automatically – with hardly any attention or intentional control. Characteristically, the development of such skills proceeds through a series of stages, in each of which there is a *progressive integration of actions into larger units.* (e.g. J. R. Anderson, 1985; Fitts & Posner, 1967).

During the initial stage of learning a skill, when there is little integration of the relevant patterns of action, the performer is aware of each step in a required sequence – and each step is usually performed as a discrete unit. One has to initiate and control one's actions intentionally and one is able to verbally describe the necessary sequence of motions. One may, moreover, guide oneself by talking aloud (. . . needle under top of loop . . . wool around bottom . . . pull wool through . . .). One also carefully observes the results of one's actions, and gives particular attention to areas where mistakes usually occur (. . . watch it! . . . not around top . . . around bottom . . . ). With repeated practice, however, actions become less discrete, and are integrated into larger units (. . . knit one . . . purl two . . .). Eventually these larger units become further integrated and are fused into smoothly co-ordinated elegant whole sequences (. . . two rows rib . . .).

When whole patterns of action have become automatic, one is often no longer conscious of performing the elemental actions. Elemental actions, if they proceed according to expectations, have very little conscious outcome. Indeed, if one is required to explain how an elemental unit is performed, one might have to derive a verbal description by forming a mental image, or by actually performing the whole pattern of actions, while giving conscious attention to what one is doing.

What probably happens at a neuronal level in the development of sensory-motor skill is that a system of lowered thresholds develops from consistent repetition of a particular pattern of neural responses, so that any stimulus entering the system causes the particular combination of elements to run off automatically as a unit. Although the outcomes of such neural patterns may include some conscious experience, the neural thresholds may eventually become so low and the system so responsive that the execution of the pattern requires very little attention and causes hardly any subjective experience. Extra input (provided by intentional investment of attention) may be needed to produce conscious experience.

I shall henceforth call automatic patterns of action such as those mentioned above 'routines', and assume that

1.  routines are originally built from elemental innate 'reflexes' (as Piaget suggests all cognitive schemas to be);
2.  routines become constantly modified through feedback;
3.  all actions, thoughts and feelings, depend to some extent on the operation of routines;
4.  routines can proceed without intentional control (but may also be initiated and directed by intentional control);
5.  among the *possible* outcomes of routines are motor reactions, somatic reactions, and conscious experience.

Well-developed specialized routines are obviously essential to sensory-motor skills. They allow smoothly integrated configurations of responses, constituting swift, well-timed, elegant, precise movements, which stand in some contrast to clumsy, over-complicated complexes of discrete halting manoeuvres that are characteristic of unpractised performers. Moreover, as one can carry out routines without much attention, they allow attention to be focussed on the demands of the particular situation and circumstances, without detracting from one's performance.

One is inclined to applaud the apparently miraculous automatically controlled performance of well-practised sportsmen, jugglers and trapeze artists, but automaticity is not only important for the performance of extraordinary skills. It is essential to all co-ordinated sensory-motor activity. As the French poet Paul Valéry (1940/1954) suggested, it is indeed credible

that our simplest act, our most familiar gesture could not be performed, that the least of our powers might become an obstacle to us if we had to bring it before the mind and know it thoroughly in order to exercise it. (p. 93)

Three closely related characteristics of routines are especially important to the following discussions. The first is their *tendency to be triggered automatically* (in the absence of attention) by certain configurations of stimuli. This tendency may sometimes disrupt controlled performance – by causing involuntary responses to stimuli that should be ignored.

Second is their tendency to *run off to completion unconsciously*. However, even if one is not conscious of initiating and performing routines, one may be conscious of their results – especially if the results are not as expected.

A third important characteristic of routines is their differential *tendency to generalize*. Generalizability in this case implies that a routine is triggered by various sets of stimuli with similar features, and that the routine varies to some extent from one occasion to another. This tendency is seldom recognized because automaticity is usually associated with inflexibility. Not all routines generalize to the same extent, however. Those developed for laboratory experiments may be relatively inflexible – involving rather precise sets of responses to specific sets of stimuli. Those developed through natural interaction with the environment may allow a relatively wide range of more-or-less-equivalent sequences of responses to roughly similar sets of stimuli – especially when they are acquired through experience and practice *in a relatively wide variety of contexts* (e.g. J. R. Anderson, 1985).

Flexible routines may well be described in terms of generalizable schemas or 'production systems'. In contrast to the concept of 'stimulus-response' systems (which suggests that bonds develop between specific stimuli and specific responses) the concept of production systems allows that whole sets of actions occur in response to whole configurations of events (e.g. Newell, 1973). This implies that various configurations of stimuli with similar features may trigger similar routines that vary to some extent from one occasion to another. Recognizing that various routines may have common elements, Shiffrin and Schneider (1977) explained that 'the same nodes may appear in different automatic sequences, depending on the context. For example, a red light might elicit a braking response when the perceiver is in a car and elicit a walking, halting, or traffic scanning response when the perceiver is a pedestrian' (p. 156).

These authors nevertheless suggested that automatic responses, once learned, follow exactly the same pattern. Although this may be relatively true, the exact form of even simple routines obviously differs to some extent from one occasion to the next – according to the context. Actions involved in even the simple routine of typing the word 'the', may vary according to the preceding action and the current posture of the typist. Moreover, *feedback* relating to prevailing conditions is likely to affect the activity, adjusting it to the present situation.

## The correspondence between thought and sensory-motor activity

So far we have focussed mainly on the practical or sensory-motor aspects of automaticity, but there are various similarities between the characteristics of action and thought that are relevant to our present interest in the subject of automatic processing.

For one, it is apparent that intellectual skills, like sensory-motor skills, involve the operation of *automatically controlled sets of integrated responses*. Those routines that have no obvious motor outcomes I shall call 'mental routines'. And there is good reason to believe that the development of mental skill proceeds along much the same lines as does sensory-motor skill.

In the early stages of cognitive development there is probably relatively little integration of discrete units of sensations but, through repeated experience, a child gradually becomes able to integrate sensations automatically into composite perceptions – developing a sort of 'perceptual short-hand' so that complexes of sensations can be perceived as single concepts. Moreover, with repeated exposure to regularities in the environment, sets of repeatedly and systematically related perceptions become progressively integrated into *increasingly large units*. When one has become thoroughly familiar with the regularities in a common experience, one perceives a whole pattern, even if many of the units are absent. A few cues are often sufficient to trigger a mental routine or 'schema' such as the automatic perception of the 'meaning' of a familiar complex pattern of events.

Extraordinary mental skills may be attributed to the development of special mental routines that enable the performer to integrate or 'chunk' certain types of information into meaningful patterns. It has been shown, for example, that the performance of chess masters can be distinguished from that of amateurs in terms of the degree to which they integrate information relating to the position of various pieces on the chess board (e.g. Chase & Simon, 1973; De Groot, 1965; Posner & McLeod, 1982). Unlike most of us, a chess master does not have to plan his next move by consciously considering the position of each piece and imagining the various consequences of each feasible move. On the basis of vast and varied experience, the master has a wide repertoire of well-learned strategies for dealing with various patterns. De Groot demonstrated another interesting difference between chess masters and amateurs. After looking for only five seconds at a board upon which pieces were positioned during a game, the masters were able to remember the positions of more than twenty pieces: amateurs remembered the positions of only four or five. If, however, pieces were arranged at random, the masters remembered no more than the amateurs. One may conclude that when pieces are arranged at random, masters are *unable to integrate* the positions of individual pieces into a meaningful pattern.

One marvels at the virtuosity of masters such as skilled chess players and arithmeticians, but one tends to take for granted the intellectual virtuosity displayed by us all in the course of everyday life. Every moment of waking life one is automatically fitting various sensory experiences, memories and emotional feelings, into a growing body of perceptions, concepts and knowledge. In general *the more experience one has in a relevant area, the better able one is to integrate the units automatically.* Furthermore, practice increases the potential amount of relevant information one will be able to hold in memory, and in the active stream of consciousness. If you are hesitant about the validity of this statement, consider the following two sets of twelve symbols. When glancing at sets 1 and 2 below, you will no doubt integrate the first set into a meaningful pattern and remember it with ease. Most of us will find it difficult to integrate the second set, and will soon forget it.

1.   DECEMBER 1989
2.   δφψχμβξρ λκνπ

Like sensory-motor routines, mental routines may be disrupted by focussing attention on the elements. Whereas attention to automatically controlled sensory-motor actions impedes smooth and effective motor performance, attention to items of mental routines tends to impede the smooth sequence of thought. The reader has, no doubt, discovered this when concentrating too hard on recalling a well-known telephone number or the spelling of a word.

In addition, like sensory-motor routines, mental routines are especially generalizable when they are developed through *varied experience.* Practising intellectual skills under a variety of conditions allows one to respond automatically to a variety of *roughly similar* sets of stimuli. Everyday examples are to be seen in the use of one's home language, which is a very generalized skill. One understands what is being said in one's home language when it is spoken in a variety of accents because one has heard it spoken in various voices and accents. One understands that various sentences have the same meaning although the words differ, because one has been exposed to various syntactical constructions. However, those who have attended classes in a foreign language, and have spoken the language only with their teacher, are likely to realize when they tour the country where the language is spoken in a variety of accents and dialects that their comprehension of the foreign language is not generalizable.

## Automatic bases of creative production

All this talk about automaticity may seem a far cry from creativity. Automaticity, after all, implies repetition of what has already been done, whereas creativity implies the introduction of something new. It is indeed frequently suggested that automaticity and creative acts are mutually exclusive. Among those who have made a distinction between automatically controlled and creative acts are Koestler (1964) and R. W. Weisberg (1986). In his masterful work on creativity, Koestler has gone to some pains to distinguish between creativity and mental acts supported by automaticity, referring to the creative act as a *defeat* of automaticity or habit by originality. His failure to acknowledge that every act involves some automaticity, and his failure to recognize the role of automatic habits in creativity are sad omissions. One is left with the impression that learning is inimical to creative thinking – which has obviously dangerous implications. Without automaticity, thinking would indeed be *uncreative*, as it would tend to concentrate on trivial detail. Elegance and integration would be lacking.

It is strange to discover that Koestler's failure to appreciate the value of automaticity in creativity is not simply an oversight, for he does in fact consider the role of automaticity in unconscious processes, making the point that

The intervention of unconscious processes in the creative act is a phenomenon quite different from the automatization of skills; and our unawareness of the sources of inspiration is of a quite different order from the unawareness of what we are doing while we tie our shoestrings or copy a letter on the typewriter. In the creative act there is an *upward* surge from some unknown fertile, underground layers of the mind; whereas the process I have described is a *downward* relegation of the controls of skilled techniques. (1964, p. 156; italics in original)

Koestler does not explain the origin and nature of the 'unknown fertile, underground layers of the mind', nor does he indicate what an 'upward surge' (as distinct from a 'downward relegation') involves. One is, moreover, surprised by Koestler's statement to the effect that one way of *escaping from* automatized routines of thinking and behaving is to plunge into dreaming or dreamlike states when the 'codes of rational thinking are suspended'.

When plunging into dreams or dreamlike states, one is not escaping from automatized codes of thought. One is resorting to them. When plunging into dreamlike states automaticity has its way – without disruption by intentional inputs.

Despite suggestions by Koestler and others, it has been recognized that creativity may involve the adaptation of old patterns to new situations (e.g. Schank, 1988). And there is, moreover, good reason for suggesting that creativity is dependent on various types of automatically controlled routines. For one, the employment of well-established routines frees attention from basic procedures to focus on the unusual or unique aspects of complex tasks. Moreover, routines imbue relevant products with elegance. Highly creative products, whether paintings, musical compositions, literary works, mechanical inventions, new methods or theoretical conceptions are elegant – not clumsy. This elegance may be attributed to automatic integration of elements.

It is often claimed that people who apply themselves diligently to their work are likely to develop virtuosity or technique, but will not be creative. This is only partly true. Creativity depends on technique, although, of course, it goes beyond it. Routines provide creators with the symbols and the language of their culture: they provide sensory-motor skill for artists, heuristics for scientists, vocabulary for poets. Creators who have built up a wide repertoire of automatic sensory-motor routines for achieving certain effects are free to devote their attention to considering what particular effects, message or emotion they intend to depict, without bothering about what overt actions to perform; they are enabled by linguistic routines to express the meaning of what they intend to convey, elegantly and pertinently, without concentrating on syntax or vocabulary.

Moreover, creative products have style, and the particular style of a creator is often clearly recognizable in all his or her products. This too reflects pervasive influences of automatic routines.

Automaticity, I believe, further contributes to creativity by engendering what we have come to know as 'intuition'. It is widely recognized, even by scientists, that intuition is essential to creative thinking. Among famous scientists who have subscribed to this idea was Einstein, who pointed out that there is no logical path to the discovery of elementary laws in science, only intuition. As Poincaré (1913) explained 'pure logic would never lead us to anything but tautologies . . . It is by logic that we prove. It is by intuition that we discover' (p. 208). Wilson (1972) illustrated the scientists' respect for intuition in this personal anecdote about the great Enrico Fermi:

Years ago, as a graduate student, I was present at a three-way argument between Rabi, Szilard, and Fermi. Szilard took a position and mathematically stated it on the blackboard. Rabi disagreed and rearranged the equations to the form he would accept. All the while Fermi was shaking his head. 'You're both wrong', he said. They demanded proof. Smiling a little he shrugged his shoulders as if proof weren't needed. 'My intuition tells me so', he said. I had never heard a scientist refer to his intuition, and I expected Rabi and Szilard to laugh. They didn't. The man of science, I soon found, works with the procedures of logic so much more than anyone else that he, more than anyone else, is aware of logic's limitations. Beyond logic there is intuition. (p. 14)

Although few would deny the importance of intuition in creativity, little has been offered in the way of clear explanation of the source and role of intuition. The term 'intuition' is often used simply for referring to insights that do not appear to follow logically from given information, and are therefore considered inexplicable. Such insights are sometimes otherwise labelled as 'instinctive' and are often attributed to inborn propensities and/or to the functioning of the right hemisphere – with the implication that it stands in contrast to learning. Several writers have referred to intuition as something 'felt' rather than known with the implication that it involves emotional empathy (e.g. Bastik, 1982; Hadamard, 1945). However, in terms of what we know of automaticity, there is good reason for attributing intuitive thinking to the operation of mental routines, unconsciously triggered by configurations of exogenous and/or endogenous stimuli. More specifically, intuition may be viewed as unconsciously triggered *automatic integration of relevant elements of information*, and an 'intuitive feeling' may be seen as part of the experiential outcome of such processes – somewhat equivalent to a feeling of recognition. This view is very much in line with Bruner's (1960) suggestion that 'intuitive thinking characteristically does not advance in careful well-planned steps. Indeed it tends to involve manoeuvres based on an implicit perception of the total problem. The thinker arrives at an answer which may be right or wrong, with little if any awareness of the process by which he reached it' (pp. 57–58).

The foregoing discussions lead one to realize that what one refers to as 'intuition' is not simply 'inborn', as often suggested. It is acquired through varied practice, which develops one's ability to integrate a relatively wide range of relevant information without even knowing what items of information one has used, or how and why one has integrated them. One is merely *conscious of the outcome* of the automatic processes.

Creators are likely to develop well-established bases for intuition because they are constantly involved with their subject of interest, and this practice would lead to the establishment of routines that enable them to integrate relevant actions and items of information. Moreover, creators work independently rather than following prescribed curricula and instructions, which favours the acquisition of a relatively wide repertoire of *generalizable routines*. In contrast, people who have obediently adhered to prescribed paths would be likely to acquire routines that are not very generalizable, but confined to a relatively limited range of stimuli – and would therefore be less 'intuitive'.

As explained in what follows, generalization is not, however, necessarily advantageous. It may have both adverse and creative effects.

### Verbal slips and slips of action

One of the adverse effects of generalizable routines is that they provide a basis for inappropriate responses, slips of the tongue or absent-minded slips of action.

Interesting work in this area provides insights into the nature and determinants of such errors (which is of considerable importance to anyone wishing to explore the unconscious aspects of mental processing). Freud suggested that slips (like primary-process thinking) are determined by hidden or unacceptable motives. The validity of this suggestion is often apparent – for example in the case of the employee who explained that she had not come to work because her grandmother had *lied*. Motley (1987) has shown, however, that not all verbal slips result from an attempt to hide unacceptable truths – but neither are they merely random combinations of words or sounds.

Verbal slips reflect displacement of elements in the speaker's well-learned verbal routines. They result from the automatic re-arrangement or substitution of elements in well-known phrases or words. Among the amusing examples offered by Motley are the use of the phrases 'As American as motherpie and applehood' and 'comprinter puteout' (for 'computer printout'). Motley explained that verbal slips characteristically reflect competition between choices that have a common element. This can clearly be seen in the use of the word 'perchaps' which reflects a turning made at the wrong point when confronted by the options 'perchance' and 'perhaps'.

Absent-minded errors of action are discussed in interesting articles on 'slips of action' by Reason (1979, 1984), who noted that such slips typically occur when the action programmes are well-learned, and *certain elements of action or meaning are common to more than one well-learned routine*. Among the common everyday errors described by Reason are those involving the substitution of inappropriate objects into an action routine – such as spreading shaving-cream on one's toothbrush. Also typical is the inadvertent substitution of one routine for another. For example, one of Reason's subjects responded to a knock at the door by lifting the phone and bellowing 'come in' into the receiver. A wrong turning may then be taken at a common juncture – as apparently happened to a person who went upstairs to change for dinner and, having removed his clothes, automatically began donning his pyjamas (rather like the person who used the word 'perchaps'). Another common mistake is the inadvertent interchange of parts of routines. For example, one of Reason's subjects, who was in the habit of throwing her dog two biscuits before setting out in the morning, found herself throwing her earrings to the dog, while trying to affix a dog biscuit to an ear (somewhat like the person who spoke of motherpie and applehood).

Absent-minded slips of action are most likely to occur when attention is diffused or is claimed elsewhere; when the person concerned is daydreaming, and/or ongoing actions are relatively free from intentional control. They may also result from pathological problems involving attention disorders, such as schizophrenia or brain damage.

It is feasible that something similar may apply to *thought* when attention is diffused and thought patterns are relatively free of intentional control. These conditions may be conducive to 'slips of thinking' that are the covert counterparts of verbal slips or slips of action. And this brings us back to the subject of 'primary-process thinking'.

*The relation between automatic routines and primary-process thinking*

Primary-process thinking, you will recall, is a meandering procession of images, covert verbalizations and emotional feelings that occurs typically when the person concerned is daydreaming, on the verge of sleep, dreaming or in a psychotic state. Attention is diffused and intensity of response to stimuli in the environment is diminished, so that one is relatively unaware of stimuli in the environment. It is described by psychoanalysts in terms of 'displacement' and 'condensation' of thought elements, where imagined objects or actions become substituted for or symbolized by others, and fragments of remote ideas tend to become merged.

As we have seen, this type of thinking has traditionally been explained in terms of eruptions from 'deeper', 'primitive', 'unsocialized', 'unspoiled', 'childlike' or instinctive levels of the mind – or even in more mystical terms relating to universal memories of mankind and being in touch with cosmic truths.

Primary-process thinking can, however, simply be explained in terms of the experiential outcomes of a jumble of interacting automatic mental routines triggering and diverting one another. This type of thinking may indeed be described as an ongoing mess of 'slips of thinking' which entail inappropriate substitutions of mental objects or actions, or diversion from one set of automatically controlled mental actions to another. The output of one mental routine might act as a trigger for the initiation of another, or one routine might be *altered in progress by another containing a similar component.* Especially where automatic sequences of thinking have certain elements in common, intersections may occur, and the fragments of two or more routines may even run off in sequence.

Slips of overt action, as Reason explains, are the exception rather than the rule. This is at least partly because maladaptive initiation of sensory-motor routines is soon bound to interfere with one's interaction with the environment and call upon conscious control. This does not, however, apply to the same extent with slips of thinking, as their immediate outcomes are covert. As slips of thinking are less immediately maladaptive and less constrained by the immediate demands of reality than slips of action are, they are therefore likely to occur more freely. Consequently thought tends to wander more than action does.

The foregoing discussion indicates that the bizarre disorganized aspects of primary-process thinking may be attributed to fragmentation and reorganization of the fragments of mental routines. The same may be said of adaptive aspects of primary-process thinking, such as divergent thinking, remote associations and other mental processes to which creativity has been attributed. All these may be seen as reorganization of fragments of existing routines. Valéry explained simply how such automatic reorganization may come to the aid of a poet like himself:

> The same mental event which psychologically is or should be assimilated to a waste product, which is caused by fatigue, or local exhaustion, or a bit of chance, a local reaction comparable to a lapsus linguae, can, in another situation, take on a literary value . . . It can give a very successful effect, very new, which the consciousness appreciates, receives, notes. (Quoted by Grubbs, 1968, p. 96)

When primary-process thinking is explained in terms of automaticity and in particular slips of thinking, the implications are very different from those drawn from traditional theory. According to traditional theory, the unconscious basis of primary-process thinking lies in inborn, instinctual, untamed, natural aspects of personality functioning, and is relatively independent of learned reactions. As instincts or primitive drives reflect the universal tendencies of the species (i.e. are similar in all members of the species), traditional explanations of the creative value of primary-process thinking therefore offer little explanation for individual differences. Accordingly, individual differences in creativity have been attributed to *the amount* of primary-process thinking in which people typically engage. However, when we consider primary-process thinking in terms of automaticity, the tremendous variation in creativity of individuals may be attributed to the fact that routines are well-established products of experience.

In the previous chapter the question arose as to why creative people might employ primary-process thinking to greater effect than others do. The answer is now clear. It is because from an early age, creators engage persistently and independently in activities relating to their field of work, and thereby acquire a potentially valuable store of automatic routines. Such people are more creative than others, *not* because they are more inclined than others to engage in primary-process thinking, but because *the content* of their primary-process thinking is more relevant to creative endeavour. The good store of raw material – the routines upon which their primary-process thinking draws – is rich with possibilities. When creators do engage in primary-process thinking, the probability of coming up with an effective combination of existing ideas is relatively high.

The foregoing discussion leads to the conclusion that the unconscious bases of individual differences in creativity depend largely on habitual experiences and thought. It leads one to recognize that the question of 'how' people think is relatively unimportant to individual differences in creativity – because the processes involved in and principles governing thinking are universal. But not so the content. The content of thought, especially the content of automatically initiated and controlled thought patterns, varies greatly from one person to another. Simply speaking, one cannot expect new scientific insights from people who never think about science, or artistic ideas from people who never take an interest in art.

Though necessary, routines are not, however, sufficient to creative inspiration. There is obviously more involved in creative problem-solving than fortuitous, haphazard interaction of automatic routines. Some guiding endogenous influence must act upon the differential initiation of the particularly relevant automatically controlled thought patterns. Something of this sort was implied by Hobbes (1651/1969), who mentioned that even in the wild ranging of unguided thought 'one may sometimes perceive the way of it' (p. 69).

Poincaré, who viewed inspiration as forming new combinations of old ideas, wondered why useful combinations were particularly inclined to emerge from unconscious sources. He pointed out that there are infinite numbers of combinations of elements that could be formed, yet it seems that those that are useful to the solution of a problem spring into the conscious stream of thought; and he asked a most provocative question:

Does it follow that the subliminal self, having divined by a delicate intuition that these combinations would be useful, has formed only these, or has it rather formed many others which were lacking in interest and have remained unconscious? (1908/1954, p. 28)

Paul Valéry (1940/1954) also puzzled over the matter, and suggested that

Sometimes we invoke what ought to exist, having defined it by its conditions. We demand it, being faced with some peculiar combination of elements all equally imminent to the mind and yet no one of which will stand out and satisfy our need. We beg of our minds some show of inequality. We hold up our desire before the mind as one places a magnet over a composite mixture of dust from which a particle of iron will suddenly jump out. In the order of mental things there seem to be very mysterious relations between *the desire and the event*. I do not wish to say that the mind's desire creates a sort of field, much more complex than a mathematic field, which might have the power to call up what suits us. (p. 101; italics in the original)

In reply to Poincaré and Valéry one might suggest that the content of the conscious stream of thought is not simply comprised of a *random* selection of automatically controlled routines from one's repertoire. It is not simply determined by the nature of one's repertoire of automatic routines, but also by *mental models of one's intentions and goals*. In accordance with this suggestion one would agree with P. C. Elliot (1986) that the physiological bases for creativity should not be sought in the right hemisphere (or in a balance between the functioning of the two hemispheres). If any physiological region is of particular importance to creativity, it is the *prefrontal lobe – the seat of will, planning and purpose.*

And this leads us to consider relevant findings of research on the characteristics of the conscious stream.

## Facts and ideas about the conscious stream of thought

In the last decade several techniques have been developed for tapping the content of ongoing thought in a real-life situation. Typical procedures include thought-sampling techniques which require subjects to go about their daily lives carrying electronic bleepers that emit signals at random intervals. On hearing the bleeper, subjects briefly record what they were thinking immediately before the interruption.

The following are to be found among the findings of such studies (*inter alia* by Klinger, 1978; Pope, 1978; Singer, 1978):

1.  in the course of their daily life, most people draw a great deal of thought material from long-term memory;
2.  their thinking relates relatively more to endogenous material and is relatively more independent of external stimuli than was previously realized;
3.  most people do not recall much of what they have thought about;
4.  rather than being bizarre, the content and flow of endogenous mentation has a great deal in common with what generally happens in the course of the person's daily life, and most thoughts are fairly specific rather than vague;
5.  although a surprising amount of the content of fantasies relates to wishes and needs, the fantasies are not necessarily wish-fulfilling and drive-reducing as Freud suggests. Singer (1978) describes them rather as fanciful explorations of the future that provide adaptive *preparations for future action*;
6.  the course of moment-to-moment thoughts is determined by motivational 'current concerns'.

Of special relevance to the present discussion are that thoughts are influenced by *current concerns* and that most of the content of endogenous mentation is *soon forgotten*. First we will consider the nature and operation of current concerns.

Klinger (1978) defined 'current concern' in terms of 'the state of the organism between the time it becomes committed to pursuing a goal and the time it either gains the goal or abandons the pursuit' (p. 249). He further stated the principle that 'at any given moment, the next thematic content of thought is induced by the combination of a current concern and a cue related to that concern' (p. 250). It is important to realize that a 'cue' may emanate from external stimuli, or from events in the current stream of thought.

The validity of Klinger's suggestions has been well supported by findings from various types of psychological studies, which show that the current content of thought is constantly influenced by cues relating to current concerns. (Hoelscher, Klinger & Barta, 1981; Klinger, 1978; Klinger, Barta & Maxheimer, 1980). It is, moreover, especially important in the present context to note that certain stimuli gain special meaning and arousal value in the light of such a concern. In other words, *stimuli relating to a current concern are likely to capture attention and enter the current stream of thought.* If one's thought is dominated by a particular concern, then anything one encounters and thinks about stands a good chance of becoming associated with that concern. A falling apple might draw the attention of an astronomer working on a problem of gravity, a botanist working on a project concerning ripening of fruit, a farmer concerned with shortage of labour and a peasant with a hungry family.

The notion of the dynamic effects of current concerns, which are sometimes referred to as 'unfinished business' is not entirely new. Freud (1900/1973a) reported that one is inclined to dream about activities that were prevented from reaching completion during the day, whereas those things that had been brought to a conclusion seldom entered dreams:

Unsolved problems, harassing cares, overwhelming impressions, continue the activity of our thought even during sleep . . . the thought impulses continued into sleep [include] . . . those which have not been completed during the day, owing to some accidental cause . . . Those which have been left uncompleted because our mental powers have failed us, that is unsolved problems . . . We need not underrate the psychic intensities introduced into sleep by these residues of the day's waking life, especially those emanating from the group of unsolved issues. It is certain that these excitations continue to strive for expression during the night. (pp. 451–452)

Writing about the experience of trying to recall a forgotten name, William James (1890, vol. I) described the experience of a gap, within which is a form 'beckoning us in a given direction' (p. 251). Thoughts of wrong names are rejected immediately, said James, as they do not properly fill the gap. The idea of a dynamic 'gap' was further developed by, for example, Wertheimer (1945) and Henle (1974), who suggested that a gap caused by an unsolved problem may be intensely active. Wertheimer explained that a gap left by an unsolved problem sets up tensions, with vectors in the direction of a solution that produces harmony between the parts and the whole. Henle pointed out that the gap not only beckons in a given direction but demands solution. Max Planck (1949), the eminent physicist, offered an account of personal experience of such a demand, describing some problems as 'very stubborn, they just refuse to let us in peace' (p. 52). In a similar vein, Nobel Prize winner Szent-Györgyi (1962) confessed 'somehow, problems get into my blood and they don't give me peace, they torture me. I have to get them out of my system, and there is but one way to get them out – by solving them' (p. 176).

The concept of the dynamic potency of gaps or 'unfinished business' is reminiscent of the work of Zeigarnik (1927), who suggested that people are generally better able to recall unfinished tasks than completed ones. It was Zeigarnik's opinion that frustration caused by an unfinished plan arouses a motive in that direction. In a somewhat similar vein, Karl Lewin (1935) proposed that any intention to reach a goal produces a tension, which is preserved when the goal is blocked.

As a whole, findings of research on memory for unfinished tasks have been inconclusive (see van Bergen, 1968). This is (at least partly) because they have mainly been derived from experiments conducted in very artificial situations. In a real-life situation the validity of Zeigarnik's suggestions is more likely to be upheld, as illustrated by the following story told by Boring (1957).

Lewin was involved in an intense protracted conversation with friends in a restaurant in Berlin. In the background hovered their waiter. Eventually Lewin called him over, asked how much they owed him, and paid. As the waiter retreated and conversation continued, Lewin had an idea. He called the waiter back and asked how much he had paid him. The waiter no longer remembered. He had completed his task.

Although the modern conception of unfinished business has much in common with earlier ideas relating to unsolved problems or unfinished plans, it provides additional insights as to how ability to generate effective ideas is affected by personality characteristics. 'Unfinished business' refers to more than isolated unfinished tasks. It implies that the course of the current train of thought is continually influenced by *a number of* current concerns, even when the person is not engaged in thinking about them (Gilhooly, 1982). It is therefore to be expected that, if a person has a relatively narrow range of concerns, the dynamic effects of various concerns would act in similar rather than conflicting directions – and the content of the experience emerging into consciousness will be more predictable than it would be if the person has a range of competing concerns. As eminent creators *typically have few concerns besides their work, and perhaps undefined emotional feelings that seek release through mastery and the experience of beauty*, it is therefore highly probable that the content of the conscious stream would be somehow related to the professional problems with which they are currently engaged.

## A reconsideration of the nature of inspiration

In the light of the foregoing sections, we are now able to cast aside traditional notions of the precipitation of inspiration by invasion of (external) supranatural forces or invasion of (internal) instinctive forces from 'the unconscious mind', and explain sudden inspiration in terms of the operation of a constant concern about certain goals, and a wide repertoire of automatic cognitive routines in a particular domain of interest.

The first-hand reports of inspiration presented in previous chapters showed they are often dramatic. As the notion of inspiration still carries some of the romantic mystical connotations brought down through history, it is possible that these tales are somewhat dramatized in the telling. For this reason one usually fails to recognize that the spontaneous eruption of unbidden thoughts into the conscious stream is not peculiar to creative individuals. It is an unexceptional, indeed universal, phenomenon. As Olton (1979) remarked, nearly everyone seems to have had such an experience, and folklore advises us to 'sleep on the problem', if we cannot solve it directly.

What I am suggesting is that the celebrated experience of creative inspiration is probably merely an instance of what is sometimes referred to as 'pop-ups'. Other forms of this phenomenon include the humble experience of spontaneous retrieval of memories that have eluded one.

Referring to such spontaneous retrievals of forgotten information, Underwood (1979) explained that 'memories of events which have been inactive for some period of time do not seem to be activated when we are busy, that is, when a rapid succession of information is achieving its conscious state. When engaged with a long car drive, or taking a long walk, such memories do become activated more often' (p. 107).

Underwood further suggested that a relaxed state not only causes generation of remote memories, but also allows one to become aware of them. This is in line with the fact that at a low level of arousal attention is diffused and directed toward endogenous stimuli. Although Underwood referred particularly to the spontaneous intrusion of memory sequences, it also happens that single facts (such as someone's name) that have eluded one suddenly intrude into awareness when one is not concentrating on the subject. Reason and Lucas (1984) found that 30.4 per cent of memory blocks are resolved by such 'pop-ups', occurring when one is not concentrating on the subject.

Searching memory for a *known fact* is not likely to be regarded as equivalent to generating a new idea (Olton, 1979). Nevertheless any thoughts or images, however novel they may be, must be influenced by the tendencies that past experience has left in the neural structures. Although a thought may not be an intact memory sequence it is nevertheless comprised of fragments of 'memory', 'knowledge' or routines, which may become fragmented and re-integrated. As so frequently asserted, a creative idea is a new combination of 'old' concepts or re-integration of fragments of familiar thought patterns that have become divorced from their original context.

The experience of a 'brilliant idea' presenting itself suddenly while the person concerned is in a car, bath or bed is also a universal phenomenon. It not only happens to eminent men but also to unexceptional people that a 'brilliant idea' presenting itself in the dark reaches of the night is sometimes exposed in the light of morning as banal, impractical – or merely an old idea.

Poincaré (1908/1954) confessed:

Often this feeling [of illumination] deceives us without being any the less vivid, and we only find out when we seek to put on foot the demonstration. I have especially noticed this fact in regard to ideas coming to me in the morning or evening in bed while in a hypnagogic state. (p. 27)

Even if a new idea is indeed valid, its value is relative. For every brilliant creative inspiration that has captured the imagination of the chroniclers of cultural history, there are no doubt thousands of 'inspirations' which are never reported because their content is trivial and of no importance for anyone besides the person concerned. It is also likely, in the light of findings relating to everyday thought (e.g. those by Klinger, 1978; Pope, 1978; and Singer, 1978), that incidents of this nature are forgotten by the person concerned unless they have some enduring relevance (or the person has been asked to record such incidents).

The probability that information will be remembered depends on the current level of arousal as well as on the significance of the event (e.g. Deutsch & Deutsch, 1963; Norman, 1968). It has long been noted (see, e.g., Rapaport, 1950) that the content of primary-process thinking is soon forgotten. On the other hand, research has confirmed that clearest memories are those for events which were surprising, consequential or emotional (Rubin and Kozin, 1984). And consequential or surprising stimuli are arousing (e.g. Berlyne, 1971; Kahneman, 1973; Walley & Weiden, 1973).

What the foregoing discussion implies is that 'inspiration' is not the prerogative of the creative individual. It is also a normal occurrence in the lives of unexceptional individuals. Creative inspiration is not, however, an ordinary event. It is distinguished from a trivial insight or the sudden recognition of a simple fact by *the content. And it is the significance of the content that calls upon arousal and attention, and makes the experience memorable.*

The trouble with past attempts to explain the phenomenon of creative inspiration is that it has been viewed in terms of a tendency to engage in *extraordinary processes* that are peculiar to creative activity, whereas the processes involved are ordinary although the *content* is extraordinary.

### Insight in context

Having considered the age-old question of how 'incubation' leads to 'inspiration', we finally return to the reality that the creative process is not merely a matter of sudden inspiration – as Gruber (1974) and R. W. Weisberg (1986) have pointed out. Nor, apparently, does it follow the traditional problem-solving or hypothesis-forming processes as well as one would suppose. In reality, significant creative achievements often have no clear beginning and ending, and may involve rather uneventful labour for months or years, during which there are certain valid insights and some which are neither valid nor useful. Creative ideas are often developed slowly, step by step, not only through a sequence of inspirations, but also through deliberately consciously-guided analysis and synthesis, induction and deduction, and trial and error.

The creative process is, moreover, not merely cumulative. It involves qualitative transformations of existing knowledge. Examples of such qualitative reorganization of knowledge and shifts of ideas occurring during the development of creative insight were carefully demonstrated by Gruber (1974), who made an intensive analysis of Darwin's notebooks. This work provided support for Whitehead's contention that 'ideas often come suddenly to individuals, but they usually have a long history' (quoted by Whyte, 1978, ix). Gruber revealed that Darwin had all the facts he needed for a long time before he was able to put them together to form his theory. The notion of creative thinking as a sequence of ideas through formation of alternative hypotheses followed by a rational choice between them is 'a rationalistic myth', said Gruber; original hypotheses are discovered with difficulty by anyone. It is hard enough to find one reasonable hypothesis, never mind two or more. From Darwin's working notebooks it is clear that he tended to give up one hypothesis and substitute another, sometimes remaining completely at a loss until his ideas matured sufficiently to permit the formulation of yet another idea. As Gruber (1974) and Weisberg (1988) explained, the theory of evolution progressed, step by step, from a theory that was rather a simple variation of existing knowledge to a theory that changed the world. Even in its final form Darwin's work remains largely intuitive and speculative, and although it is still foremost in the biological sciences, it might be considered merely anecdotal if presented for the first time today (Wolf, 1981).

Although many have attempted to explain the nature of the processes involved in creative thinking, few scientists or psychologists have considered the flounderings between the insights. The vague meanderings of creative achievers do not make for quantifiable data, and are usually ignored. Indeed most of the vicissitudes of creative endeavour are probably forgotten even by the creators themselves once their goals have been attained. The exciting moments, the solving of important problems and sudden insights are worth telling, retelling and recording. The rest is consigned to oblivion (unless it survives in notebooks).

Therefore, although there may be *some* truth in the dramatic tales of the inspirations of famous creators, such as that of Newton and the falling apple, these stories do not tell the *whole* truth. Newton did not suddenly happen on the laws of universal gravitation in his mother's orchard. He had pondered on them at length. As Richard Westfall (1983) explained, the story of the apple

vulgarizes universal gravitation by treating it as a bright idea. A bright idea cannot shape a scientific tradition ... Universal gravitation did not yield to Newton at his first effort. He hesitated and floundered, baffled for the moment by overwhelming complexities. (p. 155)

On being asked how he had discovered the law of gravitation, Newton replied:

By thinking on it continually. (Westfall, 1983, p. 41)

On another occasion he described the nature of his creative thinking by explaining

I keep the subject constantly before me, and wait till the first dawnings open slowly, by little and little, into a full and clear light. (Westfall, 1983, p. 41)

# Epilogue

During the latter half of this century, and particularly the last decade, a number of serious attempts have been made to debunk the myths that have imbued the terms 'genius' and 'inspiration' with their mystical connotations. Agassie (1985), Amabile (1983, 1985), Hennessey and Amabile (1988), Perkins (1981, 1983, 1985), R. W. Weisberg (1986), to name but a few, have argued that every normal person is potentially capable of productive creative thinking. Perkins (1981) pointed out that creation in the arts and sciences is a natural, comprehensible extension and orchestration of ordinary everyday abilities of perception, understanding, memory and so forth (as the last four chapters of this book also imply). Indeed Darwin said something to the same effect about a century ago, when he suggested that anyone endowed with ordinary capabilities could have written his book on evolution if given sufficient time, diligence and patience.

However, although most people may be capable of writing Darwin's book, the fact of the matter is that few write anything at all. And extremely little of what *is* written compares in importance with Darwin's work.

Debunking 'myths' relating to genius, though necessary, makes demands on the debunkers. The first, I have mentioned, is the demand to rescue the baby of fact while throwing out the bath water of invalid explanation. The second demand is that of replacing the deposed myths with explanations that correspond better with the facts. These demands are not always well met, and this century has seen several explanations offered for productive creativity that appear to have little more correspondence with the facts about creative achievers (or with general principles governing human behaviour) than the deposed myths did. Before concluding, I will briefly discuss two: (1) the suggestion that genius is determined by extraordinary *concrete* brain structures; and (2) the suggestion that creative skills operate in the *abstract*.

To replace the myth that genius is determined by supernatural powers, the suggestion was offered that it is determined by extraordinary brain material. In 1907 the brain of Charles Babbage, which had been preserved in alcohol for thirty-six years and had shrunk to two-thirds of its original size, was carefully examined in an attempt to discover the nature of his genius. Babbage's biographer, Halacy (1970), attributed the failure of this operation to reveal anything of note to the fact that scientific skill had not yet advanced to the point where the human intellect could be 'weighed and measured'.

A long time later, in 1978, a small notice in the *New York Times* referred to a rather similar investigation. It revealed that on 18 April 1955, a few hours before Einstein's body was cremated (without ceremony), his brain had been removed and entrusted to Dr Thomas Harvey, the pathologist at Princeton hospital where Einstein had died. Dr Harvey announced that a team of experts would examine the tissues and fluids of the organ for clues to the source of Einstein's genius. At the outset of this investigation he remarked that Einstein's brain looked just like anybody else's. After twenty-three years, when it had been reduced to slivers coloured with various stains, he was still much of the same opinion.

The notice also included the following extract of an interview with Dr Harvey:

When all is said and done then, is it just an ordinary brain? 'No', Dr Harvey says. He had met Einstein, spoken with him just before the great man's death. 'No', he says again. 'One thing we know is that it was not an ordinary brain.' (*New York Times*, Sunday, 31 December 1978, p. 17)

It depends, of course, what one means by an 'ordinary' brain, but from what we know of neurology, it would be reasonable to suggest that, even *in vivo*, neither Babbage's nor Einstein's brains would differ in any observable physical sense from the (ordinary) brains of those who examined them. The reason is that the brains of extraordinary men like Babbage and Einstein differ from those of others not in the development of extraordinary *tissue* but in the development of neural patterns of reaction underlying extraordinary *tendencies* that are manifest in thoughts, desires, aspirations and activities.

To replace the myth that creativity is a matter of extraordinary endowment, came the suggestion that it is not only ordinary but universal. It is now widely held that *all* people are potentially creative – and to actualize this potential one only needs to learn how to 'think' (to use the 'whole' of one's brain properly).

It is now frequently pointed out that academic performance neither promotes nor predicts life performance, and it has been suggested that, to build 'mankind's ultimate capital asset' one would do better to foster creativity and use creativity rather than academic performance as a predictor of life performance (e.g. Torrance, 1988). Accordingly modern educationalists are setting out to teach children creative thinking skills. The advisability of doing so is supported by what we have heard from Zuckerman's subjects, the Nobel Prize winners who testified that their most influential masters taught them thinking styles rather than facts (see chap. 5).

We must not, however, forget that these subjects referred specifically to domain relevant thinking styles taught them by masters in that field.

The notion of simply teaching children to 'think creatively' allows that creativity may be fostered in the abstract. It suggests that people may acquire certain mental skills that enable them to think creatively about anything. Not everyone agrees as to what these creative skills entail. Some suggest that creative thinking rests on imagination rather than logic or reason. Johnson-Laird (1987) has pointed out that this distinction is invalid, as imagination requires reasoning. Some believe that creative thinking requires critical thinking, and some hold that critical thinking is inimical to spontaneous creativity. Attempts to foster creative thinking skills include encouraging trainees to express their feelings spontaneously; to solve puzzles by using analogies (and/or their imaginations); to think divergently, laterally, associatively, visually rather than verbally, empathetically, and/or whatever else the teacher conceptualizes as 'creative'. It is tacitly assumed, or explicitly claimed, that such styles of thinking (which are alleged to be 'typical of people like Einstein, etc.') will be transferred to the workplace in whatever domain of creative endeavour the trainee is involved.

It may well be important for children to learn to be open-minded and empathetic, and to develop general reasoning skills in the course of their education – as a preparation for effective living and learning. But it is necessary to realize that an effective person is not necessarily productively creative. General reasoning skills are not sufficient for productive creativity. To be useful, reasoning needs to be anchored in relevant information, and there is little reason to believe that the type of creativity that Toynbee called 'mankind's ultimate capital asset' will be promoted through teaching children to think reasonably (imaginatively or in whatever way) about trivia. To imagine that puzzle-solving in the classroom will naturally transfer to weighty problem-solving in the workplace, or that artistic constructive activities in the classroom will transfer to scientific creativity in adult life, is making a very long leap of faith. There is no evidence to support the idea that 'creative thinking skills' transfer from one domain to another, and there is in fact some evidence to the contrary. For example, Spencer and Weisberg (1986) showed that, *even at a low level*, analogical thinking is context-dependent. If teachers are to continue teaching thinking skills in the abstract, then the question of transfer to various domains is an extremely important theme for future research.

As the last four chapters have explained, the processes involved in creative thinking are indeed universal. There is little question about that. But creativity is not a simple result of special types of thinking. It requires thinking about special content – it requires thinking about important questions. And the ability to ask those questions and think about them effectively rests on the acquisition of a wide range of versatile domain-relevant skills and knowledge.

In other words, people must *learn laterally* before they can think laterally.

As De Bono (e.g. 1980) has pointed out, knowledge and thinking skills are interdependent. Usually this type of comment is made to remind one that academic knowledge is not sufficient to promote or predict creative life performance. Recently, however, it has seemed necessary to remind educators that thinking skills are also not enough to predict life performance. Even if one tried to predict capacity to make a contribution to mankind's ultimate capital asset by using a composite of indices representing IQ, academic performance and creative-thinking skills, one would be leaving a very important factor out of one's reckoning: the most salient characteristic of creative achievers – persistent motivation.

Those who see creativity as a divine gift or genetic bequest may know that this bounty will be selectively bestowed by benevolent nature. Those who view it as the outcome of the development of a whole and healthy personality may have faith that it will emerge through benevolent nurture. Those who regard it as the manifestation of special mental processes may trust that it will be fostered through teaching people to think.

But those who require that creativity implies excellence, and assess it in terms of the capacity to produce something of original cultural value, are not likely to be so easily assured. They are likely to find that creative ability is no spontaneous emergence of inherent qualities; no special intellectual process; no gift – but a hard-earned prize. They are likely to discover that before the Gates of Excellence the High Gods have placed sweat – the sweat of labour – often mingled with the sweat of pain.

# References

Adler, A. (1927). *Practice and theory of individual psychology*. New York: Harcourt Brace & World.

(1935). The fundamental views of individual psychology. *International Journal of Individual Psychology, 1,* 5–8.

Agassie, J. (1985). The myth of the young genius. *Interchange, 16,* 51–60.

Albert, R. S. (1969). Genius: Present-day status of the concept and its implications for the study of creativity and giftedness. *American Psychologist, 24,* 743–753.

(1971). Cognitive development and parental loss among the gifted, and the creative. *Psychological Reports, 29,* 14–26.

(1975). Towards a behavioural definition of genius. *American Psychologist, 30,* 140–151.

(1978). Observations and suggestions regarding giftedness, familial influence and the attainment of eminence. *Gifted Child Quarterly, 22,* 201–211.

(1980). Family positions and the attainment of eminence: a study of special family positions and special family experiences. *Gifted Child Quarterly, 24,* 87–95.

(1983). Genius: Signs and outcomes. In R. S. Albert (Ed.), *Genius and eminence* (p. 45). Oxford: Pergamon Press.

Albert, R. S., & Runco, M. A. (1986). The achievement of eminence: A model based on a longitudinal study of exceptionally gifted boys and their families. In R. J. Sternberg & J. E. Davidson (Eds.), *Conceptions of giftedness* (pp. 332–367). Cambridge: Cambridge University Press.

Allport, G. W. (1961). *Pattern and growth in personality*. New York: Holt, Rinehart & Winston.

Altus, W. (1966). Birth order and its sequel. *Science, 151,* 44–48.

Amabile, T. M. (1983). *The social psychology of creativity*. New York: Springer-Verlag.

(1985). Motivation and creativity: Effects of motivational orientation on creative writers. *Journal of Personality and Social Psychology, 48,* 393–399.

Anderson, B. F. (1975). *Cognitive psychology*. New York: Academic Press.

Anderson, C. C., & Cropley, A. J. (1966). Some correlates of originality. *Australian Journal of Psychology, 18,* 218–227.

Anderson, J. R. (1985). *Cognitive psychology and its implications.* New York: Freeman.

Andreasen, N. C., & Canter, A. (1974). The creative writer: Psychiatric symptoms and family history. *Comprehensive Psychiatry, 5,* 123–131.

Ansbacher, H. L. (1971). Alfred Adler and humanistic psychology. *Journal of Humanistic Psychology, 11,* 53–63.

Apter, M. J. (1982). *The experience of motivation.* London: Academic Press.

Arieti, S. (1976). *Creativity: the magic synthesis.* New York: Basic Books.

Arlin, P. K. (1975). Cognitive development in adulthood: A fifth stage? *Development Psychology, 11,* 602–606.

Arnold, J. (1972). Creativity in engineering. In P. Smith (Ed.), *Creativity: An examination of the creative process* (pp. 33–46). Freeport: Books for Libraries Press. (Originally published 1959.)

Auden, W. H. (1956). *Selected essays.* London: Faber & Faber.

Austin, J. H. (1978). *Chase, chance, and creativity.* New York: Columbia University Press.

Babbage, C. (1969). *Passages from the life of a philosopher.* London: Kelley. (Originally published 1864.)

Bachtold, L. M., & Werner, E. E. (1970). Personality profiles of gifted women: Psychologists. *American Psychologist, 25,* 234–243.

(1973). Personality profiles of creative women. *Perceptual and Motor Skills, 36,* 311–319.

Bacon, F. (1980). Of marriage and single life. In T. S. Kane & L. J. Peters (Eds.), *Writing prose* (pp. 149–150). New York: Oxford University Press. (First published 1685.)

Bailin, S. (1984). Can there be creativity without creation? *Interchange, 15,* 13–22.

(1985). On originality. *Interchange, 16,* 6–13.

Barron, F. (1963). The needs for order and for disorder as motives in creative activity. In C. W. Taylor & F. Barron (Eds.), *Scientific creativity: Its recognition and development* (pp. 153–160). New York: Wiley.

(1968). *Creativity and personal freedom.* Princeton, NJ: D. van Nostrand.

(1988). Putting creativity to work. In R. J. Sternberg (Ed.), *The nature of creativity: Contemporary psychological perspectives* (pp. 76–98). Cambridge: Cambridge University Press.

Barron, F., & Harrington, D. M. (1981). Creativity, intelligence, and personality. *Annual Review of Psychology, 32,* 439–476.

Bastik, T. (1982). *Intuition: How we think and act.* Chichester: John Wiley.

Beard, G. (1874). *Legal responsibility in old age.* New York: Russel.

Beck, A. T., Sethi, B. B., & Tuthill, R. W. (1963). Childhood bereavement and adult depression. *Archives of General Psychiatry, 9,* 295–302.

Becker, G. (1983). The mad genius controversy. In R. S. Albert (Ed.), *Genius and eminence* (pp. 36–39). Oxford: Pergamon Press.

Beittel, K. R. (1964). On the relationships between art and general creativity: A biased history and projection of the partial conquest. *School Review, 72,* 272–288.

Bell, E. T. (1937). *Men of mathematics.* London: Gollancz.

Bellak, L. (1958). Creativity: Some random notes to a systematic consideration. *Journal of Projective Techniques, 22,* 363–380.

Belth, M. (1977). *The process of thinking.* New York: David McKay.

Berlyne, D. E. (1950). Novelty and curiosity as determinants of exploratory behaviour. *British Journal of Psychology, 41,* 68–80.

(1971). *Aesthetics and psychobiology.* New York: Appleton-Century-Crofts.

Berrington, H. (1983). Prime ministers and the search for love. In R. S. Albert (Ed.), *Genius and eminence* (pp. 358–373). Oxford: Pergamon Press.

Berry, C. (1981). The Nobel scientists and the origins of scientific achievement. *British Journal of Sociology, 32,* 381–391.

Binet, A., & Henri, V. (1896). La psychologie individuelle. *L'Année Psychologique, 2,* 411–465.

Blatt, S. J., & Stein, M. I. (1957). Some personality, value, and cognitive characteristics of the creative person. *American Psychologist, 12,* 406.

Bloom, B. S. (1963). Report on the creativity research by the examiners' office of the University of Chicago. In C. W. Taylor & F. Barron (Eds.), *Scientific creativity: Its recognition and development* (pp. 251–264). New York: Wiley.

Bloom, B. S., & Sosniak, L. A. (1981). Talent development vs schooling. *Educational Leadership, 15,* 86–94.

Bogen, J. E. (1969). The other side of the brain. *Bulletin of the Los Angeles Neurological Society, 34,* 73–105, 135–162.

Bogen, J. E., & Bogen, G. M. (1976). Creativity and the bisected brain. In A. Rothenberg & C. R. Hausman (Eds.), *The creativity question* (pp. 256–261). Durham, NC: Duke University Press.

Boismont, A. B. de (1853). *Hallucinations: The rational history of apparitions, visions, dreams, ecstasy, magnetism, and somnambulism.* Philadelphia: Lindsay & Blakiston.

Boring, E. G. (1957). *A history of experimental psychology.* New York: Appleton Century Crofts

Bowers, P. (1979). Hypnosis and creativity: The search for the missing link. *Journal of Abnormal Psychology, 88,* 564–572.

Bramwell, B. S. (1948). Galton's 'Hereditary genius' and three following generations since 1869. *Eugenics Review, 39,* 146–153.

Briskman, L. (1980). Creative product and creative process in science and art. *Inquiry, 23,* 83–106.

Brown, F. (1968). Bereavement and lack of a parent in childhood. In E. Miller (Ed.), *Foundations of child psychiatry* (pp. 437–455). Oxford: Pergamon Press.

Bruner, J. S. (1960). *The process of education.* Boston: Harvard University Press.

Bühler, K. (1918). *Die geistige Entwicklung des Kindes.* Jena: Fischer.

Bullock, A., & Stallybrass, O. (Eds.) (1977). *The Fontana dictionary of modern thought.* London: Collins.

Bullough, V., Bullough, B., & Mauro, M. (1981). History and creativity: Research problems and some possible solutions. *Journal of Creative Behavior, 15,* 102–116.

Bunge, M. (1967). *Scientific research* (Vol. 1). New York: Springer.

Bush, M. (1969). Psychoanalysis and scientific creativity. *Journal of the American Psychoanalytic Association, 17,* 136–191.

Callaway, W. R. (1969). A holistic conception of creativity and its relation to intelligence. *Gifted Child Quarterly, 13,* 237–241.

Campbell, D. T. (1960) Blind variation and selective retention in creative thought as in other knowledge processes. *Psychological Review, 67,* 380–400.

Cannon, W. B. (1976). The role of hunches in scientific thought. In A. Rothenberg & C. R. Housman (Eds.), *The creativity question* (pp. 63–69). Durham, NC: Duke University Press.

Cattell, J. McK. (1903). A statistical study of the eminent men. *Popular Science Monthly, 6,* 359–377.

Cattell, J. McK., & Brimhall, D. R. (1921). *American men of science.* Garrison: Science Press.

Cattell, R. B. (1950). The principal culture patterns discoverable in the syntal dimensions of existing nations. *Journal of Social Psychology, 32,* 215–253.

(1963). The personality and motivation of the researcher from measurements of contemporaries and from biography. In C. W. Taylor & F. Barron (Eds.), *Scientific creativity: Its recognition and development* (pp. 119–131). New York: Wiley.

(1971). *Abilities and their structure, growth and action.* Boston: Houghton Mifflin Co.

Cattell, R. B., & Butcher, H. J. (1972). The prediction, selection and cultivation of creativity. In H. J. Butcher & D. E. Lomax (Eds.), *Readings in human intelligence* (pp. 172–192). London: Methuen.

Cattell, R. B., & Drevdahl, J. E. (1955). A comparison of the personality profile of eminent researchers with that of eminent teachers and administrators. *British Journal of Psychology, 44,* 248–261.

Chall, J., & Mirsky, A. F. (Eds.) (1978). *Education and the brain.* Chicago: National Society for the Study of Education.

Chambers, J. A. (1964). Relating personality and biographical factors to scientific creativity. *Psychological Monographs: General and Applied, 78,* Whole, No. 584.

Charlesworth, W. R. (1976). Ethology of intelligence. In L. B. Resnick (Ed.), *The nature of intelligence* (pp. 147–168). Hillsdale, NJ: Erlbaum.

Chase, W. G., & Simon, H. A. (1973). The mind's eye in chess. In W. G. Chase (Ed.), *Visual information processing* (pp. 215–281). New York: Academic Press.

Chassel, L. M. (1916). Test for originality. *Journal of Educational Psychology, 7,* 317–329.

Chatterjea, R. G., & Mitra, A. (1976). A study of brainstorming. *Manas, 23,* 23–28.

Churchill, W. S. (1983). *My early life: A roving commission.* Glasgow: Collins. (Originally published 1930.)

Clark, B. (1979). *Growing up gifted.* Columbus, Ohio: Merrill.

Clark, C. H. (1958). *Brainstorming.* New York: Doubleday.

Clark, R. D., & Rice, G. A. (1982). Family constellations and eminence: The birth orders of Nobel Prize winners. *The Journal of Psychology, 110,* 281–287.

Clark, R. W. (1971). *Einstein: The life and times.* New York: World Publishing Co.

(1975). *The life of Bertrand Russell.* London: Jonathan Cape.

(1977). *Edison: The man who made the future.* London: MacDonald & James.

Clifford, P. I. (1958). Emotional contacts with the external world manifested by a selected group of highly creative chemists and mathematicians. *Perceptual and Motor Skills, 8,* 3–26.

Cocteau, J. (1954). The process of inspiration (B. Ghiselin, Trans.) In B. Ghiselin (Ed.), *The creative process: A symposium* (pp. 79–80). Berkeley: University of California Press.

Cofer, C. N., & Appley, M. H. (1964). *Motivation: Theory and research.* New York: Wiley.

Cohen, I. B. (1979). Einstein and Newton. In A. P. French (Ed.), *Einstein: A centenary volume* (pp. 40–42). London: Heinemann.

Cole, S. (1979). Age and scientific performance. *American Journal of Sociology, 84,* 958–977.

Coleridge, S. Taylor (1954). Prefatory note to 'Kubla Khan'. In B. Ghiselin (Ed.), *The creative process: A symposium* (pp. 83–84). Berkeley: University of California Press. (Written circa 1797.)

Corballis, M. C. (1980). Laterality and myth. *American Psychologist, 35,* 284–295.

Cox, C. M. (1926). *The early mental traits of three hundred geniuses.* (Vol. 2 of L. M. Terman's Genetic studies of genius.) Stanford: Stanford University Press.

Craik, K. (1943). *The nature of explanation.* Cambridge: Cambridge University Press.

Cropley, A. J. (1967). *Creativity.* London: Longman.

Cross, P. G., Cattell, R. B., & Butcher, H. J. (1967). The personality pattern of creative artists. *British Journal of Educational Psychology, 37,* 292–299.

Csikszentmihalyi, M. (1982). Toward a psychology of optimal experience. In L. Wheeler (Ed.), *Review of Personality and Social Psychology, 3,* 13–36.

(1988). Society, culture, and person: A systems view of creativity. In R. J. Sternberg (Ed.), *The nature of creativity: Contemporary psychological perspectives* (pp. 325–339). Cambridge: Cambridge University Press.

Curie, M. S. (1936). *Pierre Curie.* New York: MacMillan.

Darwin, F. (Ed.) (1929). *Autobiography of Charles Darwin*. London: Watts.

Dashiell, J. F. (1925). A quantitative demonstration of animal drive. *Journal of Comparative Psychology, 5*, 205–208.

Davis, R. A. (1954). Note on age and productive scholarship of a university faculty. *Journal of Applied Psychology, 38*, 318–319.

Dearborn, G. V. (1898). A study of imagination. *American Journal of Psychology, 5*, 183–190.

De Bono, E. (1980). *Teaching thinking*. Harmondsworth: Penguin.

Deci, E. L. (1975). *Intrinsic motivation*. New York: Plenum Press.

De Groot, A. D. (1965). *Thought and choice in chess*. The Hague: Mouton.

De Haan, R. F., & Havighurst, R. J. (1961). *Educating gifted children*. Chicago: University of Chicago Press.

Dellas, M., & Gaier, E. L. (1970). Identification of creativity. *Psychological Bulletin, 73*, 55–73.

Dennis, W. (1954). Bibliographies of eminent scientists. *Scientific Monthly, 79*, 180–183.

(1955). Variations in productivity among creative workers. *Scientific Monthly, 80*, 277–278.

(1956). Age and productivity among scientists. *Science, 123*, 724–725.

(1966). Creative productivity between the ages of 20 and 80 years. *Journal of Gerontology, 21*, 1–8.

De Quincey, T. (1950). *Confessions of an English opium-eater together with selections of the autobiography [1785–1803] of Thomas de Quincey* (E. Sackville-West Ed.). London: The Cresset Press.

Deutsch, J. A., & Deutsch, D. (1963). Attention: Some theoretical considerations. *Psychological Review, 70*, 80–90.

Dewey, J. (1910). *How to think*. Boston: Heath.

Dickinson, G. L. (1973). The Greek view of woman. In G. Tate (Ed.), *From discovery to style* (pp. 41–48). Cambridge, MA: Winthrop.

Dillon, J. T. (1982). Problem finding and solving. *Journal of Creative Behavior, 16*, 97–111.

Dirac, P. A. M. (1963). The evolution of the physicist's picture of nature. *Scientific American, 208*, 45–53.

Dreistadt, R. (1968). An analysis of the use of analogies and metaphors in science. *Journal of Psychology, 68*, 97–116.

(1969). The use of analogies and incubation in obtaining insights in creative problem solving. *Journal of Psychology, 71*, 159–175.

Drevdahl, J. E. (1956). Factors of importance for creativity. *Journal of Clinical Psychology, 12*, 21–26.

(1964). Some developmental and environmental factors in creativity. In C. W. Taylor (Ed.), *Widening horizons in creativity: The proceedings of the fifth Utah Creativity Research Conference* (pp. 170–202). New York: Wiley.

Drevdahl, J. E., & Cattell, R. B. (1958). Personality and creativity in artists and writers. *Journal of Clinical Psychology, 14*, 107–111.

Ducas, H., & Hoffman, B. (1979). *Albert Einstein: The human side.* Princeton: Princeton University Press.

Duncker, K. (1945). On problem solving. *Psychological Monographs, 58,* Whole: No. 270.

Dunnette, M. D., Campbell, J., & Jaastad, K. (1963). The effects of group participation on brainstorming effectiveness for two industrial samples. *Journal of Applied Psychology, 47,* 10–37.

Easterbrook, J. A. (1959). The effect of emotion on cue utilization and the organization of behavior. *Psychological Review, 66,* 183–201.

Edison, T. A. (1968). *The diary and sundry observations of Thomas Alva Edison* (D. D. Runes Ed.). New York: Greenwood Press. (First published 1948.)

Ehrenwald, J. (1984). *Anatomy of genius. Split brains and global minds.* New York: Human Sciences Press.

Ehrenzweig, A. (1962). Unconscious mental images in art and sciences. *Nature, 194,* 1008–1012.

Eiduson, B. T. (1962). *Scientists: Their psychological world.* New York: Basic Books.

Eindhoven, J. E., & Vinacke, W. E. (1952). Creative processes in painting. *Journal of General Psychology, 47,* 139–164.

Einstein, A. (1979a). Excerpts from 'Ideas and opinions' (1921). In A. P. French (Ed.), *Einstein: A centenary volume* (pp. 302–305). London: Heinemann. (Originally published in 1921.)

(1979b). *Autobiographical notes* (P. A. Schlipp Ed. & Trans.). La Salle: Open Court Publishing Co. (Originally published, 1949.)

Einstein, A., & Infeld, L. (1938). *The evolution of physics.* New York: Simon & Schuster.

Eisenman, R. (1987). Creativity, birth order, and risk taking. *Bulletin of the Psychonomic Society, 25,* 87–88.

Eisenstadt, J. M. (1978). Parental loss and genius. *American Psychologist, 33,* 211–223.

Elliot, J. M. (1964). Measuring creative abilities in public relations and in advertising work. In C. W. Taylor (Ed.), *Widening horizons in creativity: The proceedings of the fifth Utah Creativity Research Conference* (pp. 396–400). New York: Wiley.

Elliot, P. C. (1986). Right (or left) brain cognition, wrong metaphor for creative behaviour: It is prefrontal lobe volition that makes the (human/humane) difference in the release of creative potential. *Journal of Creative Behavior, 20,* 202–214.

Ellis, H. A. (1904). *A study of British genius.* London: Hurst & Blackwell.

Emery, O. B., & Csikszentmihalyi, M. (1982). The socialization effects of cultural role models in ontogenetic development and upward mobility. *Child Psychiatry and Human Development, 12,* 3–19.

Erikson, E. H. (1950). *Childhood and society.* New York: Norton.

Everitt, C. W. F. (1983). Maxwell's scientific creativity. In R. Aris, H. T. Davis, & R. H. Steuwer (Eds.), *Springs of scientific creativity* (pp. 71–141). Minneapolis: University of Minnesota Press.

Eysenck, M. W. (1984). *A handbook of cognitive psychology*. London: Lawrence Erlbaum Associates.

Feldman, D. H. (1984). A follow up of subjects scoring above 180 IQ in Terman's 'Genetic studies of genius'. *Exceptional Children, 50,* 518–523.

(1986). *Nature's gambit: Child prodigies and the development of human potential.* New York: Basic Books.

(1988). Creativity: Dreams, insights, and transformation. In R.J. Sternberg (Ed.), *The nature of creativity: Contemporary psychological perspectives* (pp. 271–297). Cambridge: Cambridge University Press.

Ferri, E. (1976). *Growing up in a one-parent family.* Slough: NFER Publishing Co.

Fischer, K. W., & Pipp, S. L. (1984). Development of the structure of unconscious thought. In K. S. Bowers & D. Meichenbaum (Eds.), *The unconscious reconsidered* (pp. 88–148). New York: Wiley.

Fitts, P. M., & Posner, M. I. (1967). *Human performance.* Belmont, CA: Brooks Cole.

Flanagan, D. (1972). Creativity in science. In P. Smith (Ed.), *Creativity: An examination of the creative process* (pp. 103–109). New York: Books for Libraries Press.

Flaubert, G. (1974) Letters to Louise Colet. In J. Hersey (Ed.), *The writer's craft* (pp. 322–342). New York: Knopf. (Written in 1851.)

Flescher, I. (1963). Anxiety and achievement of intellectually gifted and creatively gifted children. *Journal of Psychology, 56,* 251–268.

Freeman, J., Butcher, H. J., & Christie, T. (1971). *Creativity: A selective review of research* (2nd edn). London: Society for Research into Higher Education.

French, A. P. (Ed.) (1979). *Einstein: A centenary volume.* London: Heinemann.

Freud, A. (1937). *The ego and mechanisms of defense.* London: Hogarth.

Freud, S. (1973a). *The interpretation of dreams* (J. Strachey, Ed. & Trans.). The standard edition of the complete psychological works of Sigmund Freud (vols. 4 & 5). London: The Hogarth Press. (Originally published in 1900.)

(1973b). *Creative writers and daydreaming* (J. Strachey, Ed. & Trans.). The standard edition of the complete psychological works of Sigmund Freud (vol. 9, p. 143). London: The Hogarth Press. (Originally published in 1908.)

(1973c). *Leonardo da Vinci* (J. Strachey, Ed. & Trans.). The standard edition of the complete psychological works of Sigmund Freud (vol. 11, pp. 59–137). London: The Hogarth Press. (Originally published in 1910.)

(1973d). *23rd Introductory lecture on psychoanalysis* (J. Strachey, Ed. & Trans.). The standard edition of the complete psychological works of Sigmund Freud (vol. 16, pp. 358–377). London: The Hogarth Press. (Originally published in 1917.)

(1973e). *An autobiographical study* (J. Strachey, Ed. & Trans.). The standard edition of the complete psychological works of Sigmund Freud (vol. 20, pp. 7–74). London: The Hogarth Press. (Originally published in 1925.)

(1973f). *Dostoevski and parricide* (J. Strachey, Ed. & Trans.). The standard edition of the complete psychological works of Sigmund Freud (vol. 21, pp. 177–196). London: The Hogarth Press. (Originally published in 1928.)

Friedenthal, R. (1965). *Goethe, his life and times.* London: Weidenfeld & Nicolson.

Fromm, E. (1955). *The sane society.* New York: Rinehart.

Gallagher, J. J., & Courtright, R. D. (1986). The educational definition of giftedness and its policy implications. In R. J. Sternberg & J. E. Davidson (Eds.), *Conceptions of giftedness* (pp. 93–111). Cambridge: Cambridge University Press.

Galton, F. (1869). *Hereditary genius.* New York: Appleton.

Gardner, H. (1973). *The arts and human development.* New York: Wiley.

(1983). *Frames of mind: The theory of multiple intelligences.* New York: Basic Books.

Gardner, J. W. (1973). Facts and fancies about talent. In G. Tate (Ed.), *From discovery to style* (pp. 160–165). Cambridge, MA: Winthrop.

Garmezy, N., & Rutter, M. (Eds.) (1983). *Stress, coping and development in children.* New York: McGraw-Hill.

Gedo, J. E. (1972). On the psychology of genius. *International Journal of Psychoanalysis, 53,* 199–203.

(1983). *Portraits of the artist.* New York: The Guilford Press.

Gerard, R. W. (1954). The biological basis of imagination. In B. Ghiselin (Ed.), *The creative process: a symposium* (pp. 236–259). Berkeley: University of California Press.

Gerwin, D. G. (1974). Information processing, data inferences, and scientific generalization. *Behavioral Science, 19,* 314–325.

Getzels, J. W., & Csikszentmihalyi, M. (1975). From problem solving to problem finding. In I. A. Taylor & J. W. Getzels (Eds.), *Perspectives in creativity* (pp. 90–116). Chicago: Aldine.

Getzels, J. W., & Jackson, P. W. (1961). Family environment and cognitive style: a study of the sources of highly creative adolescents. *American Sociological Review, 26,* 351–359.

(1962). *Creativity and intelligence.* New York: Wiley.

(1963). The highly intelligent and the highly creative adolescent: A summary of some research findings. In C. W. Taylor & F. Barron (Eds.), *Scientific creativity: Its recognition and development* (pp. 161–172). New York: John Wiley.

Ghiselin, B. (Ed.) (1954). *The creative process: A symposium.* Berkeley: University of California Press.

(1963). The creative process and its relation to the identification of creative talent. In C. W. Taylor & F. Barron (Eds.), *Scientific creativity: Its recognition and development* (pp. 355–364). New York: John Wiley.

Gibbon, E. (1966) (G. Bonnard, Ed.). *Memoirs of my life.* London: Nelson. (Written in 1789.)

Gibson, C. R. (1970). *Heroes of the scientific world.* New York: Books for Libraries Press (Originally published, 1913.)

Gilhooly, K. J. (1982). *Thinking: Directed, undirected and creative.* London: Academic Press.

Gilligan, C. (1982). *In a different voice: Psychological theory and women's development.* Cambridge, MA: Harvard University Press.

Goertzel, M. G., Goertzel, V., & Goertzel, T. G. (1978). *Three hundred eminent personalities.* San Francisco: Jossey-Bass.

Goertzel, V., & Goertzel, M. G. (1962). *Cradles of eminence.* London: Constable.

Goldberg, S. (1983). Albert Einstein and the creative act: The case of special relativity. In R. Aris, H. T. Davis, & R. H. Steuwer (Eds.), *Springs of creativity* (pp. 232–253). Minneapolis: University of Minnesota Press.

Goldstein, K. (1939). *The organism: A holistic approach to biology derived from pathological data in man.* New York: American Book Co.

Gordon, W. J. J. (1961). *Synectics: The development of creative capacity.* New York: Harper.

Götz, K. O., & Götz, K. (1979). Personality characteristics of successful artists. *Perceptual and Motor Skills, 49,* 919–924.

Gough, H. G. (1964). Identifying the creative man. *Journal of Value Engineering, 2,* 5–12.

Gough, H. G., & Woodworth, D. G. (1960). Stylistic variations among professional research scientists. *Journal of Psychology, 49,* 87–98.

Gowan, J. C. (1972). *Development of the creative individual.* San Diego: Robert R. Knapp.

Gray, C. E. (1966). A measurement of creativity in Western civilization. *American Anthropologist, 68,* 1384–1417.

Greene, G. (1969). *Collected essays.* Harmondsworth: Penguin.

Gregory, J. (1965). Anterospective data following childhood loss of a parent. *Archives of General Psychiatry, 13,* 99–120.

Grubbs, H. A. (1968). *Paul Valéry.* New York: Twayne.

Gruber, H. E. (1974). *Darwin on man: A psychological study of creativity.* London: Wildwood House.

　　(1986). The self construction of the extraordinary. In R. J. Sternberg & J. E. Davidson (Eds.), *Conceptions of giftedness* (pp. 247–263). Cambridge: Cambridge University Press.

Gruber, H. E., & Davis, S. N. (1988). Inching our way up Mount Olympus: The evolving-systems approach to creative thinking. In R. J. Sternberg (Ed.), *The nature of creativity: Contemporary psychological perspectives* (pp. 243–270). Cambridge: Cambridge University Press.

Guilford, J. P. (1950). Creativity. *American Psychologist, 5,* 444–454.

　　(1963). Intellectual resources and their values as seen by scientists. In C. W. Taylor & F. Barron (Eds.), *Scientific creativity: its recognition and development* (pp. 101–118). New York: Wiley.

　　(1964). Progress in the discovery of intellectual factors. In C. W. Taylor (Ed.), *Widening horizons in creativity: the proceedings of the fifth Utah Creativity Research Conference* (pp. 261–297). New York: Wiley.

　　(1967). *The nature of human intelligence.* New York: McGraw-Hill.

　　(1970). Creativity: Retrospect and prospect. *Journal of Creative Behavior, 4,* 149–168.

(1971). Some misconceptions regarding measurement of creative talents. *Journal of Creative Behavior, 5,* 77–87.

(1975). Creativity: a quarter century of progress. In I. A. Taylor & J. W. Getzels (Eds.), *Perspectives in creativity* (pp. 37–59). Chicago: Aldine Publishing Co.

(1976). Factor analysis, intellect and creativity. In A. Rothenberg & C. R. Hausman (Eds.), *The creativity question* (pp. 200–208). Durham, NC: Duke University Press.

(1982). Transformation abilities and functions. *Journal of Creative Behavior, 17,* 75–82.

Hadamard, J. S. (1945). *The psychology of invention in the mathematical field.* Princeton, NJ: Princeton University Press.

Haefele, J. W. (1962). *Creativity and innovation.* New York: Reinhold.

Haensley, P., Reynolds, C. R., & Nash, W. R. (1986). Giftedness: Coalescence, context, conflict, and commitment. In R. J. Sternberg & J. E. Davidson (Eds.), *Conceptions of giftedness* (pp. 128–148). Cambridge: Cambridge University Press.

Halacy, D. (1970). *Charles Babbage: Father of the computer.* New York: Crowell-Collier.

Hamilton, E. (1960). The lessons of the past. In R. Thruelson & J. Kobler (Eds.), *Adventures of the mind* (pp. 69–80). London: Gollancz.

Hammer, E. F. (1964). Creativity and feminine ingredients in young male artists. *Perceptual and Motor Skills, 9,* 414.

Hammer, M., & Zubin, J. (1968). Evolution, culture, and psychopathology. *Journal of General Psychology, 78,* 154–175.

Hankoff, L. D. (1975). The hero as madman. *Journal of the History of the Behavioral Sciences, 11,* 315–333.

Hardy, G. H. (1969). *A mathematician's apology.* Cambridge: Cambridge University Press.

Harlow, H. F. (1953). Mice, monkeys, men and motives. *Psychological Review, 60,* 23–32.

Harmon, L. R. (1963). The development of a criterion of scientific competence. In C. W. Taylor & F. Barron (Eds.), *Scientific creativity: Its recognition and development* (pp. 44–52). New York: Wiley.

Hartman, E. (1975). Dreams and other hallucinations: An approach to the underlying mechanism. In R. K. Siegel & L. J. West. *Hallucinations: Behavior, experience, and theory* (chap. 3). New York: Wiley.

Hathaway, S. R., & Monachesi, E. G. (1963). *Adolescent personality and behavior.* Minneapolis: University of Minnesota Press.

Haviland, J. M. (1984). Thinking and feeling in Woolf's writing: from childhood to adulthood. In C. E. Izard, J. Kagan, & R. B. Zajonc (Eds.), *Emotions, cognition, and behavior* (515–546). Cambridge: Cambridge University Press.

Hayward, F. H. (1974). *Professionalism and originality.* New York: Arno Press.

Hellman, L. (1969). *An unfinished woman.* Boston: Little Brown.

Helmholz, H. von (1896). *Vorträge und Reden*. Braunschweig: Vieweg und Sohn.

Helson, R. (1967). Sex differences in creative style. *Journal of Personality, 35,* 214–233.

——— (1971). Women mathematicians and the creative personality. *Journal of Consulting and Clinical Psychology, 36,* 210–211; 217–220.

Helson, R., & Crutchfield, R. S. (1970). Creative types in mathematics. *Journal of Personality, 38,* 177–197.

Hendrick, I. (1943). The discussion of the 'instinct to master'. *Psychoanalytic Quarterly, 12,* 561–565.

Henle, M. (1974). The snail beneath the shell. In S. Rosner & L. E. Abt (Eds.), *Essays in creativity* (pp. 23–44). Croton-on-Hudson, NY: North River Press.

Hennessey, B. A., & Amabile, T. M. (1988). The conditions of creativity. In R. J. Sternberg (Ed.), *The nature of creativity: Contemporary psychological perspectives* (pp. 1–38). Cambridge: Cambridge University Press.

Henry, J. P., & Meehan, J. P. (1981). Psychosocial stimuli, physiological specificity, and cardiovascular disease. In H. Weiner, M. A. Hofer & A. J. Stunkard (Eds.), *Brain, behavior and bodily disease* (pp. 305–333). New York: Raven Press.

Herr, E. L., Moore, G. D., & Hasen, J. S. (1965). Creativity, intelligence, and values: A study of relationships. *Exceptional Children, 32,* 114–115.

Hershman, D. J. & Lieb, J. (1988). *The key to genius*. New York: Prometheus Books.

Herzberg, A. (1929). *Psychology of philosophers*. New York: Harcourt Brace.

Hilgard, E. R. (1962). Impulsive versus realistic thinking: An examination of the distinction between primary and secondary processes in thought. *Psychological Bulletin, 59,* 477–488.

Hill, J. C. (1976). The unconscious and the scientific method. *Reiss Davis Clinical Bulletin, 13,* 45–48.

Hobbes, T. (1969). *Leviathan*. Oxford: Collins. (Originally published in 1651.)

Hocevar, D. (1981). Measurement of creativity: Review and critique. *Journal of Personality Assessment, 45,* 450–464.

Hock, A. (1960). *Reason and genius: Studies in their origin*. Connecticut: Greenwood Press.

Hodgson, J. W., & Fischer, J. L. (1979). Sex differences in identity and intimacy development in college youth. *Journal of Youth and Adolescence, 8,* 37–49.

Hoelscher, T. J., Klinger, E., & Barta, S. G. (1981). Incorporation of concern and nonconcern related verbal stimuli into dream content. *Journal of Abnormal Psychology, 90,* 88–91.

Hoffman, B. (1972). *Albert Einstein: Creator and rebel*. New York: Plume.

Hogan, P. (1975). *Creativity in the family* (Part 2 of Creative Psychiatry). New York: Geigy Pharmaceuticals.

Holden, C. (1987). Creativity and the troubled mind. *Psychology Today, 21,* 9–10.

Hollingdale, R. (1965). *Nietzsche, the man and his philosophy.* Baton Rouge: Louisiana State University Press.

Holt, R. R. (1966). Measuring libidinal and aggressive motives and their controls by means of the Rorschach test. In D. Levine (Ed.), *Nebraska symposium on motivation* (pp. 1–47). Lincoln: University of Nebraska Press.

(1967). The development of the primary process. In R. R. Holt (Ed.), *Motives and thought: Psychoanalytic essays in honour of David Rapaport* (pp. 345–383). New York: Universities Press.

Holton, G. (1962). *Introduction to concepts and theories in physical science.* Reading, MA: Addison Wesley.

(1971). On trying to understand scientific genius. *The American Scholar, 41,* 95–110.

(1986). *The advancement of science and its burdens.* Cambridge: Cambridge University Press.

Horn, J. L., & Donaldson, G. (1977). Faith is not enough: A response to the Baltes-Schaie claim that intelligence does not wane. *American Psychologist, 32,* 369–373.

Horney, K. (1937). *Neurotic personality of our times.* New York: Norton.

Houssay, B. (1961). My struggle for science. *World Health, 36,* 36.

Howe, M. J. A. (1982). Biographical evidence and the development of outstanding individuals. *American Psychologist, 37,* 1071–1081.

Hudson, L. (1970). The question of creativity. In P. E. Vernon (Ed.), *Creativity: Selected readings* (pp. 217–234). Harmondsworth: Penguin.

(1975). *Human beings: The psychology of human experience.* New York: Anchor Press.

Huesmann, L. R., & Cheng, C. M. (1973). A theory of mathematical functions. *Psychological Review, 80,* 125–138.

Hutt, C. (1972). *Male and female.* Harmondsworth: Penguin.

Illingworth, R. S., & Illingworth, C. M. (1969). *Lessons from childhood: Some aspects of early life of unusual men and women.* Edinburgh: Livingstone.

Jackson, N. E., & Butterfield, E. C. (1986). A conception of giftedness designed to promote research. In R. J. Sternberg & J. E. Davidson (Eds.), *Conceptions of giftedness* (pp. 151–181). Cambridge: Cambridge University Press.

Jackson, P. W., & Messick, S. (1973). The person, the product and the response: Conceptual problems in the assessment of creativity. In M. Bloomberg (Ed.), *Creativity: Theory and research* (pp. 339–356). Connecticut: College and University Press.

James, W. (1890). *Principles of psychology* (vols. 1 & 2). London: Macmillan.

Jarvik, L. F., & Chadwick, S. B. (1973). Schizophrenia and survival. In M. Hammer, K. Salzinger & S. Sutton (Eds.), *Psychopathology* (pp. 57–73). New York: Wiley.

Jewkes, J., Sawers, D., & Stillerman, R. (1958). *The sources of invention.* London: Macmillan.

John, E. R., & Schwartz, E. L. (1978). The neurophysiology of information processing and cognition. *Annual Review of Psychology, 29,* 1–29.

Johnson, D. M. (1955). *The psychology of thought and judgment.* New York: Harper & Row.

Johnson-Laird, P. N. (1983). *Mental models.* Cambridge: Cambridge University Press.

  (1987). Reasoning, imagining and creating. *Bulletin of the British Psychological Society, 40,* 121–129.

Jones, E. (1953). *Sigmund Freud: His life and work* (vol. 1). New York: Basic Books.

Juda, A. (1949). The relationship between highest mental capacity and psychic abnormalities. *American Journal of Psychiatry, 106,* 296–307.

Kacerguis, M. A., & Adams, G. R. (1980). Erikson stage resolution: The relationship between identity and intimacy. *Journal of Youth and Adolescence, 9,* 117–126.

Kahneman, D. (1973). *Attention and effort.* Englewood Cliffs, NJ: Prentice Hall.

Kant, I. (1952). *The critique of judgment* (J. C. Meredith, Trans.). Oxford: Oxford University Press.

Karlsson, J. L. (1970). Genetic association of giftedness and creativity with schizophrenia. *Hereditas, 66,* 177–182.

  (1978). *Inheritance of creative intelligence.* Chicago: Nelson-Hall.

Kenmare, D. (1960). *The nature of genius.* London: Peter Owen.

Klinger, E. (1978). Modes of normal conscious flow. In K. S. Pope & J. L. Singer (Eds.), *The stream of consciousness* (pp. 225–258). New York: Plenum Press.

Klinger, E., Barta, S. G., & Maxheimer, M. E. (1980). Mathematical correlates of thought content frequency and commitment. *Journal of Personality and Social Psychology, 39,* 1222–1237.

Koch, S. (1981). The nature and limits of psychological knowledge: lessons of a century qua 'Science'. *American Psychologist, 36,* 251–269.

Koestler, A. (1964). *The act of creation.* New York: Macmillan.

  (1986). *The sleepwalkers.* Harmondsworth: Penguin. (Originally published 1959.)

Kretchmer, E. (1931). *The psychology of men of genius.* London: Kegan Paul.

Kris, E. (1952). *Psychoanalytic explorations in art.* New York: Wiley.

Kroeber, A. L. (1944). *Configurations of cultural growth.* Berkeley: University of California Press.

Kubie, L. S. (1958). *Neurotic distortion of the creative process.* Kansas: Kansas University Press.

Kuhn, T. S. (1970). *The structure of scientific revolutions.* Chicago: University of Chicago Press.

Kuniyoshi, Y. (1954). East to west. In B. Ghiselin (Ed.), *The creative process: A symposium* (pp. 54–55). Berkeley: University of California Press.

Langley, P., & Jones, R. (1988). A computational model of scientific insight. In R. J. Sternberg (Ed.), *The nature of creativity: Contemporary psychological perspectives* (pp. 177–201). Cambridge: Cambridge University Press.

Langley, P., Simon, H. A., Bradshaw, G. L., & Zytkow, J. M. (1987). *Scientific discovery: Computational explorations of the creative process.* Cambridge, MA: MIT Press.

Lavie, P., & Tzischinsky, O. (1985). Cognitive asymmetry and dreaming: Lack of relationship. *American Journal of Psychology, 98,* 353–361.

La Voie, J. C. (1976). Ego identity formation in middle adolescence. *Journal of Youth and Adolescence, 5,* 371–385.

Lazarus, R. S. (1974). Cognitive and coping processes in emotion. In B. Weiner (Ed.), *Cognitive views of human motivation* (pp. 21–33). New York: Academic Press.

Lehman, H. C. (1947). National differences in creativity. *American Journal of Sociology, 52,* 475–488.

(1953). *Age and achievement.* Princeton: Princeton University Press.

Lehman, H. C., & Witty, P. A. (1931). Scientific eminence and church membership. *Scientific Monthly, 33,* 544–549.

Lenat, D. B. (1983). The role of heuristics in learning by dicovery: Three case studies. In R. S. Michalsky, J. G. Carbonell, & T. M. Mitchell (Eds.), *Machine learning: An artificial intelligence approach* (pp. 243–306). Los Altos, CA: Morgan Kaufman.

Levine, S. (1983). A psychological approach to the ontogeny of coping. In N. Garmezy & M. Rutter (Eds.), *Stress, coping and development in children* (pp. 107–131). New York: McGraw-Hill.

Levy, J., Trevarthen, C., & Sperry, R. W. (1972). Perception of bilateral chimeric figures following hemisphere deconnection. *Brain, 95,* 61–78.

Lewin, I., & Glaubman, H. (1975). The effects of REM deprivation: Is it detrimental, beneficial or neutral? *Psychophysiology, 12,* 349–353.

Lewin, K. (1935). *A dynamic theory of personality.* New York: McGraw-Hill.

Lichtenstein, P. E. (1971). Genius as productive neurosis. *The Psychological Record, 21,* 151–164

Lombroso, C. (1895). *The man of genius.* New York: Charles Scribner's Sons.

Lowell, A. (1954). The process of making poetry. In B. Ghiselin (Ed.), *The creative process: A symposium* (pp. 110–112). Berkeley: University of California Press.

Luchins, A. S. (1942). Mechanization in problem solving behavior. *Psychological Monographs, 54,* Whole No. 248.

Lundberg, U., & Frankenhauser, M. (1978). Psychophysiological reactions to noise as modified by personal control over stimulus intensity. *Biological Psychology, 6,* 51–59.

Luria, A. R. (1984). *The working brain: an introduction to neuropsychology* (B. Haigh, Trans.). Harmondsworth: Penguin. (Originally published, 1973.)

MacDonald, D. K. C. (1964). *Faraday, Maxwell and Kelvin.* London: Heinemann.

MacKinnon, D. W. (1961). Fostering creativity in students of engineering. *Journal of Engineering Education, 52,* 129–142.

(1962a). The nature and nurture of creative talent. *American Psychologist, 17,* 484–495.

(1962b). The personality correlates of creativity: A study of American architects. In Nielsen, G. S. (Ed.), *Proceedings of the fourteenth international congress on applied psychology.* Copenhagen: Munksgaard (vol. 2, 11–39).

(1965). Personality and the realization of creative potential. *American Psychologist, 29,* 273–281.

(1978). *In search of human effectiveness.* New York: Creative Education Foundation.

(1983). The highly effective individual. In R. S. Albert (Ed.), *Genius and eminence.* Oxford: Pergamon Press. (Originally published in 1960)

Mackworth, N. H. (1965). Originality. *American Psychologist, 20,* 51–66.

Maddi, S. R. (1965). Motivational aspects of creativity. *Journal of Personality, 33,* 330–347.

Maddi, S. R., & Berne, N. (1964). Novelty of productions and desire for novelty as active and passive forms of the need for variety. *Journal of Personality, 32,* 270–277.

Maharshi, M. Y. (1966). *The science of being and art of living.* Los Angeles: International SRM Publications.

Maier, N. R. F. (1931). Reasoning in humans. The solution of a problem and its appearance in consciousness. *Journal of Comparative Psychology, 11,* 181–194.

Maier, N. R. F., & Burke, R. J. (1967). Influence of timing of hints on their effectiveness in problem solving. *Psychological Reports, 20,* 3–8.

Manchester, W. (1983). *The last lion: Winston Spencer Churchill – Visions of glory.* London: Michael Joseph.

Mansfield, R. S., & Busse, T. V. (1981). *The psychology of creativity and discovery.* Chicago: Nelson Hall.

Marcia, J. E., & Friedman, M. F. (1970). Ego-identity status in college women. *Journal of Personality, 38,* 149–263.

Marks, L. E. (1984). Synaesthesia and the arts. In W. R. Crozier & A. J. Chapman (Eds.), *Cognitive processes in perception of art* (pp. 427–447). Amsterdam: Elsevier.

Martindale, C. (1981). *Cognition and consciousness.* Homewood, IL: The Dorsey Press.

Maslow, A. (1954). *Motivation and personality.* New York: Harper.

(1967). The creative attitude. In R. L. Mooney & T. A. Rasik (Eds.), *Explorations in creativity* (pp. 43–57). New York: Harper & Row.

(1968). *Toward a psychology of being* (2nd edn). New York: Van Nostrand, Reinhold.

(1972). A holistic approach to creativity. In C. W. Taylor (Ed.), *Climate for creativity: Research Conference on Creativity* (pp. 287–293). New York: Pergamon Press.

(1976). Creativity in self-actualizing people. In A. Rothenberg & C. R. Hausman (Eds.), *The creativity question* (pp. 86–92). Durham NC: Duke University Press.

Maugham, S. (1958). *Points of view.* London: Heinemann.

Mayr, E. (1970). *Populations, species, and evolution.* Cambridge, MA: Harvard University Press.

McAdams, D. P., & Bryant, F. B. (1987). Intimacy motivation and subjective mental health in a nationwide sample. *Journal of Personality, 55,* 395–413.

McClelland, D. C. (1961). *The achieving society.* New York: Van Nostrand.

(1963). An aspect of scientific performance. In C. W. Taylor & F. Barron (Eds.), *Scientific creativity: Its recognition and development* (pp. 184–192). New York: Wiley.

McCurdy, H. G. (1957). The childhood patterns of genius. *Journal of the Elisha Mitchell Science Society, 73,* 448–462.

McGrath, J. E. (1970). *Social and psychological factors in stress.* New York: Holt, Rinehart & Winston.

McKellar, P. (1957). *Imagination and thinking.* New York: Basic Books.

McNeil, T. (1971). Prebirth and postbirth influence on the relationship between creative ability and recorded mental illness. *Journal of Personality, 39,* 391–406.

Mednick, S. A. (1962). The associative basis of the creative process. *Psychological Review, 69,* 220–232.

Mednick, S. A., & Mednick, M. T. (1964). An associative interpretation of the creative process. In C. W. Taylor (Ed.), *Widening horizons in creativity: the proceedings of the fifth Utah Creativity Research Conference* (pp. 54–68). New York: John Wiley.

Merrifield, P. R., Gardner, S. F., & Cox, A. B. (1964). *Aptitudes and personality measures related to creativity in seventh-grade children.* Reports of the Psychological Laboratories of the University of Southern California, No. 28.

Merrifield, P. R., Guilford, J. P., Christensen, P. R., & Frick, J. W. (1962). The role of intellectual factors in problem solving. *Psychological Monographs, 76,* (Whole No. 529).

Merton, R. K. (1968). The Matthew effect in science. *Science, 159,* 56–63.

(1973). *The sociology of science.* Chicago: University of Chicago Press.

Mohan, J. & Tiwana, M. (1987). Personality and alienation of creative writers: A brief report. *Personality and Individual Differences, 8,* 449.

Moles, A. (1968). *Information theory and esthetic perception* (J. E. Cohen, Trans.). Urbana: University of Illinois Press.

Montessori, M. (1912). *The Montessori method.* New York: Frederick A. Stokes.

Moszkowski, A. (1970). *Conversations with Einstein* (H. L. Brose, Trans.). New York: Horizon Press.

Motley, A. (1987). What I meant to say. *Psychology Today, 21,* 25–28.

Moulin, L. (1955). The Nobel Prizes for the sciences from 1901–1950: An essay in sociological analysis. *British Journal of Sociology, 6,* 246–263.

Murphy, G. (1958). The creative eras. In G. Murphy (Ed.), *Human potentialities* (pp. 142–157). New York: Basic Books.

Murray, H. A. (1938). *Explorations in personality.* New York: Oxford University Press.

Murray, H. A., & Kluckhohn, C. (1953). Outline of a conception of personality. In C. Kluckhohn, H. A. Murray, & D. Schneider (Eds.), *Personality in nature, society and culture* (2nd edn, pp. 3–49). New York: Knopf.

Myden, W. (1959). Interpretation and evaluation of certain personality characteristics involved in creative production. *Perceptual and Motor Skills, 9,* 139–158.

Neruda, P. (1977). *Memoirs.* New York: Farrar, Straus, Giroux.

Newell, A. (1973). Productive systems: Models of control structures. In W.C. Chase (Ed.), *Visual information processing* (pp. 463–526). New York: Academic Press.

Newell, A., Shaw, J. C., & Simon, H. A. (1962). The process of creative thinking. In H. Gruber, G. Terrel & M. Wertheimer (Eds.), *Contemporary approaches to creative thinking* (pp. 43–62). New York: Atherton Press.

Nicholls, J. G. (1972a). Some effects of testing procedures on divergent thinking. *Child Development, 42,* 1647–1651.

(1972b). Creativity in the person who will never produce anything original or useful. *American Psychologist, 27,* 717–727.

Nichols, R. C. (1964). Parental attitudes of mothers of intelligent adolescents and creativity of their children. *Child Development, 32,* 502–510.

(1967). The origin and development of talent. *Phi Delta Kappa,* June, 492–495.

Nichols, R. C., & Holland, J. L. (1963). *Prediction of the first year college performance of high aptitude children.* Minneapolis: Center for Continuation Study.

Nicolson, H. (1947). The health of authors. *Lancet, 2,* 709–714.

Nietzsche, F. (1954). Composition of 'Thus spake Zarathustra'. In B. Ghiselin (Ed.), *The creative process: A symposium* (pp. 208–211). Berkeley: University of California Press.

Nisbet, J. F. (1912). *The insanity of genius: And the general inequality of human faculty physiologically considered.* London: Stanley Paul.

Nissen, H. W. (1930). A study of exploratory behavior in the white rat by means of the obstruction method. *Journal of Genetic Psychology, 37,* 361–376.

Noller, R. B., & Parnes, S. J. (1972). Applied creativity: The creative studies project (Part 3). *Journal of Creative Behavior, 6,* 275–294.

Norman, D. A. (1968). Toward a theory of memory and attention. *Psychological Review, 75,* 522–536.

Noy, P. (1969). A revision of the psychoanalytic theory of the primary process. *International Journal of Psychoanalysis, 50,* 155–178.

Oden, M. (1968). A 40-year follow up of giftedness: Fulfillment and unfulfillment. *Genetic Psychology Monographs, 77,* 71–74, 78–86.

Ohlsson, S. (1984). Restructuring revisited. *Scandinavian Journal of Psychology, 25,* 65–78; 117–129.

Olton, R. M. (1979). Experimental studies of incubation: Searching for the elusive. *Journal of Creative Behavior, 13,* 9–23.

Oppenheimer, J. R. (1956). Analogy in science. *American Psychologist, 11,* 127–135.

Ornstein, R. E. (1972). *The psychology of consciousness.* New York: Harcourt Brace Jovanovich.

Orwell, G. (1957). *Selected essays.* New York: Doubleday Anchor.

Osborn, A. F. (1953). *Applied imagination.* New York: Charles Scribner's Sons.

Pais, A. (1979). Einstein, Newton, and success. In A. P. French (Ed.), *Einstein: A centenary volume* (pp. 35–37). London: Heinemann.

Parnes, S. J. (1967a). *Creative behavior guidebook.* New York: Scribner.

(1967b). *Creative behavior workbook.* New York: Scribner.

Patrick, C. (1935). Creative thought in poets. *Archives of Psychology, 26,* 1–74.

(1937). Creative thought in artists. *Journal of Psychology, 5,* 35–73.

Pearson, K. (1914). *Life, letters and labours of Francis Galton.* Cambridge: Cambridge University Press.

Peck, R. F. (1958). What makes a man creative? *Personnel, 35,* 18–23.

Perkins, D. N. (1981). *The mind's best work.* Cambridge MA: Harvard University Press.

(1983). Novel remote analogies seldom contribute to discovery. *Journal of Creative Behavior, 17,* 223–239.

(1985). Reasoning as imagination. *Interchange, 16,* 14–26.

(1988). The possibility of invention. In R. J. Sternberg (Ed.), *The nature of creativity: Contemporary psychological perspectives* (pp. 362–385). Cambridge: Cambridge University Press.

Pezdek, K. (1987). Television comprehension as an example of applied research in cognitive psychology. In D. E. Berger, K. Pezdek, & W. P. Banks. *Applications of cognitive psychology* (pp. 3–16). Hillsdale NJ: Erlbaum.

Piers, E. V., Daniels, J. M., & Quackenbush, J. F. (1960). The identification of creativity in adolescents. *Journal of Educational Psychology, 51,* 346–351.

Pine, F. (1959). Thematic drive content and creativity. *Journal of Personality, 27,* 136–151.

Planck, M. (1949). *Scientific autobiography and other papers* (F. Gaynor, Trans.). New York: Philosophical Library.

Plato (circa 300 BC/1976). Inspiration. In A. Rothenberg & C. R. Hausman (Eds.), *Aspects of consciousness* (vol. 1, pp. 67–89). London: Academic Press.

Podhoretz, N. (1967). *Making it.* New York: Random House.

Poincaré, H. (1908/1954). Mathematical creation. In B. Ghiselin (Ed.), *The creative process: A symposium* (pp. 22–31). Berkeley: University of California Press.

(1913). *The foundations of science.* New York: Science Press.

Polanyi, M. (1964). *Personal knowledge*. New York: Harper & Row.

Pope, K. S. (1978). How gender, solitude, and posture influence the stream of consciousness. In K. S. Pope & J. L. Singer (Eds.), *The stream of consciousness* (pp. 259–299). New York: Plenum Press.

Popper, K. R. (1972). *Objective knowledge*. Oxford: Oxford University Press.

Posner, M. I., & McLeod, P. (1982). Information processing models – in search of elementary operations. *Annual Review of Psychology, 33,* 477–514.

Prentky, R. A. (1980). *Creativity and psychopathology: A neurocognitive perspective.* New York: Praeger.

Prince, G. M. (1970). *The practice of creativity.* New York: Harper.

Rank, O. (1945). *Will therapy and truth and reality.* New York: Alfred Knopf.
   (1960). *Art and artist* (C. F. Atkinson, Trans.). New York: Knopf. (Originally published 1932.)

Rapaport, D. (1950). On the psychoanalytic theory of thinking. *International Journal of Psychoanalysis, 31,* 161–170.

Raskin, E. (1936). Comparison of scientific and literary ability: a biographical study of eminent scientists and men of letters of the nineteenth century. *Journal of Abnormal and Social Psychology, 31,* 20–35.

Reason, J. (1979). Action not as planned. In G. Underwood & R. Stevens (Eds.), *Aspects of consciousness* (vol. 1, pp. 67–89). London: Academic Press.
   (1984). Absent mindedness and cognitive control. In J. E. Harris & P. E. Morris (Eds.), *Everyday memory, actions and absent mindedness* (pp. 111–132). London: Academic Press.

Reason, J., & Lucas, D. (1984). Using cognitive diaries to investigate naturally occurring memory blocks. In J. E. Harris & P. E. Morris (Eds.), *Everyday memory actions and absent mindedness* (pp. 51–70). London: Academic Press.

Renzulli, J. S. (1979). The enrichment triad model: a guide for developing defensible programs for the gifted and talented. In J. C. Gowan, J. Khatena, & E. P. Torrance (Eds.), *Educating the ablest* (pp. 111–127). New York: Peacock.

Renzulli, J. S., Owen, S. V., & Callahan, C. M. (1974). Fluency, flexibility and originality as a function of group size. *Journal of Creative Behavior, 8,* 107–113.

Richards, R. L. (1981). Relationships between creativity and psychopathology: An evaluation and interpretation of the evidence. *Genetic Psychological Monographs, 103,* 261–324.

Richards, R. L., Kinney, D. K., Benet, M., & Merzel, A. P. (1988). Assessing everyday creativity: Characteristics of the lifetime creativity scales and validation with three large samples. *Journal of Personality and Social Psychology, 54,* 476–485.

Roe, A. (1946). The personality of artists. *Educational and Psychological Measurement, 6,* 401–408.
   (1951a). A psychological study of eminent biologists. *Psychological Monographs: General & Applied, 65,* Whole: No. 331.

(1951b). A psychological study of physical scientists. *Genetic Psychology Monographs, 43,* 121–239.

(1953). A psychological study of eminent psychologists and anthropologists, and a comparison with biological and physical scientists. *Psychological Monographs: General and Applied, 67,* Whole: No. 352.

(1965). Changes in scientific activities with age. *Science, 150,* 313–318.

(1970). A psychologist examines sixty-four eminent scientists. In P. E. Vernon (Ed.), *Creativity: Selected readings* (pp. 23–51). Harmondsworth: Penguin.

Rogers, C. R. (1959). A theory of therapy, personality, and interpersonal relationships, as developed in the client-centered framework. In S. Koch (Ed.), *Psychology: a study of a science* (vol. 3, pp. 184–256). New York: McGraw-Hill.

(1976). Toward a theory of creativity. In A. Rothenberg & C. R. Hausman (Eds.), *The creativity question* (p. 296). Durham, NC: Duke University Press. (Originally published in 1954.)

Rokeach, M. (1965). In pursuit of the creative process. In G. A. Steiner (Ed.), *The creative organization* (pp. 66–88). Chicago: University of Chicago Press.

Rosegrant, J. (1982). Primary process patterning in college students' inkblot responses. *Journal of Personality Assessment, 46,* 578–581.

Ross, E. D., & Mesulam, M. M. (1979). Dominant language functions of the right hemisphere. *Archives of Neurology, 36,* 144–148.

Rossman, B. B., & Horn, J. J. (1972). Cognitive, motivational and temperamental indicants of creativity and intelligence. *Journal of Educational Measurement, 9,* 265–286.

Rossman, J. (1931). *The psychology of the inventor: A study of the patentee.* Washington: The Inventor's Publishing Co.

Rothenberg, A. (1976). The process of Janusian thinking. In A. Rothenberg & C. R. Hausman (Eds.), *The creativity question* (pp. 311–327). Durham, NC: Duke University Press.

(1986). Artistic creation as stimulated by superimposed versus combined-composite visual images. *Journal of Personality and Social Psychology, 50,* 370–381.

(1987). Einstein, Bohr, and creative thinking in science. *History of Science, 25,* 147–166.

Rothenberg, A., & Greenberg, B. (1974). *The index of scientific writings on creativity: Creative men and women.* Hamden, CT: Anchor Books.

Rousseau, J. J. (1957). *Emile.* London: Dent. (Originally published in 1762.)

Royce, J. R. (1957). Toward the advancement of theoretical psychology. *Psychological Reports, 3,* 401–410.

Rubin, D. C., & Kozin, M. (1984). Vivid memories. *Cognition, 16,* 81–95.

Russell, B. (1967). *The autobiography of Bertrand Russell.* London: Allen & Unwin.

Rutter, M. (1983). Stress, coping, and development. In N. Garmezy & M. Rutter (Eds.), *Stress, coping and development in children* (pp. 1–41). New York: McGraw-Hill.

Ryle, G. (1982). *On thinking.* Oxford: Basil Blackwell.

Samuels, M., & Samuels, N. (1975). *Seeing with the mind's eye*. New York: Random House.

Sarnoff, D. P. (1962). *Personality dynamics and development*. New York: Wiley.

Sarnoff, D. P., & Cole, H. P. (1983). Creativity and personal growth. *Journal of Creative Behavior, 17,* 95–102.

Schachtel, E. G. (1959). *Metamorphosis*. New York: Basic Books.

(1973). Perception as creative experience. In M. Bloomberg (Ed.), *Creativity: Theory and research* (pp. 298–324). New Haven, CT: College & University Press.

Schachter, S. (1963). Birth order, eminence and higher education. *American Sociological Review, 28,* 757–768.

Schank, R. C. (1988). Creativity as a mechanical process. In R. J. Sternberg (Ed.), *The nature of creativity: Contemporary psychological perspectives* (pp. 220–238). Cambridge: Cambridge University Press.

Schlesinger, A. M. (1960). The decline of heroes. In R. Thruelson, & J. Kobler (Eds), *Adventures of the mind* (pp. 95–106). London: Gollancz.

Schorsch, A. (1979). *Images of childhood: an illustrated social history*. New York: Mayflower Books.

Seligman, M. E. P. (1975). *Learned helplessness: on depression, development and death*. San Francisco: Freeman.

Selye, H. (1960). What makes basic research basic? In R. Thruelsen & J. Kobler (Eds.), *Adventures of the mind* (pp. 135–147). London: Gollancz.

Shapero, H. (1954). The musical mind. In B. Ghiselin (Ed.), *The creative process: A symposium* (pp. 41–45). Berkeley: University of California Press.

Shapiro, R. J. (1968). Creative research scientists. *Psychologia Africana, Monograph Supplement, 4,* Whole.

Shear, J. (1982). The universal structures and dynamics of creativity. *Journal of Creative Behavior, 16,* 155–174.

Shiffrin, R. M. & Schneider, W. (1977). Controlled and automatic human information processing: II Perceptual learning, automatic attending, and a general theory. *Psychological Review, 84,* 127–190.

Simon, H. A. (1966). Scientific discovery and the psychology of problem solving. In R. G. Colodny (Ed.), *Mind and cosmos: essays in contemporary science and philosophy* (pp. 22–40). Pittsburgh: University of Pittsburgh Press.

Simonton, D. K. (1976). Biographical determinants of achieved eminence: A multivariate approach to the Cox data. *Journal of Personality and Social Psychology, 33,* 218–226.

(1978). The eminent genius in history: the critical role of creative development. *The Gifted Child Quarterly, 22,* 187–200.

(1979). Multiple discovery and invention: Zeitgeist, genius, or chance? *Journal of Personality and Social Psychology, 37,* 1603–1616.

(1983). Creative productivity and age: A mathematical model based on a two-step cognitive process. *Developmental Review, 3,* 97–111.

(1984). *Genius, creativity, and leadership: Historiometric inquiries*. Cambridge, MA: Harvard University Press.

(1985). Quality, quantity, and age: the careers of ten distinguished psychologists. *International Journal of Aging and Human Development, 21,* 241–254.

(1988). Creativity, leadership, and chance. In R. J. Sternberg (Ed.), *The nature of creativity: Contemporary psychological perspectives* (pp. 386–426). Cambridge: Cambridge University Press.

(in press). *Scientific creativity.* Cambridge: Cambridge University Press.

Simpson, E. (1987) *Orphans: Real and imaginary.* New York: Weidenfeld & Nicolson.

Singer, J. L. (1978). Experimental studies of daydreaming and the stream of thought. In K. S. Pope & J. L. Singer (Eds.), *The stream of consciousness* (pp. 187–223). New York: Plenum Press.

Singer, J. L., & McCraven, V. G. (1961). Some characteristics of adult daydreaming. *Journal of Psychology, 51,* 151–164.

Skager, R. W., Schultz, C. B., & Klein, S. P. (1967). The prediction of academic achievement at a school of design. *Journal of Educational Measurement, 4,* 105–117.

Skinner, B. F. (1976). A behavioral model of creation. In A. Rothenberg & C. R. Hausman (Eds.), *The creativity question* (pp. 267–273). Durham, NC: Duke University Press.

Slater, P. E. (1961). Toward a dualistic theory of identification. *Merrill Palmer Quarterly, 7,* 113–126.

Sorokin, P. A. (1951). *Social philosophies of an age of crisis.* Boston: Beacon Press.

Spearman, C. (1927). *The abilities of man.* New York: Macmillan.

(1931). *The creative mind.* New York: Appleton.

Spencer, R. M., & Weisberg, R. W. (1986). Context dependent effects on analogical transfer. *Memory and Cognition, 14,* 442–449.

Spender, S. (1954). The making of a poem. In B. Ghiselin (Ed.), *The creative process: A symposium* (pp. 113–126). Berkeley: University of California Press.

Sperry, R. W. (1969). A modified concept of consciousness. *Psychological Review, 76,* 532–536.

Stanley, J. C., & Benbow, C. P. (1986). Youths who reason exceptionally well mathematically. In R. J. Sternberg & J. E. Davidson (Eds.), *Conceptions of giftedness* (pp. 361–387). Cambridge: Cambridge University Press.

Stein, M. I. (1962). Creativity and the scientist. In B. Barber & W. Hirsch (Eds.), *The sociology of science* (pp. 329–343). New York: Free Press.

(1974). *Stimulating creativity* (vols. 1 & 2). New York: Academic Press.

Stein, M. I., & Heinze, S. J. (1960). *Creativity and the individual.* New York: Free Press.

Steinkraus, W. (1985). Artistic creativity and pain. In M. H. Mitias (Ed.), *Creativity in art, religion and culture* (pp. 42–63). Amsterdam: Rodopi.

Sternberg, R. J. (1986). *Intelligence applied.* San Diego: Harcourt Brace Jovanovich.

(1988). A three-facet model of creativity. In R. J. Sternberg (Ed.), *The nature of creativity: Contemporary psychological perspectives* (pp. 125–147). Cambridge: Cambridge University Press.

Stoke, S. M. (1950). An inquiry into the concept of identification. *Journal of Genetic Psychology, 76,* 163–189.

Storr, A. (1983). *The dynamics of creation.* Harmondsworth: Penguin.

Street, W. R. (1974). Brainstorming by individuals, coacting and interacting groups. *Journal of Applied Psychology, 59,* 433–436.

Suler, J. R. (1980). Primary process thinking and creativity. *Psychological Bulletin, 88,* 144–165.

Suler, J. R., & Rizziello, J. (1987). Imagery and verbal processes in creativity. *Journal of Creative Behavior, 21,* 1–6.

Sutton-Smith, B., & Rosenberg, B. G. (1970). *The sibling.* New York: Holt, Rinehart & Winston.

Szent-Györgyi, A. (1962). On scientific creativity. *Perspectives in Biology and Medicine, 5,* 173–178.

Tardif, T. Z., & Sternberg, R. J. (1988). What do we know about creativity? In R. J. Sternberg (Ed.), *The nature of creativity: Contemporary psychological perspectives* (pp. 429–440). Cambridge: Cambridge University Press.

Tauber, E. S., & Green, M. R. (1959). Prelogical experience, basic machine. *Scientific American, 203,* 60–68.

Taylor, C. W. (1963). Some possible relations between communication abilities and creative abilities. In C. W. Taylor and F. Barron (Eds.), *Scientific creativity: Its recognition and development* (pp. 53–76). New York: Wiley.

(1988). Various approaches to and definitions of creativity. In R. J. Sternberg (Ed.), *The nature of creativity: Contemporary psychological perspectives* (pp. 99–121). Cambridge: Cambridge University Press.

Taylor, C. W., Albo, D., Holland, J. & Brandt, G. (1985). Attributes of excellence in various professions: Their relevance to the selection of gifted/talented persons. *Gifted Children, 29,* 29–34.

Taylor, C. W., Smith, W. R., & Ghiselin, B. (1963). The creative and other contributions of one sample of research scientists. In C. W. Taylor & F. Barron (Eds.), *Scientific creativity: Its recognition and development* (pp. 53–76). New York: Wiley.

Taylor, C. W., Smith, W. R., Ghiselin, B., & Elison, R. L. (1961). Explorations in the measurement and prediction of contributions of one sample of scientists. Technical Reports. ASD-TR-61-96. Aeronautical Systems Division, Personnel Laboratory, Lackland Air Force Base, Texas.

Taylor, D. W. (1963). Variables related to creativity and productivity among men in two research laboratories. In C. W. Taylor & F. Barron (Eds.), *Scientific creativity: Its recognition and development* (pp. 228–250). New York: Wiley.

Taylor, D. W., Berry, P. C., & Block, C. H. (1958). Does group participation when using brain-storming facilitate or inhibit creative thinking? *Administrative Science Quarterly, 3,* 23–47.

Taylor, I. A. (1972). The nature of the creative process. In P. Smith (Ed.), *Creativity: An examination of the creative process* (pp. 51–101). New York: Books for Libraries Press. (Originally published, 1959.)

Tchaikowsky, P. I. (1970). Letters: reprinted in P. E. Vernon (Ed.), *Creativity* (pp. 57–60). Harmondsworth: Penguin. (Originally published 1906.)

Terman, L. M. (1925). *Mental and physical traits of a thousand gifted children* (vol. I of Genetic studies of genius). Stanford: Stanford University Press.

(1926). Genius and stupidity: A study of some of the intellectual processes of seven 'brighter' and seven 'stupid' boys. *Pedagogical Seminary, 13,* 307–373.

(1947). Psychological approaches to the study of genius. *Papers on Eugenics, 4,* 3–20.

Terman, L. M., & Oden, M. H. (1959). *The gifted child grows up: twenty-five years' follow-up of the superior child* (vol. 4 of L. M. Terman's Genetic studies of genius). Stanford: Stanford University Press.

Thurstone, L. L. (1950). *Creative talent.* Chicago: Chicago University Press.

Thurstone, L. L., & Jenkins R. L. (1929). Birth order and intelligence. *Journal of Educational Psychology, 20,* 641–651.

Toder, N., & Marcia, J. E. (1973). Ego identity status and response to conformity pressure in college women. *Journal of Personality and Social Psychology, 26,* 287–294.

Torrance, E. P. (1962). *Guiding creative talent.* Englewood Cliffs, NJ: Prentice Hall.

(1967). Nurture of creative talents. In R. L. Mooney & T. Rasik (Eds.), *Explorations in creativity* (pp. 185–195). New York: Harper & Row.

(1974). *Torrance tests of creative thinking: Norms-technical manual.* Lexington, MA: Personnel Press/Ginn.

(1979). *The search for satori and creativity.* New York: Creative Education Foundation.

(1987). Future career image as a predictor of creative achievement in a 22-year longitudinal study. *Psychological Reports, 60,* 574.

(1988). The nature of creativity as manifest in testing. In R. J. Sternberg (Ed.), *The nature of creativity: Contemporary psychological perspectives* (pp. 42–75). Cambridge: Cambridge University Press.

Toynbee, A. (1964). Is America neglecting her creative minority? In C. W. Taylor (Ed.), *Widening horizons in creativity: The proceedings of the fifth Utah Creativity Research Conference* (pp. 3–9). New York: Wiley.

Treffinger, J., Isaksen, S. K., & Firestien, R. L. (1982). *Handbook of creative learning.* New York: Center for Creativity Training.

Trollope, A. (1974). From an autobiography. In J. Hersey (Ed.), *The writer's craft* (pp. 239–254). New York: Knopf.

Tsanoff, R. A. (1949). *The ways of genius.* New York: Harper & Brothers.

Underwood, G. (1979). Memory systems and conscious processes. In G. Underwood & R. Stevens (Eds.), *Aspects of consciousness* (vol. 1, pp. 91–121). London: Academic Press.

Valéry, P. (1954). The course in poetics: First lesson. In B. Ghiselin (Ed.), *The creative process: A symposium* (pp. 92–105). Berkeley: University of California Press. (Originally published in 1940.)

Vallery-Radot, R. (1937). *The life of Pasteur* (R. L. Devonshire, Trans.). New York: Sun Dial Press.

Van Bergen, A. (1968). *Task interruption.* Amsterdam: North-Holland Publishing Co.

Van Zelst, R. H., & Kerr, W. A. (1951). Some correlates of technical and scientific productivity. *Journal of Abnormal and Social Psychology, 46,* 470–475.

Veroff, J., Atkinson, J. W., Feld, S. C., & Gurin, G. (1960). The use of thematic apperception to assess motivation in a nationwide interview study. *Psychological Monographs, 74,* (Whole No. 499).

Vidal, G. (1977). *Matters of fact and fiction.* London: Heinemann.

Visher, S. S. (1948). Environmental backgrounds of leading American scientists. *American Sociological Review, 13,* 65–72.

Walberg, H. J. (1988). Creativity as learning. In R. J. Sternberg (Ed.), *The nature of creativity: Contemporary psychological perspectives* (pp. 340–361). Cambridge: Cambridge University Press.

Walberg, H. J., Rasher, S. P., & Parkerson, J. (1979). Childhood and eminence. *Journal of Creative Behavior, 13,* 225–231.

Walberg, H. S., Rasher, S. P., & Hase, K. (1978). IQ correlates with high eminence. *Gifted Child Quarterly, 22,* 196–200.

Wallace, B., & Fisher, L. E. (1983). *Consciousness and behavior.* Boston: Allyn & Bacon.

Wallach, M. A., & Kogan, N. (1965). *Modes of thinking in young children: A study of the creativity-intelligence distinction.* New York: Holt, Rinehart & Winston.

Wallas, G. (1926). *The act of thought.* London: Watts.

Walley, R. E., & Weiden, T. D. (1973). Lateral inhibition and cognitive masking: A new psychological theory of attention. *Psychological Review, 80,* 284–302.

Walters, J., & Gardner, H. (1986). The crystallizing experience: Discovering an intellectual gift. In R. J. Sternberg & J. E. Davidson (Eds.), *Conceptions of giftedness* (pp. 306–331). Cambridge: Cambridge University Press.

Washburn, M. C. (1978). Observations relevant to a unified theory of meditation. *Journal of Transpersonal Psychology, 10,* 45–65.

Waterman, A. S. (1982). Identity development from adolescence to adulthood. *Development Psychology, 18,* 341–358.

Weil, A. (1972). *The natural mind.* Boston: Houghton-Mifflin.

Weisberg, P. S., & Springer, K. J. (1961). Environmental factors in creative function. *Archives of General Psychiatry, 5,* 64–74.

Weisberg, R. W. (1986). *Creativity: genius and other myths.* New York: Freeman.

(1988). Problem solving and creativity. In R. J. Sternberg (Ed.), *The nature of creativity: Contemporary psychological perspectives* (pp. 148–176). Cambridge: Cambridge University Press.

Wertheimer, M. (1945). *Productive thinking.* New York: Harper & Row.

West, L. J. (1975). A clinical and theoretical overview of hallucinatory phenomena. In R. K. Siegel & L. J. West (Eds.), *Hallucinations: behavior, experience, and theory* (chap. 9). New York: Wiley.

Westfall, R. S. (1980). *Never at rest: A biography of Issac Newton.* Cambridge: Cambridge University Press.

(1983). Newton's development of the *Principia.* In R. Aris, H. T. Davis & R. H. Struewer (Eds.), *Springs of scientific creativity* (pp. 21–43). Minneapolis: University of Minnesota Press.

Whitbourne, S. K., & Weinstock, C. S. (1979). *Adult development: The differentiation of experience.* New York: Holt, Rinehart, & Winston.

White, J. P. (1968). Creativity and education: A philosophical analysis. *British Journal of Educational Studies, 16,* 123–137.

White, L. A. (1949). *The science of culture.* New York: Farrar, Strauss.

White, R. K. (1930). Note on the psychopathology of genius. *Journal of Social Psychology, 1,* 311–315.

White, R. W. (1959). Motivation reconsidered: The concept of competence. *Psychological Review, 66,* 297–333.

Whyte, L. L. (1973). Where do those bright ideas come from? In G. Tate (Ed.), *From discovery to style* (pp. 34–41). Cambridge, MA: Winthrop.

(1978). *The unconscious before Freud.* New York: St Martin's Press.

Wiener, N. (1953). *Ex-prodigy: My childhood and youth.* New York: Simon & Schuster.

Wild, C. (1965). Creativity and adaptive regression. *Journal of Personality and Social Psychology, 2,* 161–169.

Wilson, M. (1972). *Passion to know: The world's scientists.* New York: Doubleday.

Winchester, I. (1985). Panel discussion. *Interchange, 16,* 104–118.

Wolf, S. (1981). The role of the brain in bodily disease. In A. Weiner, & M. A. Stunkard (Eds.), *Brain, behavior, and bodily disease* (pp. 1–9). New York: Raven Press.

Woodworth, R. S. (1918). *Dynamic psychology.* New York: Columbia University Press.

Woodworth, R. S. (1938). *Experimental psychology.* New York: Holt.

Woodworth, R. S. (1958). *Dynamics of behavior.* New York: Holt.

Woodworth, R. S., & Scholsberg, H. (1954). *Experimental psychology.* New York: Rinehart.

Woody, E., & Claridge, G. (1983). Psychoticism and creativity. In R. S. Albert (Ed.), *Genius and eminence* (pp. 347–357). Oxford: Pergamon Press.

Yamamoto, K. (1964). Evaluation of some creativity measures in a high school with peer nominations as criteria. *Journal of Psychology, 58,* 285–293.

Ypma, E. G. (1968). *Prediction of the industrial creativity of research scientists from biographical information.* Doctoral dissertation, Purdue University. Dissertation Abstracts International, 1970, 30, 5731B–5732B. University Microfilms, No. 70–10, 670.

Yukawa, H. (1973). *Creativity and intuition.* New York: Kodanska International.

Zajonc, R. B. (1976). Family configuration and intelligence. *Science, 192*, 227–236.

Zeigarnik, B. (1927). Über das Behalten von erledigten und unerledigten Handlungen. *Psychologische Forschung, 9,* 1–18.

Zilboorg, G. (1972). The psychology of the creative personality. In P. Smith (Ed.), *Creativity: an examination of the creative process* (pp. 21–32). Freeport: Books for Libraries Press. (Originally published 1959.)

Zuckerman, H. (1977). *Scientific elite: Nobel laureates in the United States.* New York: The Free Press.

# Index of names

# Subject index

abilities, intellectual, 108–9, 111, 112, 202–18
absentminded errors, *see* slips
academic performance, 63, 66, 87–8, 93, 167
Adler's theory, 17–18, 72, 82, 143, 147
aesthetic reactions: 122–4, 153–9, 215; intellectual sources of, 154–6; emotional sources of, 156–8; cultural influences on, 158–9
aesthetic sensitivity, 122–4, 155
age at which first, best and last works are produced, 94–99, 101–2
ambition, aspiration, 14, 18, 61, 64, 77, 128, 132, 144, 147, 165
analogical thinking, 29, 200, 208, 212–15,
animosity, 146–7
arousal, cortical, 200–1, 228, 230, 232, 235, 254
artificial simulation of creative thinking, 190, 216–8
associative processes, 28, 189, 201, 207–16
attention, 200–1, 225, 230, 250, 253–4
automatic routines: as bases for creative production, 241–4; sensory-motor, 236–9, mental, 239–44, 247–9; generalizable 244; *see also* slips
automaticity, 108, 236–49

bath-bed-bus-syndrome, 196, 200, 253
bereavement, 74–7, 82, 166
birth order, 64–7, 164
brain, 112, 257–8; *see also* neurological structures and hemispheric specialization

career, 94–102
computers, 128, 190, 216–18

conditions of worth, 25, 180–1; *see also* evaluation
conscious stream of thought, 235–6, 249–50, 252
consciousness, 235, 249; altered states of 16, 228–31
control, need for, 123, 148–50, 167; sense of, 178
coping: through control, 167; through intellectual activity, 151–2; with inferiority, 18; with psychopathology, 117; with threat, 149; *see also* palliation
creativity: conceptions of, 2–4, 27, 35–6, 202, 204, 206–10, 259; criteria of, 1–2, 4, 11, 32, 42–5, 205; definitions of, 2, 210; tests, 45, 175, 204–6; training, 23, 25–6, 31, 36, 113, 171, 227, 259
cultural influences, 50–7, 60–4, 158, 182,
current concerns, 224, 249, 250–2

daydreaming, 13–15, 221, 223–4, 245–6
depression, 76, 115, 117, 118, 122, 149, 176
developmental pattern, 160–72, of creative women, 172–3
discipline, 19, 21, 69, 79–80, 178, 180; versus freedom, 178–80; *see also* parental style of control
divergent thinking, 28, 204–6, 210, 213
dreams and dreaming, 14, 194–6, 224–5, 228, 236, 242, 246, 250
drugs, 16, 221, 230–1

education: 25, 83; attitudes toward, 88–90, 93; evaluation of, 90; formal, 83; in the home, 68–71, 84, 163–4;